KU-351-101

UNIVERSITY REBEL

WILLIAM FREND

Portrait in the possession of Miss Philothea Thompson

UNIVERSITY REBEL

The Life of William Frend
(1757–1841)

FRIDA KNIGHT

LONDON
VICTOR GOLLANCZ LTD
1971

ISBN 0 575 00633 1

PRINTED IN GREAT BRITAIN
BY EBENEZER BAYLIS & SON LIMITED
THE TRINITY PRESS, WORCESTER, AND LONDON

William Frend to his Prosecutors, 1794:

"Foolish and inconsiderate men! What avail it that ye have deprived a student of the little solace left to him, that ye have shut against him the doors of those libraries in which your footsteps are seldom heard? that ye would bar against him every avenue to knowledge? . . . Ye have driven one student from his books, but his opinions are left behind. Ye cannot banish thought, and thought engenders thought; and future students, whilst they reprobate your meanness and your malice, will investigate the opinions which have given rise to so much persecution and blind zeal."

Sequel to An Account, 1795

THE CAMBRIDGE RAMBLE

1785

(Broadsheet in British Museum)

Of Cambridge I had heard much talk
And of the Varzity;
Adzooks! said I within my mind
I'ze go that place to see!

Next day we went to view the town
Which is a wondrous place
With Colleges I think they're call'd
In every other place;

Zuch Gardens vine (if they were mine,
I'd zet the plough a going)
There you may walk & zaunter & talk
But there's no Corn a growing.

Zome things they told us wondrous strange
Of men of great discerning:
How they could spirits raise and greek
And all by dint of learning.

I was in a fright I own downright
And zo was Brother Jack
Zo we sneaked along among the throng
And zaw the men in black.

And there was plenty every where
With big sleeves hanging down
And flat square hats upon their heads
They skip'd about the town;
They looked so zly as we passed by
So we were vastly civil—
In my mind they had design'd
Zomehow to raise the devil . . .

ACKNOWLEDGEMENTS

IT HAS BEEN possible to reconstruct the life of William Frend only through the kindness of his descendants, who trustingly lent the precious letters and papers which are the basis of this study.

To Professor W. H. C. Frend, to Miss Joan Antrobus, to Mr Charles Frend and to Mrs Nancy Baker, I owe a debt of gratitude; and most of all to Miss Philothea Thompson who generously allowed me to raid her attic and carry off a trunkful of unpublished family letters.

For allowing me access to material in their care I thank the Librarians of Christ's, Jesus, Queens' Colleges; of the University Library and of the City Library, Cambridge; of the Bodleian Library, Oxford; of Birkbeck College, University College, and Dr Williams' Library, London; of Reading University Library and of Reading Borough Library; the Goldsmith Librarian, University of London Library; the Archivists of Beds., Berks., Cambs., Hunts. and Kent County Record Offices.

My thanks are due to Lord Lytton who allowed me to include extracts from some 70 letters from Frend to Lady Byron, now in the Lovelace Collection, and to Mr Malcolm Elwin who kindly gave me access to them.

I have had much personal help from my learned friends Edward Thompson, Dr Ian Fletcher, Rev. Tony Cross (former editor, *The Inquirer*), Mrs Elizabeth Hope and John Adlard; I thank them one and all, and last but not least my husband and my daughters for their aid in transcribing letters and typing the manuscript, and for their never failing support and constructive criticism.

F.K.

CONTENTS

PREFACE

THE STORY OF William Frend is not the highly coloured drama of a famous figure; it is the brief chronicle of one of the lesser men who are the moving force of society, the stuff of whom social history is made. Frend's letters, which have lain, tied in yellowing bundles, in an old trunk in an attic for 120 years, are living chunks of the age of revolution; reading them one is carried back into that period, and shares the experiences of a campaigner in the most progressive movements of that time.

William Frend was born in 1757 and grew up during the American War of Independence, witnessed the French Revolution, the radical campaigns of the London Corresponding Society, the Napoleonic Wars, the popular upheavals of the early nineteenth century, and the technical and social changes of the 1820's and 30's—and he wrote and commented on all of these, always taking an advanced position and often suffering for it.

A brilliant mathematician and economist, linguist and statistician, Frend could have had an easy life at university; he chose instead to quarrel with the orthodox academics, becoming briefly famous by his trial in Cambridge where he raised the Unitarian banner against the evangelical Milner. Thereafter he led an independent life in London in the vanguard of the Reform movement, and in Stoke Newington, bringing up his family while an actuary in one of the first insurance companies.

He counted among his friends most of the well-known progressives of his day: the dissenters Dr Priestley, Theophilus Lindsey, Baron Maseres; the writers Coleridge, Lamb, Dyer, Crabb Robinson; the politicians Francis Place, Burdett, Brougham; the distinguished women Mrs Barbauld,

Mary Hays, Lady Byron. Frend's correspondence throws new light on many of them and their doings.

But it is for his personal view of life that it seems most worth reviving Frend's memory. Devoutly religious in an unorthodox way, he had a scientific outlook which led him to comment pungently on society, government (whether national, local, or academic) and to debunk all that he considered pompous, false or stupid. And so we find in these old letters, and in his journalism, observations on eighteenth- and nineteenth-century affairs which apply to many aspects of life in our own time—social problems, student revolts, war, struggles for independence, racial discrimination are all considered, and Frend's remarks strike one as surprisingly wise and helpful even for us today; they reveal an interesting and deeply humane character, worth, one may hope, a modest place among the more celebrated (but perhaps less lovable) people of his time.

PART I

ACADEMICS AND HERETICS

I

INTRODUCTION TO CAMBRIDGE

On 18 December 1775 Mr George Frend, wine merchant and twice Mayor of Canterbury, climbed down from the stage coach in the centre of Cambridge, followed by his eighteen-year-old son William. They had made the long journey from Kent in answer to a summons for William to attend an interview for admission to Christ's College, and he was to see the great Dr Paley there that afternoon.

Cambridge was then a busy crowded little town of some 8,000 inhabitants,[1] its normal population swollen by nearly a thousand students during university term. Its narrow streets swarmed with gownsmen, the very young jostling the old and venerable; country and townspeople alike hurried about their business, gathered at the market stalls, gazed into the windows of bookshops, hatters and clothiers; traffic rumbled through from East Anglia to the Midlands and vice versa, causing congestion on the unpaved thoroughfares.

A stone's throw from the centre, the river flowed gently between green lawns fringed by flowerbeds and weeping willows, lapping the bases of weatherbeaten bridges and old brick walls. And wherever one looked were the colleges, with their charming and varied buildings: some of them like miniature castles or monasteries, others like Tudor manors, renaissance palaces, Jacobean mansions—their courts exuding an atmosphere of domestic security, scholarly peace and welcoming warmth to the lucky person who belonged within their grey or cream or ochre-yellow walls.

As William and his father entered the tower gateway of Christ's College and crossed the cobbled court to Dr Paley's rooms, the young man must have looked enviously at the

[1] The nearest census, 1794, records a total of 8,942 resident in the parishes of Cambridge, plus 141 servants living in colleges.

narrow entrances to the student "sets" and longed to be among the privileged with a room of his own up one of the dark staircases—however small, chilly and medieval, a sanctuary and home, and haunt of his friends, during three precious years of student life.

William had always wanted to go to Cambridge: his best friends from King's School, Canterbury, had entered in October 1775, and were happily installed, James Tylden at Jesus College, and James Six (son of the inventor of the maximum and minimum thermometer) at Clare College.

William's entry had been delayed owing to his father's opposition to the idea of a scholarly career. George Frend wanted the boy to go into the flourishing family wine business, like his elder son (also George). In spite of protests William was sent at the age of seventeen, to Quebec, to learn the ins and outs of the wine trade.

While he was in Canada the War of American Independence broke out, and he was recruited into the British army. "Such was his bravery and gallant bearing", his daughter wrote long after, "that it was desired to retain him in the army; but he preferred the life of a scholar, and, journeying back to England, begged his father to let him enter the Ministry."[1]

Mr Frend agreed reluctantly—it was probably as little use arguing with eighteen-year-old William about something on which he felt strongly as it proved to be ten years later. And the father must have realized that his son, as well as being single-minded to the point of obstinacy, was singularly gifted and worthy of the best education available.

He was unable to bestow on the boy the £500 or so yearly allowance through which the Gentlemen Commoners of Cambridge ran like flame through stubble. So William had to enter as a scholar and to pass the ordeal of the college interview, and so we find him, a week before Christmas 1775, getting his first glimpse of the university and of Dr Paley, his tutor-to-be.

[1] Sophia De Morgan: *Three Score Years and Ten*, p. ix.

As he later wrote, recalling his memories of the occasion and of Paley: "The first time I saw him was on my admission at College when I deliver'd to him a letter of introduction from the then arch-deacon of Canterbury, & in a very little time got over the little agitation which a young man naturally feels at an examination . . . My father of course was not present but Paley dined with us at the Master's Lodge where there was a mixed party & he would have taken us to his rooms for supper if my father had not collected a set of youngsters with whom to spend the evening."[1]

William apparently made a good impression, and he was accepted.

That he was obviously very much in earnest about his studies, and anxious to get down to them, is shown in a letter from his friend Tylden, answering inquiries about reading while waiting to go up to college: "You desire me to give you an account of what books you are to read—as to Mathematicks, in my opinion you had much better leave them alone entirely till you return here—they will puzzle you & take up that time wh. you may at present employ to more advantage.

"Reading Mathematicks alone is like wandering in a bye way where you can seldom meet with a passenger to direct you right. Here is the Turnpike Road, the via regia ad Mathesin (to use Euclid's expression)—numbers are travelling the same path & tis hard if you can't chime in with some of them—in the mean time apply yourself strenuously to the Classicks."

From his elevated position as second-year undergraduate he admonished William, "Keep the couplet of Horace constantly in yr mind—qui student optatant etc."[2] Whether William took the advice is not known; probably he did rise early to study, but surely not only classics—mathematics being his favourite subject he was very unlikely to "leave them alone entirely".

[1] W.F. letter to Frances Frend, 21.3.1823.

[2] Tylden to W.F., 24.2.1776.

However that may have been, he duly arrived at Christ's College at the beginning of the Michaelmas term of 1776, and like all freshmen presented himself at Dr Paley's door for instructions.

He was invited to drink tea with the Doctor "& sat upwards of two hours with him tête a tête, during which he settled everything for my lodgement that night in college & the next day he put me under the care of a proper young man to introduce me into college."[1]

His father must have been glad to know that William was being befriended by Paley and "a proper young man". Many fathers were seriously worried about their sons' entering one of the ancient universities, whose reputations towards the end of the eighteenth century were unenviable. Letters to *The Gentleman's Magazine* reflected their anxiety. According to one correspondent, "the academic gown's a masquerade; the tassell'd cap and the spruce band a jest"—"The Senate-house, the libraries, and the schools, chapels, halls and colleges still exhibit an august appearance ... but on a closer survey, nothing will be found within their walls but claycold relics of departed grandeur." As for the fellow-commoners of Cambridge, "they take the lead in every disgraceful frolic of juvenile debauchery. They are curiously tricked out in cloth of gold, of silver and of purple, and feast most sumptuously throughout the year."[2] In the opinion of "T.F.", the writer, all this was largely due to the decline of the fortunes of the real aristocracy of the country, and the rise of the merchant class, who, along with the *nouveaux riches* and Indian "nabobs" were sending their sons to the university to pick up a smattering of learning, with far too much money in their pockets.

In another issue of *The Gentleman's Magazine* there is a letter from an anxious father who might have been George Frend; his son, he says, "is now about to pass through those

[1] W.F. to Frances Frend, 21.3.1823.

[2] *The Gentleman's Magazine*, January 1798.

envenomed regions of which T.F. gives so alarming a description. He *must* pass through them or he will in vain seek admission into the sacred ministry of the Church for which he is destined . . . Humble in his situation and prospects, he will be less exposed to the extremity of danger than if his rank in life entitled him to the gaudy pre-eminence of a gilded or a silken robe . . . but perils of every description will await him at every step he takes. May the Almighty God protect and preserve him!"

William managed to escape perdition, and indeed one cannot help feeling that these alarmist cries were overdone; wealthy undergraduates might have opportunity for debauchery but the ordinary student was not inevitably swept away by it. After all, there were reasonable rules, and sensible boys like Frend might be expected to obey them. One was, for instance, not permitted to keep a servant or a horse without consent (not that young Frend could have afforded either); guns and sporting dogs were forbidden, so was dining in a coffee house. The student must not run up bills of over twenty shillings at a tavern, nor ask for wine or punch after 11 p.m. He must show respect to his superiors, and attend the University sermon or pay a fine of sixpence. He was forbidden "to keep evil company, break windows, make and foment riots and disturbances"; he might play at dice and cards only for small sums and at certain times. Academic wear was compulsory within the University precincts.

A contemporary poem shows that the rules were unpopular with the better-off student who could and did evade them. Whoever had money, "still in a blue or a scarlett vest may saunter thro' the town, or strut regardless of the rules even to St Mary's or the Schools in hat or poplin gown." Moreover,

> A dog he unconcerned maintains, and seeks with gun the sportive plains
> Which ancient Cam divides;

Or to the hills on horseback strays, unasked his tutor,
or his chaise
To famed Newmarket guides.[1]

With good reason, the correspondent of *The Gentleman's Magazine* boomed away: "Cavillers may tell you that no offences are unpunished; for that every misdemenour subjects the delinquent to proportionate fines ... A fellow commoner pays for neglecting matins or vespers, 2d each time; the hours of closing gates, 3d; lectures 4d; meals in hall, one shilling ... Is it not an insult to discipline to suppose such paltry mulcts as these can curb the licentiousness of impetuous youths, whose fortunes are enormous and whose profusion is proverbial? ... the cost of one gay excursion to Newmarket ... far exceeds the accumulated forfeiture of a whole term."

If the rich young men ignored the rules and enjoyed themselves, it must be said that some of their elders and betters did not offer them a particularly edifying example. Life in college for a Fellow who was not an ardent scholar or a strong self-disciplinarian, could be very easy. As Christopher Wordsworth said, "Although there were not wanting men of learning and of purity" in either university, "the few great divines of the eighteenth century did not communicate their knowledge and enthusiasm to the younger men."

For a professor at the University to lecture was almost the exception. In Cambridge at the end of the century, the Professors of Physics, Hebrew, Greek, Casuistry, Arabic, Mathematics, Music, Mineralogy, Astronomy and the Lady Margaret Professor of Divinity, none of them troubled to give lectures. Dr Parr commented that this state of things "plainly shows that the Universities were by no means altogether dens of idleness," but that there was "a great part of the instruction of younger men which

[1] Christopher Wordsworth: *Social Life at the English Universities*, pp. 67–69.

was not covered by the efforts of the University Professors."[1]

It is pleasant to record one student's remarks showing that Dr Paley at least fulfilled his duties: "I was a constant attendant on his lectures", William Frend wrote, years later, to his daughter, "which were scarcely ever shirked by anyone as they were a treat in themselves."[2]

The deficiency of professorial lectures was supplied in part at least by the college tutors, or by "pupil-mongers". The former were reasonably well paid, having petitioned for a salary rise some years previously. The private tutors got £20 a year per pupil; they were not always scrupulously honest, passing themselves off as graduates when in fact they were not, often examining their own pupils and giving "the second wrangler first place".[3]

In 1777, the year after Frend's admission, a Grace[4] was passed which threatened that any tutor examining his own pupil would be blacklisted—but many abuses still continued.

William Frend was fortunate in not having to resort to a pupil-monger, being admirably tutored by Dr Paley, pre-eminent among Cambridge's scholars at that time.

Paley, "the most perspicacious and popular of English moralists" according to one admirer, was a Yorkshireman and his biographer ascribes "his prudential morality and racy style to his early intercourse with the shrewd peasantry". He had entered Christ's College as a sizar in 1759 and remained there after being elected a Fellow in 1766, teaching philosophy and logic. His *Principles of Moral and Political Philosophy*, published in 1783, had a very wide circulation: "It was admirably adapted to the spirit of the times, being very orthodox in its tone and very worldly in its principles ... Its pithy and intelligible chapters must have fallen like a

[1] C. Wordsworth: *op. cit.*, pp. 84–86.
[2] W.F. to Frances Frend, 21.3.1823.
[3] C. Wordsworth: *op. cit.*, pp. 112–114.
[4] Grace = University statute presented by senate member.

refreshing dew on a generation worn out by the dreary prosing of Bishop Cumberland . . . or left unsatisfied by visionary moralizing of Cudworth and of Clark."[1]

Paley's view of ethics was well suited to Cambridge University which had for seventy years been under the influence of Sir Isaac Newton—the ancient statutes and traditions surviving awkwardly alongside forward-looking Newtonian science.

Paley accepted Newton's assumption that the design of the physical world is mechanical and "expedient", and said that the design of the moral world must be so too. He emphasized self-centred expediency as the goal of moral action.[2]

The University adopted and for a very long time used Paley's work as its text book of moral philosophy, deeming that "the good sense of its practical expositions renders it a beneficial study and neutralizes the unsoundness of its theoretical principles."[3]

It must unfortunately be admitted that the combination of "unsound principles" and "good sense", led Paley throughout his career into positions of regrettable compromise. At one stage he even went so far as to confess "I cannot afford to keep a conscience".[4] His basic liberalism was reflected in his outspoken disapproval of various university statutes, particularly that which insisted that degree-takers should subscribe to the Thirty-nine Articles of the Church of England; yet (true to his doctrine of expediency) he argued in favour of subscription because "the intent of the statutes was to see that undergraduates were prepared for their degrees."[5]

And many stories show that, in spite of good intentions, Paley was too often ready to trim his sails to the prevailing wind. But whatever his shortcomings he was popular with his pupils,

[1] Paley in *Dictionary of Universal Biography* (U.B.).

[2] B. Schneider: *Wordsworth's Cambridge Education*, pp. 10, 11.

[3] Paley in U.B.

[4] Paley: *Works*, quoted by Schneider, *op. cit.*, p. 121.

[5] Schneider: *op. cit.*, pp. 121, 122. Paley: *Works*, i, p. 43.

partly perhaps because he wore his great learning so lightly.

Frend for one was devoted to him besides regarding him with "respect for a senior of acknowledg'd pre-eminence". In later years he described Paley to his daughter who had asked him for a definition of a *gentleman* as "just exactly that". Paley was "a man of the world who could converse with propriety with every man in every rank of life from the king to the beggar . . . They could not spend half an hour with him without being delighted". If Paley had been at a party of squires and squiresses, "they in their best array and he in his best wig, the odds are they would not have gone away without a hearty laugh." [1]

In an anonymous article[2] thirty years later Frend expanded on the subject of Paley's lectures: "There was no need of punishments for missing lectures, we were sufficiently punished if any circumstance prevented us from attending them." Paley "shone as a lecturer at a place where the art of lecturing is better understood than in any other part of the world. In most places . . . the lecturer delivers a kind of preachment and thinks he has done much if from his notes he has uttered a harangue, suitable to the subject however unsuitable it may be to his hearers".

Not so Paley. His lectures were evidently more like a modern seminar, to judge by Frend's picture: "You should have seen him, as we did, when he stept out of his little study into the lecture room, rolled from the door into his arm chair, turned his old scratch over his left ear, and his left leg over his right, buttoned up his waistcoat, pulled up a stocking, and fixed a dirty, cover-torn, ragged Locke upon his left knee, moistened his thumb with his lip, and then turned over the ragged leaves of his books, dogs eared and scrawled about, with the utmost rapidity . . . We were so accustomed to this preparation that it ceased to make any impression upon us; and sat each in expectation of the first question falling to his lot.

[1] W.F. to Frances Frend, 21.3.1823.

[2] *Universal Magazine*, 1805.

"On one occasion, an unfortunate freshman was asked, 'Pray, Mr B—— . . . give me an instance of a simple idea.' B——replied 'The Vice-Chancellor'. 'Very well, very well, Mr B——,' says Paley, pulling his scratch over his left ear, turning his right leg over his left, refixing his book, 'Very well, Mr B——. Pray tell me, have you ever seen the Vice-Chancellor?' Poor Mr B—— dragged forth the reluctant yes. Poor fellow, it was now all over with him: the beadles, the silver maces, the large cap, large band, great wig, solemn port, and a few goodly allusions to the dignified person of the Vice-Chancellor all came forth, and not one person who heard that lecture will ever mistake a complex for a simple idea.

"After the questions were over, Paley's position in his seat was changed: the scratch, the leg, the book, took exactly the opposite directions, the thumb was moistened as before, the leaves turned over, but nine times in ten not stopped at the place which had any reference to what he was going to say, when in the most familiar manner he discussed some subject in Locke or Clarke, or in moral Philosophy, pointing out the passages which we were to read for the next lecture day, and explaining everything in such a manner that the driest subjects were made interesting. At this time we were most of us employed in taking notes, and the manuscripts thus taken of his lectures were not only in the highest repute in our own, but were eagerly sought after in other colleges. I remember to have copied out large copy books on Locke and Clarke, on natural religion, on revealed religion, and on moral philosophy . . ."

Paley's idiosyncrasies were also amusingly described by his pupil: His untidy wig: "You might imagine that the example of such a tutor as we had, whom we all loved, and who was deserving of the respect in which he was held, would have a powerful influence upon us. Negligence in dress might be expected to become the characteristic of a christian, and our heads would be frizzed out, in imitation of Paley's scratch." His garb—"not always so smart as that of his pupils"; his fondness for fishing, in which he indulged often "on the banks of the Cam, meditating perhaps that important question, the happiness of an oyster"; his indolence ("Newton and Locke were not unfrequently in the middle of the day, the companions of his pillow"), indolence which "preserved him from that disgraceful mode of gaining preferment—rooting." He was indeed the author of the term "Rooting, an expression much used in the university of Cambridge; denoting that baseness and servility of character which, like swine rooting in a dunghill, will perform the basest acts for a rich patron to gain his protection, and a good benefice."[1]

Frend, fortunate in having so remarkable a man as tutor, absorbed a great deal of moral philosophy and logic from him. At the same time he worked hard at mathematics, logic and Greek for which he had no great love but which was, of course, a compulsory subject for anybody wishing to enter the Church.

[1] *Universal Magazine*, 1805.

2

STUDENTS AND TEACHERS

"AT THE UNIVERSITY my conduct resembled that of most other young men who attain to . . . the honours of the place", Frend wrote in 1795.

He "passed many hours in company", but "indulged much in solitary walks. When alone my time was dedicated to reading and thinking."[1]

One can get a more detailed picture of what Frend's routine and recreation must have been from the accounts of undergraduate life by his friend Henry Gunning and by Christopher Wordsworth (younger but also a contemporary). These show that whatever today's differences, in essence Cambridge student life has not changed so very much.

In the late eighteenth century a student might rise early and work, or he might lie in and breakfast at 9 o'clock on tea and toast (a verse about a 1792 undergraduate describes how "Friend Warren takes appointed seat/pours tea on sugar very sweet . . . and from Brown George[2] toasts slice of bread"). He would then go off to lectures or tutorials or to read in one of the libraries. Dinner in hall was usually between 12 and 1 o'clock, and after dinner the students flocked to the philosophical disputations which began at 2 p.m. (These were a form of intellectual entertainment, a public debate between eminent academic figures considered worth hearing.) On Sundays the meal was at 1.15, and the University sermon, semi-compulsory for students, at 3 p.m. The Vice-Chancellor gave weekly dinner parties, and all his company went with him to St Mary's Church.[3]

During the week those who were not attending disputa-

[1] W.F.: *Sequel to an Account of the Proceedings*, p. 128.
[2] College loaf.
[3] C. Wordsworth: *op. cit.*, p. 51.

tions went off in the afternoon for fresh air and exercise. Those who could afford it might hire a horse and go fox- or stag-hunting or to a Newmarket meeting—either of which cost about £1 5s. a time. Young Frend could not have afforded this, but he might have hired a horse for "a common ride" at 4s. 6d. Swimming was popular (and the occasional subject of tripos verses); it was permitted within the colleges' grounds.

William's favourite recreation, as we know, was walking, with or without a gun. He was no hunter but did not object to potting at birds. If he and his friends walked out along the Trumpington Road and entered on Cow Fen they would put up any number of snipe; going through the osier beds on the Trumpington side of the brook they often sent a partridge whirring away, and now and then a pheasant would scuttle off, scared, across the fen. From thence to the lower end of Trumpington village, which was one long marshy stretch, there would be plenty of snipe and in early spring a hare or two would start up from almost underfoot.[1]

For wet winter days there was no ready-made entertainment; in fact it was only during Stourbridge Fair, held just outside the town, that there was the chance of seeing a play, apart from an occasional dramatic performance by students inside a college.

The chief indoor resorts were the coffee-houses—the Union, the Johnian (in All Saints' Yard) or the Rose Inn—where one met friends and talked politics or scandal, and read the newspapers "of which swarms are constantly supplied from London". Still relevant were this and other observations of Roger North's (fifty years earlier) to the effect that "the scholars are so greedy after news, which is none of their business, that they neglect all for it . . . which is a vast loss of time . . . for who can apply close to a subject with his head full of the din of a coffee-house?" However that might be, in Frend's student days the important issues of the time, such as the American war, the Dissenters' pleas

[1] Gunning: *Reminiscences of Cambridge*, ii, p. 40.

for toleration, Parliamentary Reform—all very much in the news—were certainly given a healthy airing in the coffee-houses.[1]

To return to our undergraduate's routine, whether he had spent the afternoon on the fens or indoors, he would be expected to be back in college for chapel at 5.30; then he would probably retire to his room, "shut the outer door, take tea, and read till 10 or 11 o'clock." Few, it seems, went to supper in hall. In most colleges, supper was laid on in the Combination Room on Sundays, for the electoral Fellows who had been taking services in their country churches; at King's this convivial meal was known as "Neck or Nothing"; as "the Curates' Club" at St John's; and as "the Apostolic" at Christ's, where the supper was always tripe, dressed in different ways.

While the reverend gentlemen were enjoying their tripe, the undergraduates of Christ's would be having groups of friends to supper in their rooms, and one may be sure that young Frend joined in these "sizing parties". Each guest ordered at his own expense, from the kitchen, whatever he fancied, to be carried to the entertainer's room: "a part of fowl, a part of Apple Pie" and so on. The host supplied bread, butter, cheese, beer, a "beaker" or large tea-pot full of punch which was kept on the hob. (These tea-pots were sometimes enormous, and were supplied by the bed-makers, who charged according to size.) Wine was not allowed, and the parties were almost always well-conducted and cheerful but not rowdy.[2]

Contemporary accounts show that the students—even the most earnest—were by no means overworked, and had plenty of time for enjoyment. William Wordsworth summed up the life of an average student:

> We saunter'd, play'd, we rioted, we talk'd
> Unprofitable talk at morning hours,

[1] *Lives of the Norths*, ii, p. 292.
[2] Gunning: *op. cit.*, i, p. 41.

Drifted about along the streets and walks,
Read lazily in lazy books, went forth
To gallop through the country in blind zeal
Of senseless horsemanship, or on the breast
Of Cam sail'd boisterously; and let the stars
Come out perhaps without one quiet thought . . .[1]

In February 1776 James Tylden wrote to William Frend, that "we have had most excellent scating—I scated down to Ely on Thursday"; neither did they lack for female society; "the Miss M.——s have been with us this fortnight past, rather I believe to endeavour to get Husbands than out of chagrin at their Sister's Marriage—they did not succeed—however they were here very seasonably to keep the animal spirits from freezing this cold weather."[2]

Students also seemed to have plenty of time to beautify themselves for the ladies' benefit, at the hairdressers and barbers of whom there was no shortage in Cambridge. Frend says that "as much pains as were employed by our tutor to furnish the inside, our frizeur should take to adorn the outside of our pates." He adds that "whatever may be said of the degeneracy of the present race in one respect the younkers now at college are far superior to us, who had their rooms before them. They do not look so much like monkies; their countenance bears a manly semblance; they are not, as we were, tortured by a hairdresser, their heads filled with powder and pomatum."[3] A contemporary portrait shows Frend elegantly curled and pomaded. Though not a fop he was certainly a highly presentable young man—but like many, would gladly have dispensed with the expensive and time-consuming friseur.

Such frivolities were put aside however when the day of reckoning came, relentless in the late eighteenth century as it is today. It was rather longer drawn out at that time and

[1] W. Wordsworth: *The Prelude* III, ll. 251–258. (1805 text ed.—E. De Selincourt).

[2] Tylden to W.F., February 1776.

[3] *Universal Magazine*, 1805.

accompanied by a good deal of ritual and pantomime which was swept away by the reformers of the following century.

The Tripos, then as now the final examination, was so called after the three verse poems which had to be read by the candidates (themselves entitled "tripos"); it took place in the early morning of Ash Wednesday, starting with a service at St Mary's church.

The candidates proceeded to the Old Schools, where they took their seats along with "Proctors, Father, Disputants, Tripos, Bachelors, Sophisters and other Scholars." The Senior Proctor called on the Tripos and exhorted him "to be witty but modest withal."

The candidate made his speech; the "senior Brother" replied to it, then the Junior Brother. While the Brothers disputed on the Tripos speech the candidate's verses were handed by the Bedells to the Vice-Chancellor. Eventually the Proctor ended the proceedings "with a word or two in commendation of the Tripos if he deserved it."

Those being examined had to sit in the schools from 1 to 5 p.m. every day except Saturday and Sunday, for a month, to defend their theses against all comers. The speeches of the Tripos and the two Brothers eventually tended to become boisterous and even scurrilous.

Very often, particularly during the time of the younger Pitt, these became violently political, dealing with the Slave Trade, America, troubles in France, and so on. There were similar rituals for the contests of the Wranglers—for high mathematical proficiency—into which Frend entered (and in which he came second), and the awards of prizes and degrees were equally ceremonial.[1]

William Frend was no doubt deeply impressed by the ancient traditions and ceremonies of Cambridge. Only later, when he grievously offended against university protocol, did he become fully aware of the deep-seated prejudices, the profound complacency, and the vested interests of much of Cambridge society; but even as a student he must have

[1] C. Wordsworth: *op. cit.*, pp. 207–222.

realized how the ancient customs and ingrown traditions, the attitudes, residual from the Middle Ages, limited the scope of learning—and how university education was hamstrung by the strict tests demanded by the Alma Mater, and through her authoritarianism deprived of many intelligent and earnest seekers after truth.

William Wordsworth's indictment of the Cambridge he knew ten years later reflects this:

> Feuds, Factions, Flatteries, Enmity and Guile;
> Murmuring Submission and bald Government;
> The Idol weak as the Idolater;
> And decency and custom starving Truth;
> And blind Authority, beating with his Staff
> The Child that might have led him . . .[1]

This is perhaps unduly harsh, and it is unlikely that William Frend (who was a more serious student than Wordsworth, and enjoyed his Cambridge days without the poet's reservations and comparisons with simple country life) felt the university's shortcomings so strongly. He would have been more inclined to endorse Wordsworth's later remarks about Cambridge and an academic life:

> That something there was holden up to view
> Of a Republic where all stood thus far
> Upon equal ground, that they were brothers all
> In honour, as in one community,
> Scholars and Gentlemen, where, further more,
> Distinction lay open to all that came.[2]

There is nothing in Frend's letters to suggest that he resented academic authority; apart from Paley, he knew the dons and professors as learned figureheads, not as symbols of a repressive establishment. He knew that many scholars in

[1] W. Wordsworth: *The Prelude* III, ll. 36–41.
[2] W. Wordsworth: *The Prelude* IX, ll. 228–233.

the ancient universities were like plants in a nursery garden, transplanted at a certain stage to another part of the garden where they took deep root and spent the rest of their lives; but he did not realize the limitations this continuity imposed on university culture. Indeed, if things had turned out differently Frend might have slipped into a don's life and this story would not have been written.

As it was, the academic personalities of Cambridge were known to him, when an undergraduate, by sight as eminent or eccentric figures; when a post-graduate, as colleagues; and later still as either allies or opponents in a battle which split the university into political and religious factions undreamed of before 1780.

As we shall meet some of them again, perhaps we should give them a passing glance here. One with whom Frend was to cross swords was Dr Thomas Kipling, known more for his eccentricity than for his learning, a Fellow of St John's College and editor of various mediocre Latin texts. He became Lady Margaret Professor of Divinity, but was never known to give a lecture. The invaluable writer of Cambridge reminiscences, Henry Gunning, recounted that "he always preserved an immeasurable distance between himself and the undergraduates, and was by no means popular. He used to ride up to the Gogs every day along Hills Road, and once caused the younger members of the university much merriment by picking up an ostrich feather which a famous lady of the town had dropped on purpose to ensnare him. When he caught her up and found that it was the notorious Jemima Watson (who lived in expensive lodgings where she received some of the most fashionable men in the university), his confusion was indescribable."

Kipling appears to have been a thoroughly absurd figure, but also a very malicious and ignorant one. Gunning quarrelled with him on various occasions in the course of Disputations. "I was [he wrote] not a favourite of the Deputy Professor, who took every opportunity of annoying me in my new undertaking . . . I had not forgotten his dislike to the disjunctive syllogism, one or more of which I seldom failed to produce. On one occasion he became so angry that he threatened to give me a *descendus*." Another time, "Kipling became all at once totally inattentive both to me and the Respondent, and the Disputation appeared to be at an end for want of his interference. To my utter astonishment he began with a violent tirade against Gibbon as an enemy to our holy religion . . . I thought the doctor had taken leave of his senses, but, following the direction of his eye, I immediately discovered the cause of this unlooked-for burst of oratory; for he was obviously endeavouring to make an impression on a very fat man . . . in a grey coat with black buttons, who turned out to be the Duke of Norfolk. The Deputy Professor was so exhausted by the premature delivery of . . . his Speech, that the Disputation shortly concluded with his reading his Determination in a voice scarcely audible".[1]

Another very familiar figure in the university whom we must mention here, and shall return to later—for he and Frend were to clash dramatically within a few years of this peaceful period—was Isaac Milner, a Yorkshireman, educated at Whitby Grammar School and Queens' College. Gunning says that "the University perhaps never produced a man of more eminent abilities. It is to be regretted that he did not prosecute his mathematical studies with greater energy . . . " Like other professors Milner was exceedingly lazy about doing anything he did not fancy. He was very large, with a loud voice and a strong personality, could not bear to be thwarted, and would unmercifully browbeat anyone who opposed him.

As an examiner he was in the habit of indulging in jokes at the expense of the unfortunate borderline cases, who, when dissatisfied with their situation had caused him to be called in. Milner's voice was exceptionally loud, and, Gunning says, "combined with a peculiar shrillness, could make itself heard at a considerable distance." He called dull and stupid

[1] Gunning: *op. cit.*, i, p. 49.

men "sooty fellows", and when he had a class of these to examine he would roar out to the Moderators at the other end of the Senate-House, "In rebus fuliginosis [*sic*] versatus sum." * [1]

Milner was a Tory and Establishment man to the backbone; he had, under the influence of his brother Joseph, a Methodist historian, become an Evangelical and as such, detested the unorthodox views of the dissenters in the University; when an undergraduate he had distinguished himself by being the only one of his year to refuse to sign a petition against compulsory subscription to the Thirty-nine Articles by B.A.s. If he took up this position as a very young man on a question which most enlightened people were at least prepared to consider, how much more extreme would he become when he really thought the Church was in danger? A few years were to show.

Milner's attitude was not typical of eighteenth-century Cambridge, which was politically Whig, and traditionally less conformist than Oxford (which declared itself unashamedly *plus royaliste que le roi*) perhaps owing to Cambridge's leaning to mathematics and the natural sciences. Since the days of Erasmus and of Bacon, a long line of independent-minded men, including characters like Dr Thomas Edwards, and Dr John Jebb, in the late eighteenth century, had kept alive the tradition of free enquiry in spite of a heavy weight of conformism and orthodoxy.

During William Frend's student years there were no burning causes for controversy, and dons, professors, graduates and undergraduates co-existed, with occasional differences at administrative level over University appointments, statutes, points of scholarship, but in spite of sometimes disastrously opposing ideas and temperaments, placidly enough.

* Trans.: "I am well-versed in sooty things."

[1] Gunning: *op. cit.*, i, p. 83.

3
FELLOW OF JESUS COLLEGE

William Frend's three years at Christ's College passed peacefully and profitably; he won the prize of Second Wrangler for his year, became ordained by the Bishop of Ely, and applied to Jesus College for a Fellowship which he obtained thanks to his good record and to the recommendation of Dr Paley. A little later he was elected to the post of Tutor—a pleasant, well-paid and responsible job.

It was one which suited William admirably, and in which he saw himself spending a long, studious, useful—if not wildly exciting—life-time. He had been offered, in 1781, the post of tutor to the young son of Archduke Alexander of Russia, with a salary of £2,000 a year (a fantastic sum in those days for a man of twenty-four), "a suitable establishment", and a retiring pension of £800 a year for life. The Archduke had applied to Christ's College for a suitable candidate—someone scholarly, reliable, able to teach the ducal offspring maths, Greek, logic and other gentlemanly subjects. Frend's name was suggested by the authorities as eminently suitable, but he refused the post; he was happy at Cambridge, he had set his heart on taking orders, and he knew that however tempting the offer he did not want to devote himself to the education of one rich young man. Youthful as he was, he was determined to give the best of his talents to the service of his fellow men and women—at this stage, through the Church.

Having declined the Archduke's offer, Frend turned his attention to the minds of the Jesus College undergraduates, and to the souls of the Cambridgeshire countryfolk. He had two parishes to look after. The most important was Long Stanton, some ten miles north-west of Cambridge, a remote, lengthy, ribbon-built village lying lost in the flattest of reclaimed fenland.

The pretty Early English church stood—and still stands—on a rise, backed by the graceful trees, and as you look out of the church porch, the great spread of west Cambridgeshire stretches away from your feet, field after field of dark earth, grey stubble, green pasture, with an occasional bonfire sending up wisps of smoke, a lonely spire marking the odd fenland village in the distance.

William was "collated" to All Saints on 22 December 1783 (he was already authorized to serve as Registrar at Madingley) and in April '84 "read himself in". He took early service every Sunday morning, riding over from Cambridge while most of his colleagues were still asleep. He loved the church with its carved roof, its handsome hexagonal font and its splendid alabaster monument to the Hatton family; but it seems that he did not spend a great deal of time there, for the register of weddings, baptisms and funerals during his term of office is signed throughout by the curate (no doubt as poor, overworked and underpaid as most curates of those days). William's main interest lay in his second parish, and as soon as the service was over he mounted his horse to ride across country to Madingley, seven miles away beyond the Huntingdon Road. He arrived there in time to take the village Sunday school, which he and Miss Cotton, daughter of the Lord of the Manor, had initiated for the benefit of the Madingley children. It was the first of its kind in the area, and was an outlet for Frend's passion for education in all its aspects which was to continue all his life.

Many years later he described this Sunday school to Lady Byron, who was nearly as interested as he was in "the principle of giving instruction to the poor."

"I formed a school in a parish which supplied I think between 30 & 40 children, and my helpmate in the business was Miss Cotton . . . The children on their first entering the school were as ignorant as you cd well conceive them to be. The best of them could hardly read a sentence. However, we made a class of the best, and soon brought them to read a chapter in the Testament much better than most of the clergy; for the rest we distributed them in classes, and after teaching them their letters, they were for a time kept in short sentences, and then introduced to Watts' hymns for children.

"First they got a stanza, then a whole hymn; and miserable & wretched hand as I was at music, with a hand-organ on which I had some psalm tunes, and my miserable flute, and the still less knowledge of the blacksmith, our children in no gt length of time became such adepts in singing, that not only their parents came early to church and stayed after the service to hear them, but people came from the adjoining parishes to witness their improvement. The parish church had pews on each side, and between them was sufficient space for the boys to sit on one form, and the girls on the opposite, and there was space between for 3 or 4 persons to walk abreast. The psalmody of the church was wretched before the institution of the Sunday-school, being confined almost entirely to the clerk, assisted occasionally by the baronet; but so wretched work they made of it, that scarcely anyone was induced to join them . . .

"But the face of things was altered entirely by the children . . . they came to church at eleven and in the interval between their arrival and the beginning of the service they sang some of Watts' hymns and this they did at the conclusion of the service.

"There was no fear of absence in any of them, for not one could be persuaded to keep away but for some very urgent reason.

"I used to get to the school at 9 o'clock in the morning; Miss Cotton came, I think, at 10. In the afternoon Miss C. went at 4 and I went at 5, and the school broke up at 6.

"Our cleverest girl, from her over-spriteliness, broke in upon the discipline of the school, and her punishment was to stay away.

"Of course she did not appear at her usual place at church the next Sunday, but we were obliged to take her in the

Sunday after, as she was in danger of crying herself to death. We used in our school the common little books for reading, and some little books of the history of the Bible, with questions at the end of each lesson, which I made for this purpose; and the upper classes always read some portions of the Bible or Testament, on which they were questioned in succession, answers not being put into their mouths; but they were encouraged to think of what they read."[1]

We learn more about the Sunday school in Frend's letters to his half-sister Mary, a delicate girl of eighteen, living at home in Canterbury. He asks her to keep up her Bible reading and to put it to good use by adapting stories from the Old Testament for the edification of the Madingley children. It would, he thinks, "be a pleasing exercise to yourself to assist me . . . a great weight will be taken off my shoulders & you will have nothing but amusement.

"Could you not take your pen now & then in hand & after reading over the stories of Jacob and Joseph draw them in a few short and easy & familiar lessons for children about twelve years old? It will not fatigue you much if you will undertake it & you cannot imagine what service you will render me . . . "

He also asks her for help with needlework for the children, who he thinks should all have a school uniform: "Betsy has begg'd the favour of you in my name to get the caps, bibs & aprons as before but not worked and to pack up instructions on the nature of their manufacture, or I may perhaps run into some blunders."

Mary's reaction to the request for stories was negative: "The subject . . . seems so much beyond my capacity, so entirely out of my reach", she answers, "that I never for a moment entertain'd an idea of being able to put your plan into execution, you can do nothing now my dear Br but give me up as a stupid girl of whom you can make nothing and whose knowledge is confin'd to the meer ABC of her sex."

As to the wardrobe, she agrees to help with that, and

[1] W.F. to Lady Annabella Byron. (A.B.), Lovelace Papers, 20.9.1818.

writes that she has bought (with the guinea and a half which he sent her) "seven shifts, caps, aprons and handkerchiefs, with the materials to make them, and I ashure you thought myself a good market woman, as the cloth met with the approbation of my mother and sisters, I hope it will with yours . . . I cut out all by guess . . . tho' I am not passionately fond of cutting out, yet I ashure you, I took great pleasure in doing these, and it will be doubled if you say I have pleased you in it."

The Sunday school, the double duty in his parishes, and his teaching in the College took up most of Frend's time. On 24 April 1784 he excuses himself for not writing to Mary oftener: "My necessary occupations must take up a great portion of my attention—at present I am engag'd in three kinds of business all relating to the head & to myself of seemingly great importance."

However, he managed to relax occasionally. He describes a ball:

"We danced till 4 o'clock in the morning, every person in good spirits, everyone pleased & everyone wishing to see his neighbour in good humour." And another letter describes a jaunt up the river with friends, "taking the opportunity of a day's intermission of Lectures." He writes (June 1784) with rather heavy irony: " . . . To me who does not accustom himself to any excessive labour or to the earliest rising, you may imagine how very pleasant it must be to labour at the oar for ten or twelve hours & with additional exercise to be indulged with only half of his usual rest. This was my case at five on Wednesday evening. We went on the water, continued there six hours, entertain'd with the conversation of Bargemen . . . returning at five o'clock the next morning . . . I am but just recovered from my jaunt."

Then there were the University's end-of-the-year festivities, into which he threw himself with gusto: "You may have an idea of the agreeable manner of spending our time to a quiet Fellow of a College when I tell you that every day has given me some amusement chiefly at Musick and mix'd

Parties. We had three Concerts and a Ball, two private Musical Parties, Musick in the Church & as an exercise at Promenades every evening upon a Common where there are temporary Booths for the Fair . . . I am now heartily tired & wish for repose yet at the moment the cloth is laid in my rooms & I expect a party to dinner." On 7 July he wrote: "The Company began to separate yesterday & in a few days scarce a solitary Gownsman will be left in the streets;" adding that he had been in the Senate House the previous day (Degree Day ceremony, no doubt) and had perceived some of his relations, the Salt family, from London, in the crowd.

Frend's letters of this period abound with references to shadowy cousins, and more solid sisters and brothers. The Frend family were close knit, and took great interest in each other's doings. George, the elder brother, who went into the family wine business, wrote from time to time in a rumbustious style very unlike William's own:

"Well, do you fag pretty smartly, driving post for a Bishoprik I suppose, whip & spur, these sleeves and large wig put all you young cushion thumpers upon your metal, success attend you my lad. We are all upon the same scent, independence is what we aim at . . ."

Occasionally, George travelled on business to Portugal, and in a letter of 1779 described his journey: meeting a foreign frigate at sea, "ships were soon clear'd, guns ready, matches lighted & the devil to pay. Poor Marianne, [his wife], bore all like a heroine till the Surgeon began to prepare his instruments & talk'd of a removal to the Cock pit. I was to use a delicate expression between a sh-t & a Sweat but up I march'd upon Deck . . ." However, the strange ship turned out to be "a large Dutchman with a Van Trump upon his rudder almost as big as Bell Harry" and George reached Portugal unscathed.[1] Later, George's letters to his younger brother concerned family business, and expressions of disapproval at William's politics. At this time,

[1] George Frend to W.F., 23.2.79.

the main topics of the family's correspondence were their health and social activities. Frend's letters to Mary offer her much good advice on everything from spelling to clothes, from how to manage her money to how to handle her admirers. Mary responded very well, accepting his counsel in a mock humble vein: "How good you are—I think it is the most disagreeable thing in the world to find fault . . . How much ought I not then to be obliged to those people who will condescend to tell me of mine . . ."

When she described her meeting with a German Baron, William wrote back (24 April 1784), "I imagine the Baron has already thrown himself at your feet & in broken accents declar'd his tender passion. Perhaps he has attained the happy answer and my sister is now the Baronne de Einzenvanschillenhellerdlingdorff . . . Joking apart, German Barons are as common as Country Squires, poorer & prouder in general, every sharper takes up this title when he is on his travels. Yours may not be a counterfeit but . . . I shd be apt to pay very little regard to his pretensions. In your next pray give me some further account of this gentleman for a German Baron on his travels, pretending to some principality, has just tricked a friend of mine out of 12 thousand pounds."

When in May that year Mary set out for the London season, Frend showed himself much concerned: Where should she stay? "I wish you were going to a house more adapted to your purpose . . . " than the "dreary lane in which Mr Salt resides"; what should she see and do? "You will of course see the usual resorts of company and entertainment . . . You will be carried to the play houses"; rather than go to the Pitt "go seldomer and go into the Boxes." At the Opera "You will find very genteel company and it is the proper place, by all means go there."

He asked Mary to send him details of her sightseeing: "Have you been to Kensington gardens? The walk in them is very pleasant . . . take a view of the Old Garden, it is kept in very good order and will enable you to form an idea of the superiority of the present taste over that of the last century." To which Mary replied (2 May) that she had indeed visited the gardens: "the place was so crowded with company I was quite enchanted with it; the ladies all dressed so elegantly—one scarcely saw a plain woman in the Garden." It was all much more sophisticated than Canterbury: "I am sure Paint is a great addition to the face—everybody here looks handsome, and I am told that allmost everybody uses art of some kind or another." She thought *The Careless Husband* "a frightful play & I was heartily glad when it was over", but was greatly edified "by seeing Kemble perform the part of Cato—there is not a sentiment in that but must improve every one who hears it."

Frend sent Mary tickets for "the Great Handel Commemoration Concert" and wrote of his great anxiety "at not hearing from you within a few days after the first performance in honour of Handel."

William evidently wanted his sister to make the most of her London season, but was very anxious that she should not be swept off her feet by all the fashionable finery around her. He gave qualified approval to her being "at the Drawing Room"—"to a person not us'd to such sights the view of the first Nobility in their best looks & best dresses is very brilliant & to one who also can moralize what numberless thoughts must occur on beholding the trappings & tinsels of a court?"

The poor weaver, he reminded her, deserved far more credit than the wealthy Duchess "with a feather on her head" who was wearing the so much admired creation! Whether Mary could "moralize" is doubtful, but it is certain that William was a master of the art, perhaps particularly at this time, when he was composing a couple of sermons every week. Yet though his moralizing was long-winded and sometimes dreadfully boring, he often had his tongue in his cheek, and was not intentionally a spoilsport. On the contrary, we find him congratulating his sister "on having made very good use of your time" and being acquainted "with the best places about & in town."—"I agree with you intirely in preferring Ranelagh to Vauxhall", says he, "though the former is nothing but an eternal circle of company following one another's tails like so many blind asses in a Mill"; but he owns that "I begin to find myself a very incompetent judge of fashionable scenes & have scarce a desire to be present at them."

It is clear from the letters that followed that William was becoming concerned with less frivolous matters. In 1785 he was writing to Mary about questions of history and books, of religion, and above all of education—the subject nearest his heart, which was stimulated at this period by his practical experiences of teaching young men in college, and of the Madingley Sunday school.

He gave Mary good advice about her reading, warning her off novels and recommending alarmingly heavy history books—Rollin and Bossuet being, he decided, particularly suited to her needs—and methods of self-education, such as "reading an hour a day with Jane", thus "gathering sufficient material for reflection & conversation for the whole day."[1]

Poor Mary who was not physically strong tried to act on his advice, but confessed in a letter in December, that "I have not persever'd in my historical reading, either the Bible or Rollin . . . Jane's absence from Cant'y for seven weeks oblig'd me to lay aside a study I thought myself so fond of, and on her return the coldness of the weather would not permit us to rise as we used to do to read an hour before breakfast." She hopes that when William next comes to Canterbury he will take her studies in hand, which "will go on so well guided by your presence as to fully compensate for our idleness in the winter, but I fear we are both of us too old to make any very surprising progress. Jane's birthday was last Thursday, when she was, Oh mercy, twenty years old. Mine is next month and I am one year younger. She, you know, has a lover & other things to think of, but for my

[1] W.F. to Mary Frend, 13.11.85.

own part I am shock'd at finding myself so old and knowing so little."

* * *

The correspondence of these years shows us one side of William Frend: the solicitous brother, anxious about his sister's physical, spiritual and cultural welfare, striving to improve her mind, taking an incidental interest in trivial social and domestic happenings, while conscientiously and contentedly pursuing his own work. The other side—the independent outspoken searcher after truth—emerges later, in the stress of political and religious struggles. As yet he had not become involved in the wider issues which were to rouse his social conscience and upset his quiet life.

Like other open-minded academics he knew that the Dissenters laboured under unjust restrictions, and that Parliamentary Reform was a crying need; Major Cartwright's 1780 Reform Campaign had stirred the surface of life even in Cambridge, and Dr Jebb's resignation from the university, when his "Grace" to relax the restrictions on Dissenters was rejected in 1774, provided food for thought.

But many of Frend's colleagues had high hopes of the young William Pitt, to whom Nonconformists and Reformers alike had rallied during the General Election of 1784, in view of his record of support for reform, and of his strong words in Parliament on the prevalent corrupt royal influence. It was thought that Pitt might bring in a bill to repeal the Test Acts, and there was widespread discussion on this up and down the country not excluding Cambridge.

Whether Frend joined in the debate is doubtful—up to 1786 his letters betray little interest in political controversy; but it is clear that the talk around him of religious freedom, and of different forms of worship, started him thinking about things that he had hitherto taken for granted, and looking afresh at his faith.

While not questioning the basic tenets of Christianity he

began to wonder whether the priesthood, the rites, the compulsory subscription to the Articles, were really necessary to the practice of Christ's teaching, and whether the dogma and rules evolved by the Church were justified in every case by the gospels. Doubts even arose in his mind as to the worship of the Trinity.

Frend was experiencing the same qualms as other churchmen of different denominations of the period. Since the early eighteenth century anti-Trinitarianism had been an issue among Presbyterian, Independent and Baptist ministers—though rarely among Church of England men like Frend. By the 1780's some Baptist and most Independent congregations had become firmly Trinitarian and Methodist; many joined John Wesley, who was still at 83 years old extremely active and had in 1784 founded the Methodist Conference and Church; some followed the calvinistic Whitefield and Selina Countess of Huntingdon (though the harsh doctrine of pre-destination had less popular appeal than the Wesleyan call "repent-and-ye-shall-be-saved").

By 1786 two new movements were attracting the discontented followers of both establishment and nonconformist churches: one was the "new methodists" campaign, led by Joseph Milner and later by his younger brother Isaac and William Wilberforce. (In 1785 Isaac Milner converted Wilberforce while on a continental tour. On one occasion their carriage was "in danger of instant destruction on the very brink of a precipice"; they "were saved by the timely exertions of Mr Milner" and they firmly believed by the intervention of the Deity.) [1]

These evangelicals believed in spiritual "reform" through the conversion of the rich and powerful, and were politically conservative. The other movement, which attracted many Baptists and most Presbyterians, was the Unitarian movement, radical and independent, inaugurated by Theophilus Lindsey, a former orthodox clergyman, who opened his chapel in Essex Street off the Strand in London in 1774. Dr

[1] Mary Milner: *Life of Isaac Milner*, p. 25.

Joseph Priestley, the eminent chemist and discoverer of oxygen, provided the dynamism in pamphlets and sermons preaching the goodness of God to man, the human nature of Jesus, and the use of reason in religion.

At a time when atheism, or even deism, was rare—thinkers such as Thelwall and Holcroft who had come under the influence of the French *encyclopédistes* being very exceptional—many serious men turned to the most rational religion available, one which rejected dogma and doctrine. As later Unitarians wrote, "We are convinced that no doctrines can ultimately prevail among a people allowed to think and examine for themselves," and "Our faith is rational."[1]

Unitarianism rejected the mystery of the Three-In-One, of Original Sin and of Atonement. It denied too that eternal salvation was dependent upon correctness of belief—man must be free to speculate without fear of punishment, and an all-loving God would admit all souls to Heaven.

It was a simple optimistic faith which required man to use his reason in relation to scriptural authority. This is what William Frend was seeking, although at this stage it was an unformulated need.

Frend only knew that he had doubts about dogma and doctrine; and being a person of strong purpose, not content with half measures, he determined to see for himself whether the Bible, the foundation of his religion, affirmed church dogma and doctrine—whether, in particular, it demanded the worship of three persons in one God.

He already knew some Hebrew, but he applied himself to studying it seriously so as to read the Holy Books in the original. He spent a vacation living with a Jewish family in London to learn the language and this led to a lifelong interest in Jewish history and culture, and to friendship with distinguished Jews such as the economist David Ricardo, Eli Lindo, and many more.

In general, Frend's conscience was a good enough guide

[1] c.f. F. E. Mineka: *The Dissidence of Dissent.*

for his belief; but these thorny and complicated theological questions could not be answered by his own inner voice. He needed guidance, and obtained it gradually, through reading and through discussion with friends who had been in the Church and left it to become Dissenters.

Frend himself was not ready for such an irrevocable step; in the summer of 1786 his ideas were in a state of flux, and he needed above everything a rest from his problems, right away from Cambridge. He decided to go off as soon as occasion arose with a couple of good companions for a tour of the continent and a complete change of scene and ideas.

* * *

Happily for Frend, James Six and Will Tylden, his former schoolmates, were planning a journey to Italy via Paris and Switzerland that summer, and invited him to join them. He willingly accepted and they set off, well equipped with guide books, maps and "a Book of Botany"—and accompanied by William's little dog Dash—in mid-June; they crossed from Dover to Calais, in three and a half painful hours ("luckily very short") and took the diligence to Paris where they spent two days sightseeing and improving their minds. Having seen the gardens and museums, been to the theatre and to "the variétés amusantes", heard lectures on Botany and on Chymistry, as well as "disputations in Theology", they set out on foot eastwards across France.

They walked through Rheims, Chalons, Nancy—"superior to any city I have seen"—carrying their eight and twenty packets done up in bundles slung on sticks over their shoulders, "Dash frisking about us delighted with the new mode of travelling."

Occasionally they rode in covered carriages, but preferred to trudge through the countryside: "The smell of the new made hay, the contented happy looks of the country people . . . the wide extended fields with the promises of a golden harvest, the sides of the hills cover'd with vines, the delightful banks of the rivers, everything presented itself in its best colours to soften the fatigue of our march."

They walked through the pass into Alsace by Saverne (which Frend found "surpasses everything almost that I have seen. Had it but the sea of the Isle of Wight as it is seen six miles from Portsmouth, it would defy the powers of description"); they stayed a night in Strasburg, then walked to Basel, through "the richest and best cultivated country I ever set my eyes on ... a perfect garden", taking the opportunity to visit the Roman Baths at Baden, "in which Six and I were very comfortably parboil'd."

Other letters describe their walk to Constanze, and their exciting adventures in the high Alps where Tylden had a miraculous escape after falling into a crevasse.

Frend reveals his late eighteenth-century penchant for the sublime and aweful, particularly when describing the walk from Geneva to Chamonix where "frequent waterfalls were our entertainment, and Mont Blanc in the background gave a majesty to the scenery ... The mixture of Cornfields and Ice in the middle of Summer, the amazing height of Mont Blanc contrasted with the verdure of the opposite mountains ... form a picture incapable of description."[1]

At the foot of Mont Blanc the friends separated. Six and Tylden went on towards Rome,[2] while William "measured his steps back to Geneva with faithful Dash." On the way to the Grande Chartreuse, Dash strayed and was never seen again. William, desolated at his loss, found consolation in the hospitality of "many venerable fathers totally abstracted from worldly cares & yet full of civility and attention to strangers." He completed his journey from Lyons by water to Chalon, thence by diligence to Sens and by boat to Paris. From there he wrote to Mary, "the diligence will carry me to Lille in three days & three more will bring me to Calais," where he proposed to stay till he could be sure of a smooth

[1] W.F. to Mary Frend, Summer 1786.

[2] Young James Six caught a fever and died in Rome in December 1786.

crossing. For (recalling his previous ordeal) "I shall certainly not imbark in a storm."

He landed at Dover at the end of August, much invigorated by the ten-week holiday, ready to face his problems afresh, and well able, he felt, to resolve them.

But it was not going to be so easy.

4
DOUBTS AND DECISIONS

BEFORE RETURNING TO Cambridge William went to stay at Canterbury. He was restless however, could not settle down, and cut his visit home short, admitting later in a note to Mary that he "had been mistaken to leave my friends in a blustering stormy night & to exchange a College for the comfort of a family." If he had stayed longer under her good management, he said, he would not now be punished by confinement to his room. He was turbulent, and after his recent long walks "as unwilling as a headstrong freshman to be brought under the discipline of a College."

"From my inability to walk as in Switzerland", he writes, "& the glove perpetually on my hand you would suppose that the gout had attacked me . . . But do not be alarmed at the mention of an enemy I dread as much as any under the sun." He assures Mary that if temperate living can keep the enemy off "he stands very little chance of lodging his Chalk Balls in my fingers." It was not gout, but simply "a scratch in the heel wh from the awkwardness of the place was subject to continual gallings" which had kept him indoors for above a fortnight.

He expressed much concern over Mary's own health which had not been at all good. "I was sorry to find that you still remained an invalid—every morning when I took up my usual book of amusement brought you to my mind & I wished it possible to transport my chair next yours, that as we neither of us shd be ambitious of sallying forth with the noonday walkers I might have the pleasure of reading an excellent author to you, & hearing your remarks . . . Betsy naturally supposed that I should soon be reconciled to my winter life—it is well that I had paid a visit to the Chartreuse & contracted a more than ordinary desire for solitude." But, comparing his employment with that of the monks, William decided: "Mine, I think, if not as useful is capable of affording equal amusement."

The truth was that neither amusement nor solitude were what William Frend required for his peace of mind at this juncture. He did not realize that he was on the brink of a great change in his life, but a few weeks after writing that letter he was to take a decision which would make him in many senses a quite different person.

In the autumn term of 1786 then, he resumed his duties as tutor and had among his pupils at Jesus College three particularly bright freshmen—Richard Malthus, Edward Clarke and William Otter (of whom more in a later chapter). He took his part in the life of the college, meticulously carrying out the financial and social tasks that his tutorship entailed.

He still had his parishes to look after, and rode out every Sunday, enjoying the wind whistling past his ears along the Huntingdon Road and the wide views over the open fields on either side, till he turned into the lanes leading to his churches—right to Long Stanton, left to Madingley. Frend loved this village with its tall elms harbouring colonies of rooks that cawed above the cottages and the little church; he felt at home equally with the villagers and with the Lord of the Manor, Sir John Cotton, who lived in the great hall in the park. Sir John often invited William to dinner, and his daughter helped devotedly with the Sunday school. On his return to Madingley that autumn, Frend wrote to Mary that "My little parish at M. was of more consequence to me than Versailles, and the pleasure of revisiting it was in no small degree increased from the care Miss Cotton had taken of the little flock in my absence."

But although he was outwardly placidly engaged on his day-to-day tasks, Frend was at this time increasingly beset by doubts.

He put in more hours at Hebrew, delving down to the source of Biblical teaching; and through his studies he came into close contact with the learned Hebrew scholar Robert Tyrwhitt, also a Fellow of Jesus, but unlike most Cambridge dons of the time a convinced anti-Trinitarian and a firm believer in Unitarianism.

Many years later Frend described Tyrwhitt as "my very excellent friend ... who had with his Fellowship held a small living in the gift of the College; both of these he resigned and lived in College on a very scanty income till by the death of his brother it was increased to an amount far beyond what he required."

Tyrwhitt evidently strongly influenced Frend, who in a reminiscing vein told Lady Byron: "When I was invited to [Jesus] College I naturally from my prepossessions looked on him with no small degree of aversion & our acquaintance was slight till a change in my own opinions took place. Mr T. dined in the common hall & retired with the rest to the Combination room but in no case did he ever bring forward his particular religious opinions. He never went to Chapel or to any church except St Mary's where the liturgy is not used & he preached there when it came to his turn. Two of his sermons are printed & in them his Unitarian sentiments are not disguised ...

"He died universally respected, 'a benefactor to his College & to the University', leaving to the latter four thousand pounds for the promotion of Hebrew literature in any way that the University might determine." [1]

This letter suggests that Frend was well advanced in his new faith when he came to know Tyrwhitt, who confirmed many of his ideas but was not responsible for his disillusion with the Church.

What was it then that caused his spiritual upheaval and conversion? Not the influence of a colleague nor merely his study of theology, but two separate factors: the first, Frend's strong, if still latent, social conscience—he had entered the Church in the genuine belief that here was a vocation, here he could work for the good of mankind. Once within the

[1] W.F. to A.B., 15.11.1835.

Church's fold, he saw around him a contradiction of all he believed to be Christian ethics; first, the structure of the hierarchy—its exceedingly wealthy prelates, its fox-hunting parsons (who, although of course there were exceptions, worked little and tended to drink hard), the absentee incumbents pocketing as much church revenue as they could, leaving their parishes to wretchedly paid curates; the use of printed sermons by the average parson to save himself trouble; the selfishness implied by even his admired teacher Paley, who had remarked that "if there be any principal objection to the life of a clergyman . . . it is this—that it does not supply sufficient engagements to the time and thoughts of an active mind", and had recommended the study of natural history to while away the time.[1]

The unfortunate country curate, in the meantime, served several parishes, hurrying, according to Arthur Young, "through the service in a manner perfectly indecent", striding from the pulpit to his horse, and galloping away as if pursuing a fox, all for a meagre pittance and little hope of preferment.[2]

At the other end of the scale there were the enormously rich who had risen through their connections and who possessed vast lands and influence, and filled incumbencies with their relatives: to name a very few bishops (all but one of them from Cambridge) we find Porteus of Chester and London, Barrington (from Oxford) and Thurlow, of Durham (both brothers of prominent peers), North (who married two heiresses)—all promoted through "connections"; Archbishop Moore of Canterbury (who, according to the D.N.B., "appears to have dispensed his patronage with somewhat more than due regard to the interest of his own family"), William Mansel, who held the two important posts of Master of Trinity and Bishop of Bristol simultaneously, and Richard Watson, Bishop of Llandaff, who outdid them all—

[1] Paley: *Works*, Vol. vi, p. 41.
[2] Young: *Enquiry*, pp. 22–23.

being Professor of Divinity at Cambridge, Archdeacon of Ely, and rector of sixteen parishes at once! [1]

Although this was generally accepted practice it is small wonder that an honest searcher after truth should feel disgusted with the Establishment, so complacent, well heeled and completely divorced from the life of the community it was supposed to serve. Frend must have been disturbed when he became aware of the state of things; and he no doubt agreed with the Cambridge Baptist minister, Robert Robinson's, views on the Established Church, published in 1778: "Consider episcopacy as it affects property—calculate the charge of introducing, supporting, adorning, employing it. It is an enormous tax imposed on industry, to empower a few individuals to sign a few useless papers—to loll in indolence—to riot in luxury—and to defeat, among Lords, what liberal acts for religious liberty are supported by commons."[2]

Another reason for Frend's discontent was the lack of support among the clergy for "liberal acts", and the crying injustices which he saw imposed by the orthodox church on its fellow Christians, the Dissenters, in Cambridge. These were not allowed to become B.A.s unless they subscribed to the Thirty-nine Articles.

If they sought higher education in dissenting academies or with learned men of their own persuasion they were able to become ministers of their Presbyterian, Baptist or other chapels, but depended for their living on the goodwill of their flocks, and were often hounded by the local "high church" people out of their towns and villages. This manifold injustice was perhaps the most potent factor in changing Frend's views.

There were of course many within the Church who were discontented and demanded reform—but for very different reasons than Frend, and not likely to tempt him into their ranks: these, as already mentioned, were the new Methodists, who had supplanted in many communities the Wesleyan

[1] Brown: *Fathers of the Victorians*, p. 40.

[2] George Dyer: *Life of Robinson*, pp. 160–161.

(calvinistic) Methodists and were particularly thriving in Cambridge, under the leadership of Isaac Milner. At the time when Frend was assailed by misgivings, the Rev. Henry Venn wrote: "Indeed there is a pleasant prospect at Cambridge . . . Isaac Milner kept an act in the schools . . . on justification by *faith* only. The pit could not contain the masters of arts, and a greater number there was of students than has been seen there for years."

He added, " . . . the three first mathematicians in the university confessedly, Milner, Coulthurst and Farish, are all on the side of the truth."[1]

These hard-headed mathematicians might have been expected to have looked, as Frend did, at the stark facts of the situation: the glaring discrepancy between rich and poor, the harsh fate of the conscientious objectors, the need for political, ecclesiastical and social reform; but they preferred to ignore these aspects of "the truth", and raise the banner of evangelical reform—the moral elevation of the populace, through soul-saving exhortation, led by the powerful and rich. Wholly supporting the *status quo* they were the bitterest enemies of parliamentary reform, or of any kind of popular protest.

So, though professing discontent with the "high church" whom they accused not without reason of being unreligious or not serious christians, they still more disliked dissenters or anyone who believed in the need for political or social action to set the world right.

This in itself was a political attitude; and it is no wonder that when Frend became a radical activist he found himself in direct conflict with the "methodist" leader, Milner—though there is a certain irony that both should have reached their extreme positions from the same starting point: the students' bench in the mathematics school of the orthodox Whig university of Cambridge.

* * *

[1] Brown: *op. cit.*, p. 289.

Frend spent many weeks in mental strife. It was early in 1787 that he decided on the first step: "When my scruples had taken some hold on my mind", he says, "I made Miss Cotton, eldest daughter of Sir J. H. Cotton, acquainted with them. This was in the spring of the year and at her request I kept them private for about three months & then she mention'd the subject to her father.

"It was then agreed that I should put in a Curate till Michaelmas at which time I might if I persisted in my intention of quitting the Church tender my resignation to the Bishop; Michaelmas came & I gave in my resignation, receiving in return a very affectionate letter from him."[1]

The Bishop of Ely's letter survives, and is indeed very kind:

> July 18, 1787: I am sorry that for any reason short of your honest emolument you find it necessary to relinquish a preferment agreeable and creditable to you. Your Patron and Diocesan have much approved your active zeal in the situation and trust.
>
> You are the best judge for yourself of the motives on which you proceed: and an honest though erroneous conscience will at last be rewarded.
>
> I very much wish it had been in my power to quiet or soften those prejudices which seem to me to hazard present inconveniences. But no, I am a stranger to them [and] I can only recommend you in my prayers to the protection of an all-knowing and gracious Providence and subscribe myself very sincerely your faithful and humble servant
>
> James Ely.

Frend's change of outlook was, as *The Gentleman's Magazine* later remarked, "of course fatal to his advancement in the Church and in a worldly point of view destructive of all his fair prospects in life; but in this as on every other occasion,

[1] W.F. to A.B., 15.11.1835.

Mr Frend acted with his accustomed decision—he never hesitated."

"He publicly avowed the change of his opinions, painful as it must have been to him who knew that . . . he not only exposed himself to much misrepresentation and obloquy, but also risked severing those ties which bound him to affectionate relatives and friends." Happily this did not take place; "though my father felt severely the disappointment of his expectations when my prospects of success in life were cut off by the freedom of my opinions, he could never be induced to alter the current of paternal affection."[1]

Having made his decision to leave the Church of England, Frend threw himself with his usual energy into the cause of the Unitarians. He felt strongly the injustice of the university laws which excluded Dissenters from entering for the B.A. degree—a candidate was required to declare that "I am, *bona fide*, a member of the Church of England as by law established," and to "subscribe" to the Thirty-nine Articles.

Frend began that autumn to labour earnestly for the cause of religious freedom at Cambridge, distributing copies of the laws about "subscription", and also notices of a grace that he intended to introduce for the abolition of the said laws at the university.

He did not actually introduce his intended grace; not long after he had begun to work on it a similar grace was introduced on 11 December 1787, by Dr Thomas Edwards ("a learned and liberal-minded man, editor of Plutarch's works, and author of a highly critical essay on Dr Kipling's *Preface to Beza*.")[2]

To quote a contemporary commentator: "The Grace was rejected and no reason assigned for its rejection; nor was any reason urged . . . the only person who attempted a public vindication of that act of mental degradation—subscription—was Dr Kipling, a man who in every literary department in which he has made his appearance has only appeared to

[1] *The Gentleman's Magazine*, April 1841.

[2] Dyer, *op. cit.*, p. 312.

expose his insufficiency and to render himself ridiculous; another person who made himself conspicuous on this occasion was the present Dr Coulthurst, a disciple of St Austin's and Calvin's, then a fellow of Sidney College."[1]

Shortly after the rejection of Dr Edwards' grace, for which Frend had worked as vigorously as for his own, he decided to make a more public disavowal of the Church of England doctrines than he had up till then felt necessary—though his views were clear to all who knew him—and "as I had once given a public sanction to the doctrines of the church, it became me now that I had discovered my errours . . . to disavow them with equal publicity."

He did this in a pamphlet, *Thoughts on Subscription to Religious Tests*, which was published in May 1788. The development of his views can be seen in these pages, written over a period of several weeks, in which he seemed to be making up his mind as to the most effective way of winning supporters.

The beginning of the pamphlet counsels toleration and abolition of subscription by B.A.s, but after twenty-five pages the writer shows himself to be a convinced Unitarian, attacking the Thirty-nine Articles as false and unscriptural. It seems as though, in the course of writing, Frend decided that appeals to toleration could not be expected to carry the day for the cause of religious liberty, and that the time had come for him openly to avow his Unitarianism. This he proceeded to do, all the more passionately for not having spoken out before.[2]

Frend later wrote, "I was still [in Spring 1788] Tutor of the College and might have continued in that office if I had kept my opinions to myself, but a circumstance occurred some time after on which I thought it incumbent on me to avow openly the change of my opinions; this was followed by the loss of the tuition."[3]

[1] Dyer: *op. cit.*, p. 312.
[2] Frothingham: *Thesis*, Ms, p. 31.
[3] Frend: *Sequel to the Proceedings.*

The "circumstance" was, it seems, the publication of his *Thoughts*, accompanied by *A Letter to the Reverend H. W. Coulthurst DD*[1] which was naturally somewhat upsetting to his more orthodox colleagues. However the summer term of 1788 was nearing its end, and no definite steps were taken against him by the authorities. Perhaps they hoped that he would understand the embarrassing position in which he was placing them and voluntarily resign his tutorship? If so they could not have been more mistaken: Frend was determined to spread the truth as he saw it, and lost no opportunity of proclaiming his "heresies" from the housetops.

He spent a good part of the summer vacation of 1788 setting forth his ideas in a pamphlet entitled *An Address to the Inhabitants of Cambridge and its Neighbourhood, exhorting them to turn from the false worship of Three Persons to the worship of the One True God.* This was published on 10 September by a sympathetic printer, Bloom, of St Ives. It was extremely strongly worded, stating categorically that there was only one God, and that "if Jesus Christ be not God, if the Holy Ghost be not God . . . you are guilty of a breach of God's commandments in praying to them." Frend tells his readers: "Be not deceived, Brethren, religion is a personal concern—the Bible is open before you—from thence you are to form your opinions, not from the notions of your Fathers, or the custom of the times."

These words, written when Frend was already under a cloud, were undoubtedly strong meat for the average don to swallow, and it is no wonder that the Master of the College, Dr Beadon, finding Frend intractable, lost little time in arranging for his removal from the office of tutor. The order is dated 27 September 1788.

Frend immediately appealed to the Visitor (the external college arbiter, whose decisions were final) who, as always for Jesus College, was the Bishop of Ely; but as might have been expected the appeal was rejected. It was one thing for

[1] Coulthurst, friend of Milner's, "One of the three first mathematicians in the university.' Brown: *op. cit.*, p. 289.

the Bishop to like him personally and to sympathize with his crises of conscience, but quite another for him to condone the heresies that were being spread by Frend; and the latter's argument against the Master's action—that it was not in Dr Beadon's authority to promote some other Fellow to be tutor over the head of the standing tutor—was not accepted. A sharp little note in the College archives gives the Master permission to assign a new tutor whenever he deems it desirable. It also deputes "J. Plampin and Thomas Newton to have sole care and tuition of all freshmen Commoners" and "forbids such Commoners to put themselves under the tuition of any others than those so appointed."

This was a bitter blow for Frend. He loved teaching, and knew that he taught well. The appointment of Plampin in his place was salt in the wound, for he both disliked this particular colleague and thought him lazy and incompetent. The financial loss (£150) was considerable. However he was still a Fellow of the college and had enough to do in the little community to feel he was not an outcast. He had Robert Tyrwhitt to support him and at least two of the younger Fellows (Whitehead and Warren, for instance) and most of the more thoughtful undergraduates, even if he were cold-shouldered by Plampin and old Costobadie and their friends.

His *Address* brought him a number of like-minded supporters, both in and outside the university—James Lambert and Thomas Jones, both Fellows of Trinity, John Hammond of Queens', and George Dyer the scholar-poet (then teaching in a small school at Grantchester). Dyer, an avowed Unitarian who had been at Christ's Hospital with Charles Lamb, is now remembered chiefly for his eccentricities—though he would have preferred his poetry and pamphlets to survive. He was a prolific writer deeply interested in social questions, and at this time researching into *The Complaints of the Poor People of England*, published in 1791.

Frend's change of ideas had already in 1787 brought him into contact with this new circle of people, and he also discovered a whole range of novel activities, in which the leader was the celebrated nonconformist minister of St Andrew's Baptist Congregation, Cambridge, the Reverend Robert Robinson.

This most remarkable character should have a chapter to himself if space allowed, but a brief sketch must serve. The reader is recommended to go for more details to the *Life* by George Dyer,[1] who at one time lived in Robinson's home as his assistant; this book, which William Wordsworth praised as "the best biography in the English language",[2] gives an excellent picture of the man and his influence on religious and political thinking in Cambridge at that time.

Robert Robinson had in his youth been an ardent disciple of George Whitefield the Calvinist preacher, a regular attender at his Tabernacles and approved by Selina, Countess of Huntingdon.

Being a man of considerable intellect and independence he became critical of the sect's emotional and basically conservative attitude, and turned to a more rational and humane outlook. He founded an independent church in Norwich, had himself baptized by a Baptist minister, and from thenceforth considered himself a Baptist; but his deep interest in social and political questions led him towards the radicalism of the Unitarians and caused him to be deeply suspect to his erstwhile Methodist friends.

At the time Frend came to know him Robinson was the Minister of St Andrew's Baptist Congregation, and lived on an eighty-acre farm down by the river at Chesterton, where he kept cattle, pigs and sheep, grew barley, wheat and peas, and dealt as a corn and coal merchant with barges plying up and down the Cam.

[1] In September 1788 Dyer was also completing an Inquiry into the Nature of Subscription to the 39 Articles and wrote to a friend "I have drop'd my school at present & I devote myself entirely to this business." The Inquiry came out in 1789. (Letter to M. Edwards, Dissenting Minister, Northampton, in Bodleian Library, Montagu Mss.)

[2] Schneider: *op. cit.*, p. 150.

He had twelve children of his own and an adopted family of countless parishioners who brought him their social and spiritual problems to solve. He was deeply religious, with a refreshing tendency to disregard points of doctrine in favour of general truths, which brought him to cross swords with various Unitarian dogmatists. Dyer considered that Robinson's later discussions with William Frend, who had very clear-cut views on these things, "tended probably to confirm his convictions . . . and to incline him to adopt a more decided tone as to doctrines, in his public discourses; though he remained till the last, rather a friend to liberty, than to precision of religious sentiment or to strict theological language."[1]

Robinson was an indefatigable writer and an eloquent preacher. He possessed enormous energy; when engaged on a book he would rise at 3 a.m. to write, otherwise he would be up at 4, and out supervising his large and flourishing farm in every detail. His journal for 26 May 1784 records that from the time he "rang the great bell and roused the girls to milking" he did not pause in his round of inspection and ordering, with many a turn at pumping, whip-cording and picking thrown in, till the evening meeting when he preached on the text "the end of all things is at hand, be ye sober and watch unto prayer."

Before Robinson settled down as Minister of St Andrew's he travelled tirelessly about the country around Cambridge, preaching in the villages—in paddocks or orchards in summer, and in barns or dwellings in less clement seasons. When he went to Abingdon and Oxford in 1780 he had "preached to such multitudes . . . that he got violent colds. He accordingly assumed a less saintly garb, disguising himself in light clothes—white stockings—scratch wig—round beaver hat—band and buckle . . . No one could lay aside the manners of the priest with greater facility and address."[2]

In the early days of the new Meeting House at Cambridge

[1] Dyer: *op. cit.*, pp. 209–212.
[2] *Ibid.*, p. 198.

there had been a good deal of trouble at the services, caused by rowdy undergraduates who treated a morning listening to the famous preacher as "a pleasant lounge", interrupting the prayers and annoying the ladies.

The parishioners sent a letter drawing the students' behaviour to the attention of their tutor, Dr Farmer of Emmanuel. "Would you imagine, sir," they wrote, "that we scarcely ever meet without interruptions from the undergraduates; that every agreeable female in the society is exposed to the same insults as in a bawdy-house; no pew privileged from a bold intrusion; no family from insolent affronts? Is it credible that prostitutes should parade our ailes in academic habits? An unforeseen accident discovered the sex of such a one but a fortnight ago . . . " One of the visiting preachers had protested he had never seen "such heathenish impiety during divine service as in the Cambridge undergraduates."

Robinson himself took a strong line. After interruptions by two particularly obnoxious students of Emmanuel College, he insisted to the Vice-Chancellor, who was also Master of that College, that the culprits must pay the fine of £50 settled by an act of the legislature (one of the few legal protections allowed to dissenters) or ask pardon in the public papers. "The latter course was preferred", Dyer tells us. And there the matter rested. Peace and order were restored to St Andrew's.[1]

In politics Robinson was an unashamed radical, publicly and energetically defending the causes he believed in. He aired his views about parliamentary reform in a "Catechism" published in 1782 and later denounced by Burke as a dangerous piece of sedition, which gave its readers many home truths about corruption and trafficking in seats, and exposed the "canvassing, carousing, intoxication, bribery, perjury and all the usual attendants on a modern election."

He had been the prime mover in the formation of the Cambridge Constitutional Information Society, whose

[1] Dyer: *op. cit.*, pp. 71–74.

objects (wide measures of Reform) were the same as those of a similar society in London founded in 1782 by Dr Jebb, Major Cartwright and Capell Lofft, who sent Robinson a copy of their "address" as a model. At a meeting held by this Society "to celebrate the revolution of 1688" the Mayor and many local worthies were present and "they wound up and confirmed my sermons, by good revolutional songs", says Robinson. The society grew from a few dissenters "into a very large body of freeholders of liberal sentiments", and acquired for the dissenters of the Cambridge district "a great respectability because a great political weight." The society's more active members met once a quarter at an inn, and dined together, after which Robinson would "preach civil and religious liberty, and often when tea comes, theology —*not points*, but general, and, I judge, useful truths."[1]

Likewise in 1788, at the time of the widespread agitation against the slave trade, Robinson was the moving spirit in Cambridge, preaching, writing, and drawing up a petition about it which was the first in the country to be presented to the House of Commons. He made sure that the Right Honourable Members were left in no doubt about the feelings of the Cambridge petitioners, who among other things declared they "could not help observing with sorrow, that a slave trade is a dishonour to humanity, a disgrace to our national character, utterly inconsistent with the sound policy of commercial states, and a perpetual scandal to the profession of Christianity."[2]

By getting to know Robinson in 1787, Frend was inevitably drawn into the vortex of all this activity. The two men evidently took to each other: Frend "became a pretty constant attendant at Robinson's meeting", Dyer tells us, and through the Minister's good offices Frend established "a theological lecture at a private house in the town, and occasionally delivered expository discourses at Fen Stanton in a room belonging to John Curwan . . . a very worthy

[1] Dyer: *op. cit.*, p. 194.
[2] *Ibid.*, pp. 195–196.

dissenting minister, an old acquaintance of Robinson's who had lately embraced the doctrine of the unitarians."[1]

Frend was attracted to Robinson as much by mutual scholarly interests as by dissenting politics. The minister was working on a history of Baptism, a very comprehensive and erudite volume for which he needed access to learned books not only in English, Greek and Latin, but also in Italian, Spanish, Portuguese and German, all of which he learned for the purpose of covering the vast reaches of his subject.

To Frend, besides one or two other scholars, Robinson was indebted for the free use of books in the public (i.e. University) library which much facilitated his literary inquiries, and enabled him to complete his two elaborate histories. His journal describes a learned party in Jesus College, on 8 October 1788:

"Lords Day. After service, Frend, Barham, Paulus, Dyer . . . and myself drank tea with the venerable Dr Tyrwhitt. He is the grandson of Gibson, bishop of London, and stood full in the path of preferment; but conscience forbad; he resigned all, even his fellowship and now lives in college, as in a hotel, a tranquil life of literary labour and universal benevolence. Here I procured a Manuscript which Mr Frend had taken out of the public library for me. We supped at Chesterton, every hour receiving some new information."

The next day he spent examining "an ancient ms of the New Testament of Wickliffe, lent me that morning by Mr Frend, out of the cabinet of Jesus Library."

Tyrwhitt and Frend both helped Robinson in "pointing out many scarce and valuable books, both manuscripts as well as printed volumes, in the public library." And after the worthy minister's death in 1790, Frend corrected the proofs of his *Ecclesiastical Researches*—a not inconsiderable task—and saw the book through the press. Dyer gracefully says that Robinson's admirers "are much indebted" to Frend "for that accuracy with which it was presented to the public."[2]

[1] Dyer, pp. 315–316.
[2] *Ibid.*, pp. 316–318.

Of all the friends gained through his change of beliefs, perhaps the closest eventually was Theophilus Lindsey ("the father of Unitarian churchmanship"), admirer and ally of Dr Joseph Priestley, and husband of Archdeacon Blackburn's daughter Hannah. He had been a Church of England parson, but had changed his views and in 1773 given up prospects of promotion along with a comfortable home at Catterick and a cherished library, to move from Yorkshire to set up a Unitarian centre of worship in London.

Lindsey was not physically impressive—with his melancholy eyes and drooping mouth, he looked more like an unhappy bloodhound than a man of action, but he consistently showed courage and energy in defending his unpopular views. Leader in several campaigns against the Test Acts, Lindsey proved tireless in promoting meetings and petitions for religious freedom. In 1772 he rode all over the Yorkshire moors through the January blizzards, collecting single-handed 250 signatures to a petition against compulsory subscription to the Thirty-nine Articles.

Lindsey was constantly on the look-out for new adherents to the Unitarian movement, and was naturally delighted to hear of Frend's resignation from his Long Stanton living ("not very great in value but much sought after, as so securely to be served from college") and to welcome him to Essex Street Chapel on 30 December 1787. Writing to his friend William Tayleur of Shrewsbury the next day, Lindsey shows that he is impressed by the newcomer: "How far his scruples go, I cannot tell, but by his great ardour of mind, and being a Tutor of the College, he may be of great service. He does not seem to be more than 27 or 28 years old. One proof of his and his friends' zeal at Cambridge—no heretical books are admitted on the shelves of the two principal booksellers. They have therefore engaged an inferior one to have a shelf for them, and have undertaken to support him."[1]

When Frend's *Letter to Mr Coulthurst* appeared, Lindsey procured it "as soon as possible" from the publisher, and

[1] H. McLachlan: *Letters of Theophilus Lindsey*, p. 127.

wrote to Frend that "Dr Priestley being with us, we read it together with avidity & with the greatest satisfaction, as a manly proof of your own virtue and integrity & sound mind & judgement, such as must make the friends of truth rejoice & its enemies tremble; & the greatest good must accrue from your conduct & example . . . I am glad of this opportunity of saying how truly I honour you."

Frend, fighting to save his tutorship, had drawn up a statement accusing the Master of Jesus of unfair procedure, with an introduction by Micaiah Towgood, a friendly Dissenting Minister. Lindsey helped by handing the statement to the London press—*The Public Advertiser* and three other newspapers published it—and he (Lindsey) congratulated Frend on "deciding to make some stand & not to let your resignation of your station of usefulness in the college take place so lightly, upon the mere signification of the will of one man (the Master) of whose authority just doubts may be entertained, as also whether he had properly exercised it." The statement in the press "will contribute to make your cause more known, & be of service to it."

Lindsey wrote similarly to Tayleur on 26 June quoting "the current wit"—"Frend of Jesus, Friend of the Devil": "I am glad he does not tamely give up his Tutorship, as standing out a little will make the cause for which he is removed from it more attended to"; and Lindsey mentioned a letter from Frend's colleague James Lambert, who had written to him: "Our friends here, Tyrwhitt and Frend, are in good spirits. The lions begin to roar from their pulpits. The Divinity of Jesus was maintained on Sunday in full force by Mr Boycott of Caius College, and yesterday Dr Kipling, one of the Divinity Professors, thought proper to give the heretics a drubbing."[1]

Lindsey was however following events with some anxiety, and reported to Tayleur on 7 October that "many expect they will try to eject him [Frend] from his Fellowship, while others suppose they will let him alone for fear of the noise it

[1] McLachlan: *op. cit.*, p. 128.

will make, as he will certainly not be silent under persecution . . . " It was some comfort that "Mr Tyrwhitt who still lives in the College . . . will be no small check upon them, as his sentiments are so well known, and his character and connections very respectable, and his fortune also, since his brother's death, very ample."

Among bits of Cambridge news Tayleur is told that Dr Heberden, whose son was there, had remarked "that Unitarianism is spreading among the young students"; also that "Mr Coulthurst has preached another sermon at which Mr Frend was present, and he is setting about an answer but . . . he sends it up to be printed here as he is denied the University Press." A few days later, Lindsey praises Frend's "open cheerful disposition, which renders his company very agreeable."[1]

Lindsey's interest must have been of great support to Frend, and his long letters, full of respect and affection, must have warmed the younger man who was meeting with so much coolness and acerbity in his college. Especially encouraging was the letter in which Lindsey said he had sent Frend's *Address* as soon as it was published to Dr Priestley who had commented "I like Mr Frend's piece much but wish that he had deferred the publication till after the issue of his cause."[2] For Frend, new to the radical and Unitarian movement, prai e from the great Dr Priestley was doubtless both sweet and stimulating. There was more to come: a few months later the Doctor told Lindsey "I like Mr Frend's Second Address no less than his first. I greatly admire his spirit and ability and hope much from him."[3] In May 1789 he says that if Lindsey sends him "a few more copies of Mr Frend's Addresses I could dispose of them to advantage. I have an active distributor at Manchester and Unitarianism gains ground there."[4]

[1] McLachlan: *op. cit.*, p. 129.

[2] J. T. Rutt: *Life and Correspondence of Dr Joseph Priestley*, p. 11.

[3] Rutt: *op. cit.*, p. 18.

[4] *Ibid.*, p. 22.

On 6 March 1789 Lindsey thanked Frend "for the present of your Appendix [to the Address] in which you have clearly proved that Dr Beadon acted arbitrarily . . . in dispossessing you of the Tutorship, but all the demonstration in the world would never have convinced your judge of the injustice done you; nor shall I be surprised if they proceed in a short time to eject you from your fellowship, should the same favourable circumstances return as before the king's illness." He drew William's attention to the Duke of Grafton's pamphlet* about the new Association formed to carry out the anti-Dissenter policy announced in a recent King's Proclamation. This pamphlet, says Lindsey, "and Lord Stanhope's late movement in the House of Lords, & the determination of the Dissenters to renew their application to Parliament this session . . . with a new case wh I have seen in print, so strong that I think it will flash conviction in the face of every member of both houses—all these things together will work out something—not to omit your recent movement of the waters to prevent stagnation, for we here in 15 years' time are grown somewhat old and settled, though I trust we have our use."

Frend seems at this time—the beginning of 1789—to have been consumed by the importance and urgency of his discoveries; he was convinced that he had found Truth and that it was his duty to impart it to all and sundry. He re-wrote the *Address to the Inhabitants of Cambridge*, and entitled the new version *An Address to the Members of the Church of England and to Protestant Trinitarians in General etc* and sent off copies to all his acquaintances outside Cambridge; he also set out to storm the enemy's camp through the Society for the Promotion of Christian Knowledge, which he had hitherto loyally supported as an active member.[1]

From the S.P.C.K.'s minutes and the letters that have survived this passage of arms, we get a strangely vivid picture

* "Hints etc. submitted to the attention of the Clergy, Nobility and Gentry newly associated." 1789.

[1] S.P.C.K. Minute-Book, 1789. British Museum.

of the incident; we can imagine how William, provided with copies of the two-page pamphlet fresh from the press, went along to the April meeting of the Society; how he sat more or less patiently through the discussions on stipends of the clergy, overseas work, and Sunday schools; and how, as A.O.B. drew to a close and members rose to go, Frend leapt to his feet, hurrying to catch the Secretary and thrusting into his hands some of the pamphlets with a request that they should be given out to the members; we can see the Secretary peering at him with surprise and disapproval, but being left standing with the papers in his hand, while Frend went off after the members who were leaving.

Flights of fancy apart, we do know that the Secretary consulted the committee members immediately after this and that it was decided to hold a special meeting to discuss Frend and his writings. As a result, a fortnight later William received a stiff letter from the Secretary informing him that "at a very numerous meeting of the Society held on May 12th 1789 at their house in Bartlett's Buildings, certain resolutions were unanimously agreed to:

"viz: since he openly denied the Divinity of our Lord Jesus Christ, reviled the doctrine of the Trinity, renounced the Thirty-nine Articles, etc. etc." it was "the duty of this Society to testify in the strongest and most public manner their just abhorrence of these impieties." In short, Frend was to be expelled from the Society, and, among other humiliating conditions, there was to be no right of appeal, and "no arrears tendered by him were to be acceptable."

From Canterbury on 22 May, Frend replied to the Secretary of the S.P.C.K. that the resolutions were "the result of a mean and narrow spirit which would become the order of Saint Dominick but are unworthy of Englishmen and Christians . . . " He also enclosed a letter to the Society not so much defending himself but attacking *them*. In it he denied the power of the Church to decree rites, and declared that it would be treasonable to acknowledge any authority in the land other than that of the King, Lords and Commons. "The

Church was formerly a Bugbear, a Scarecrow, to frighten the poor people of this country, but Englishmen are too well acquainted with the inestimable blessing of freedom to be frightened in these days by a sound that can alarm only women and children."

He asked "by what authority ye expelled me from the Society?" Why had he had no intimation of their intentions? If expulsion were intended, why had he had no opportunity of answering for himself? If this can happen, he said, "no member of the Society is at any time safe; it being in the power of a headstrong orthodox man like himself to accuse a member of infidelity, to pack a board with headstrong men like himself, & expel every character whose principles are too upright, and whose faith in Christianity is too firm to answer the purpose of a pliant and intriguing priest."[1]

But they were not going to get rid of him so easily; he stated flatly that "I shall therefore esteem myself a member till I am informed that I am expelled by the Society, and on my return from the Continent shall claim a seat at the board."

Having fired this broadside, Frend turned his attention to his continental holiday; to get away, to relax, to see new scenes, to recuperate from two years of mental and spiritual struggle, were what he urgently needed. There were many skirmishes ahead, much tougher than the passage with the S.P.C.K. (of which we hear no more). Frend needed all his intellectual vigour to enter these, and the four months' rest was, as it were, a charging of the batteries which would enable him to forge ahead and play his full part when the time for the big battles arrived.

[1] W.F.: Reply to the Secretary, S.P.C.K. British Museum.

5
MORE FOREIGN TRAVEL

FREND WENT OFF at the beginning of June 1789, alone this time, for a prolonged stay in North West Germany. He was well provided with letters of introduction and addresses in the towns he was to pass through, and apparently looked forward to a leisurely tour of northern Europe, unaware that much of this area resembled a powder keg liable to blow up beneath his feet at any time after 14 July, catching a spark from France.

Few people in England in fact realized how explosive the situation had become across the Channel. Several young men of Frend's acquaintance had planned holidays in France—Lord Lansdowne's son was there, and Dr Price's nephew George Morgan, with two friends; and William Priestley, the Doctor's youngest son, was setting off for Paris in July in the care of John Wilkinson, Mrs Priestley's brother. They were to visit another brother, William Wilkinson, then advising the French on industrial and technical questions of smelting iron, as practised in the Wilkinson ironworks at Broseley.

After a short stay in Paris William Priestley was to travel to Germany, where his father had arranged for Frend to meet him and install him with a German family known to Frend in Frankfurt. Dr Priestley was slightly concerned, not about the political situation in France, but lest the gay life of Paris should adversely influence his son. However he decided that the boy would be all right with his two uncles, and there was M. Lavoisier the scientist who would look after him in an emergency. It was certainly somewhat worrying when Dr Price wrote to say that his nephew had been arrested and held in prison for over a week; even more so when news came of the outbreak of revolution. But notwithstanding Mrs Priestley's fears (the Doctor remained remarkably calm), her son came to no harm. After witnessing some dramatic scenes, including the taking of the Bastille, from a safe distance, Wilkinson and William Priestley left Paris with M. Lavoisier, travelled to Nantes where they stayed a few nights with him, and thence to Frankfurt.[1]

In the meantime Frend had been travelling through Belgium, untroubled by thoughts of revolution. He told his sister Mary that he slept "tolerably well" on the channel crossing, though it had been disagreeable "to get into a boat at 2 a.m., rowed to the end of the river, thence to be carried through the sand and get up the slimy steps." He had enjoyed the journey by diligence to Dunkirk, and "by Barque" to Bruges. On embarking he had "found an Englishman the exact picture of Pitt"—"His name is Lyttelton. On mentioning the likeness, he said he had often been taken for the Minister."

Of Bruges, Frend said, "there is not much to be seen—a large old town—large old churches—large old houses." He was chiefly impressed by the human beings he came across there: firstly, "a lady—formed on the model of Rubens wife—perfect features, hand & arm of snow—rings in abundance—& to make her a compleat Beauty she weighed at least—one Ton. I am now perfectly convinced that Rubens drew from nature & give every nation permission to have its own ideas of Beauty"; secondly, a Mr E. (William Edwards) to whom he had an introduction: "He has a modest fortune & a large family which he educates himself" by means of three Preceptors—"One an English Clergyman, the second a sound Papist, the third a Philosopher."

Mr E. "adopts the philosophy of Priestley & the liturgy of Lindsey." A blind Englishman, "formerly a Catholick, now a sound necessarian, enlivens the society," Frend told Mary. He was very happy: "The company was intirely a mon gout, we chatted on philosophy, on religion, on other subjects, with the utmost freedom & did not decide to cut each others throats when we happened to differ in opinion."

[1] J. Gillam: *The Crucible*, pp. 168–176.

His host, as we shall see later, was going to have an exciting time in Bruges. A long letter describing subsequent events begins, "When we last parted I little thought that Flanders would have been so soon shaken to its centre & plunged into all the horrors of civil war"—but at the beginning of June there was outward calm.

A keen-nosed tourist could however scent unrest; Frend, visiting St Peter's Abbey at Ghent observed that "The Library is one of the most elegant rooms I have ever seen. The books too, very well chosen but the building is likely to share the fate of many convents in its neighbourhood. They have no novices at present & the emperor seems determined to suppress in time these useless institutions. A large convent of the Capucins has been converted into a storehouse. The people are very bigotted in their religion & the Emperor not only endeavours to reform the church but has attacked with it the lawyers, a formidable corps. The consequence is that the country is in a very unquiet state & the greater part devoutly pray that their Sovereign may never get over his present illness."

During his two days in Brussels Frend was offered a box for a performance at the theatre ("the house good, the comedie stark naught"); he visited the palace; he admired the views around the capital, and commented that "the country is kept in the highest state of cultivation. Indeed if it were not for the religion of this country I should not despair of seeing it again possess that degree of consequence it formerly maintained in Europe."

In Louvain he met a young English student who conducted him about the town. He found "the Colleges were all shut—the greater part of the students are at Bruxelles or their own homes & instead of Professors the Soldiers preserve the discipline of the town. I wish the Emperor success but I have learned that the professors are convicted by the University of Paris of Heterodoxy." [1]

He wrote again, on 27 June, of Louvain as "a town which

[1] W.F. to Mary Frend, 8.6.1789.

formerly boasted of its university. It remains with the Emperor to determine its fate for the future. If he continues steady the reforms which occasion continual disturbances among his subjects it will be beneficial.

"At Tirlemont we found a company of soldiers on the *place* just arrived to quell a tumult, but there did not seem much occasion for them; a few persons the night before got drunk, broke each others heads & called out Long live the States, the Magistrate thought fit to send for the Military but before their arrival the rioters had retired quietly to their homes & were composing themselves after their little debauch."

Arrived at Liège—which he compared to "a Spider, whose body is the town & the suburbs the legs"—he noted that "the coals in the hills are convenient for the inhabitants but the town is dirty & the streets as narrow as those of Newcastle," and said he "was pleased here by a sight I never enjoyed in England . . . a water mill for the sawing & polishing of stone. By means of the mill thirteen saws were kept at work & forty or fifty square feet of stone polished."

At his next stop, Aix-la-Chapelle, he was shocked by the gaming that was going on. "They live here only to play morning noon & night, they play, but such an abuse of the word play ought not to be suffered, it is not an amusement but a trade & a very dull stupid trade it appeared to be. The moment you leave the gaming table if your feelings have not been properly hardened by the sight of so many miserable wretches in high life you are shocked at the appearance of the most numerous & wretched crew of beggars. They are troublesome to the last degree, every street swarms with them & they appear to be as vicious as troublesome."

From Aix, Frend took a diligence to Cologne and observed that Germany "claims the pre-eminence for badness . . . of roads, & the most tormenting construction of vehicles . . . You are scarce out of sight of the steeples when the roads would vie with the worst in the Weald of Kent." Moreover, "the drivers possess that amiable characteristic of this nation, a degree of Phlegm that thunder, hail, lightning & rain could not induce them to quicken their pace."

For about a hundred miles he had travelled post, but found this so tiring and troublesome, with changes of chaises, paying postilions and so on, that he changed to the diligence. "This is reckoned a very ungenteel mode of travelling for it is very cheap" . . . However, he "slept in it nearly as well as in a feather bed"—a remark which Mary probably took with a pinch of salt, in view of what followed: "Why," asked her brother, "have we in England good roads, good chaises, good horses, good diligences, & good accommodations on every road? Is it not the interest of every person concerned in the above articles to have everything good. And why is everything bad in this country? Because it is not the interest of any person on the road to provide any thing good except the Inns. A certain prince . . . is Post master general of the Empire. His income is very considerable & while he sleeps in down, he little imagines the jolts which his passengers suffer every moment . . .

"For the future, when an Englishman talks to me of the danger of innovation, or reformation in government, church, etc. etc. I shall recommend him a tour of five hundred miles in a post waggon & if I were able would condemn him to a penance of the last fifty that I passed over."

Frend had not been looking forward to Cologne: "Everybody says that Cologne is a most melancholy town", he wrote; "I was afraid that if I staid here three days nothing but the waters of the Rhine would put an end to my ennui." But he was fortunately not driven by boredom to suicide, and in fact enjoyed himself walking round seeing the sights; after which he proceeded to Hanau, where he stayed for nearly three months. "Let me tell you where I now am", he writes, on 27 June: "the only stranger in a watering place built by the prince of Hanau . . . You can make a considerable walk without getting 40 rods from the house. Besides here are swings, turnabouts, see-sawing boards & every other accommodation that is to be had at Jack &

Jone's fair. I am here only for a few days till the Gentleman returns with whom I shall take up my lodgings. My address is Mons. Frend, chez M., Bergstrasse, Hanau, pres de Frankfort sur Main."

When William Priestley arrived in Frankfurt Frend went over to see him and the Doctor wrote to Lindsey: "It was very fortunate that Mr Frend met my son at Fft. He is very happily situated, and with agreeable acquaintances, particularly a Mr Miles. I do not know him but Mr F. does & was to send him some of my publications." [1]

Progressive Englishmen enjoyed the intellectual climate in Germany where the European Enlightenment had at that time many followers—from Koenigsberg, Kant's base, to Frankfurt, home of Goethe, and Bonn, a centre of liberal studies where Eulogius Schneider, a fiery radical, preached and fanned young Beethoven's passion for freedom.[2]

Regrettably for us, Frend's letters to Mary do not mention current political or literary trends; they mainly consist of long and lively reports of local people and customs.

On 14 September he writes, "Here I am—still in Hanau. In Hanau! what the devil can you do in Hanau said an Englishman to me the other day. It must be damn'd dull & triste." Frend assures his sister that he is not at all triste, and describes what is going on in the little Principality.

"Last Saturday the Landgrave came to Wilhelmsbad. My host thought it incumbent on him to be one of a company of about 40 persons that went there to receive him." Frend went, for the good dinner, and to see how a German Prince travels, and gave Mary a detailed account of the court ceremonies, remarking incidentally on the snobbery of the English tourists of the "company" who were pining for an introduction to a prince. "Nine out of ten of them [German princes] are not upon a par with the greater part of our Squires & some of our rich members for Counties could buy

[1] Rutt: *Life of Priestley*, p. 42.

[2] Knepler: *Musikgeschichte*, ii, pp. 538–539.

half a dozen principalities . . . many of them are exceedingly poor & exceedingly illiterate . . . "

Another diversion was a visit to Wilhelmsbad, which, Frend says, was "the general resort of company on Wednesdays and Sundays.

"You have a very good dinner there for about 16 pence and supper for 11 pence. The company in the walks & in the hall is very miscellaneous . . . Here are but two classes, the noble & the ignoble, & as you see the former with lace cloaths, frequently a star & always desperately coarse if not dirty linen, so here princes & footmen, barons & filles de chambre are crowded together in the most democratical confusion." Still, he does not want to be unfair: "I must not leave you with a bad impression of this people. They have many good qualities, are exceedingly civil to strangers & are very partial to our country."

This letter is dated 14 September 1789—and yet there is no comment on the happenings in France, though William Priestley must have told him what he had witnessed. However Frend does report "that the Landgrave had left Wilhelmsbad in a very great hurry on account it was supposed of a rebellion at Cassel. As rebellion is so much in fashion at present on the Continent I resolved to wait a day or two before I sealed up my letter.

"For several days we had no letters here & the reports were various, at one time fifteen officers were killed, & so forth. It appears at last that there has been no rebellion, only a remonstrance which may perhaps tend to disable his highness from robbing his country of so many lands [illegible] & selling them to the English. The peasants mean to complain to the Imperial court if the Landgrave does not acquiesce in their proposals."

He tells Mary that he is setting off for Mannheim, and thence "to Paris if the roads are safe, if not I shall return by way of Holland & some time in November . . . " Perhaps for fear of upsetting her, he had not told her of the grisly sights he had seen on his outward journey, nor did he describe these or his homeward journey till many years later, when he told Lady Byron: "I travelled through the Low Countries in my way to Germany in the year '89 & there saw in many towns a gibbet erected in the market place with cannon & lighted match that immediate vengeance might be taken on any one who dared to utter a word against the existing government."[1]

From the same letter we learn that he travelled home not via Paris but through north Germany and Belgium and did in fact see something of the European ferment, and the way that the rulers were trying to keep the lid on the seething cauldron of discontent:

"On my return home [from Hanau] I dined at Mechlin at a military mess & after dinner went on the market place with some officers of the regiment of Bender to see one of its battalions eight hundred strong marching out against the Patriotes. Between seven and eight next morning six hundred of them were put hors de combat. The marching out struck me forcibly. They drew up in the great square & such a sight in general attracts multitudes in a large town but not an inhabitant was to be seen except at the corner of the square, & the soldiers were evidently the object of general detestation.

"When I got to Brussels the Archduke & Duchess had made a precipitate retreat from the place & in a short time after the Austrian government was at an end." Thus Frend learned the lesson that "to fix a gibbet in the market place, to suspend the Habeas Corpus act, to immure people in Bastilles, is far from being a solid bulwark to any administration."[2]—a lesson which he was to remember on very many occasions in the course of his long political life.

* * *

Soon after his return to England, at the beginning of December, Frend received a letter from Mr Edwards, of Bruges, telling him how narrowly he had escaped the

[1] W.F. to A.B., 13.3.1817.

[2] *Ibid.*

fighting that had broken out in Flanders, and giving him a vivid description of the events in the uprising against the Archduke's regime. In Ghent, he said, 1,100 Imperial troops had been trapped and overcome by the townspeople helped by 6 or 700 countryfolk who had been summoned by the priests (who took the lead in planning the campaign); these peasants had forced their way into the town; the guards had retreated to the barrack—"they were attacked there pell-mell; for there was neither discipline nor subordination among the insurgents," and when they made sorties to obtain provisions "they were opposed and fired upon from the windows, cellars, etc." The troops set fire to houses and "much innocent blood was shed in these nocturnal sallies."

After about three and a half days, the soldiers surrendered to the local clergy, "and were conducted by divisions to the different mendicant convents, the friars *chearfully* undertaking their guardianship, *materially* and *immaterially*." A reinforcement of troops finding that "the quarters were surrendered they retreated without the least molestation, carrying off their artillery and baggage."

Events at Bruges had not been so dramatic as at Ghent, but the quiet little town had had its share of excitement: "On the tuesday subsequent to the attack on Ghent," wrote Mr Edwards, "Bruges declared its independence & summoned a company of 150 Imperial troops to surrender. They were here in barracks. For the sake of form they suffered a fire of an hour and a half & then laid down their arms. The friars now have them in charge. One soldier was killed; another desperately wounded and since dead. Not one of the assailants, for they were most under cover, met with the least accident. So ended *our* Campaign."

Mr Edwards was not optimistic about the future: "What will be the issue of the contest I will not predict; but should not an accommodation take place, the ensuing summer will produce a struggle that will deluge the pays-bas with blood. May God avert it!"

The uprising in Belgium, of course, was unlike the French

Revolution in that it was a movement against foreign rule, not for reform and social justice. The Church saw a good chance of strengthening its power by playing the part of leader and directing the negotiations with the future rulers, when the turmoil subsided. Edwards was greatly incensed by the turn things had taken: "I had much rather be governed by a single despot," he wrote, "than that the Recollects, Carmes, Dominicans should lead me by the nose hoodwinked. Would you not smile to see these ministers of peace with their crosses and rosaries heading armies & leading them on to shed their blood in support of superstition & Intolerance? Yet, this is literally the case . . . Miracles are wrought every week & scarcely a day passes without crowded processions."

All this had happened under the name of national independence and republicanism: "Business of every sort is now suspended, & the care of the republic seems to be the sole occupation of every Weaver & Taylor in the country. Yes, my dear Sir, we dream of nothing but republic, alliances, & the universal downfall of monarchy." He protests that "No man more ardently wishes a free constitution to every country upon earth than myself; but to use a vulgar phrase, I dread being out of the frying pan into the fire.

"France is giving to the world a glorious example of freedom in Church & state; but we, alas, do not catch a single spark of that pure flame which is now separating the metal from the dross in our sister kingdom."

Mr Edwards was perturbed about the future of local Protestants and their churches: "Those who are so unfortunate as to be bewildered in the temporary darkness, must grope their way as well as they can, . . . at the risk of being well scratched by clerical brambles."

Luckily for him, "the first mover of our political machine *here* is my particular friend. He is one of the judges, & a liberal minded, well informed, man. You supped at his house, with me, & may recollect the orthodoxy of your conversation with Mme . . . I have ventured to keep up our little Sunday congregation. Were we more numerous, it might not be so safe under the present circumstances. In conversations I have lately had with some of the gentlemen who are principal actors in the present scene, I have freely expressed my surprise at & lamented the retrograde motion of their political machine, chiefly in respect to the religious freedom.

"This too, at a time when our french neighbours are making such a rapid progress in it. From my heart I wish their new constitution a speedy & peaceable establishment—enough of blood has already been shed on the occasion."[1]

In these words William Edwards expressed a sentiment which had been recently aroused in Frend, and which from that time on was to be his constant preoccupation and the motive power for his future activity.

[1] William Edwards to W.F., 11.12.1789.

6

ENTHUSIASTIC DISSENTER
(1790)

HIS EUROPEAN JOURNEY opened Frend's eyes to many things of which he had previously been vaguely aware but which had not stirred him to action. He was now burning to say and do his utmost to repair social wrongs and to promote understanding of what was happening on the continent.

Theophilus Lindsey welcomed him back to England, writing, on 14 November 1789, "Heaven be praised that we have gotten you safe again to our isle. You will hardly believe how much many known and unknown to you have been concerned lest you should have suffered for want of health, or amidst the perils and dangers now on our continent."

Frend had evidently felt that politics and France were more suitable topics for Lindsey than for his sister (to whom he hardly mentioned either in his many letters), for Theophilus says he is "obliged to you for yr brief strictures on the state of things there. The revolution in France is a wonderful work of providence in our days, & we trust it will prosper and go on and be the speedy means of putting an end to tyranny everywhere."

This letter, which gives Frend the latest news of the Essex Street circle, asks him to have his *Address* reprinted, and reports the spread of Unitarianism in the north and west of England; it is the first of many communications from Lindsey during the next two years. They reflect months of ceaseless activity in the spreading of the Unitarian doctrine through books and tracts and communications all over the country. Very often the letters are little more than an answer to a request for pamphlets or an order for reprints of sermons.

Lindsey was the publisher and director of the Unitarian book service, and very often editor and author as well; Frend was a willing co-operator and distributor, as can be seen from such extracts from the correspondence as "I expect you will receive the parcell of tracts before this reaches you, and am glad it will be in your way to dispose of them ... I cd not help throwing in some copies of Mr Toulmin's Exhortations ... the new edition which you will like; and I have more, at your service" (14.1.90); "I have sent some copies of your Account which last I believe has done much good ... Along with it were sent a few tracts, which I have always by me to give away ... " (10.3.90) —"I was not unmindful of paying the 5 guineas to Mr Disney ... and three doz of hymns were delivered to good Mr Hammond" (10.3.90).

There are a number of references to George Dyer's *Inquiry into the Nature of Subscription to the Thirty-nine Articles* (published in 1789 and being zealously pushed by Essex Street) such as "I shall take care the Dr [Priestley] has his copy of Mr Dyer" and "at coming out of the country I met with a parcel from the worthy Mr Dyer, and a letter with which I am charmed more than I can tell you, bespeaking a character of native simplicity and goodness and great ingenuity" (14 July 1790).

One matter that Lindsey mentions early in 1790 is the appointment of Gilbert Wakefield[1] as Tutor at the new Academy in Hackney:

"We have a good hope," he writes, "that Mr Wakefield will answer all expectations at our new College and raise its credit; but now the affair is over, I may tell you that *you* was the person first thought of by the Tutors & by many others, if you had been so disengaged from the University that such an offer could have been made you: for ... there was not a man who did not express an affection for you, and say that they would like to live with you ... "

[1] Gilbert Wakefield (1756–1801), scholar of Jesus College 1772, editor and translator of classics, Unitarian and polemist.

This is typical of the tone of Lindsey's letters to Frend—a combination of kind uncle, master to his disciple, protector to new boy. Theophilus' affection is very evident, and so is his pride at having made this recruit to the ranks of the Unitarian confraternity. He fostered Frend's interest by regular reports of all that was going on: the "extraordinary meeting" of the General Body of Dissenting Ministers in Dr Williams' Library in London; the decision to re-apply for a repeal of the Test Acts; their hopes that Fox would introduce the Bill, which they hoped to have debated in March.

Early in the year there was great activity up and down the country: "You see how well the Dissenters go on. The resolutions at Nottingham would particularly please you. I hope some liberal ministers of the established church will dare to step forth openly in their cause"; (this was over-optimistic—the clergy as a whole rose up in arms, and backed by the local squirearchy organized "numerous and respectable meetings" in opposition).[1]

"In the west, and in Lancashire particularly . . . the freest inquiry is going on, and of course the doctrine of the Divine Unity spreading much" (2.1.90); "You will be particularly pleased with the Scotch Assembly having so interfered in asserting their rights, which will come so well in aid of our next application for the repeal of the Test Acts" (9.1.90). And on 14 January he wrote, "this renewal of their application from the Dissenters will be of infinite service to them and to the nation by disseminating knowledge of their true principles . . . and by uniting so cordially and universally, a thing never known before."

There is a gap in the correspondence, as Lindsey was being rushed off his feet during February by preparations for the debate on Fox's Bill on 2 March. "During our late application to Parliament and since, I could as soon fly as sit down to write to Cambridge or any where . . . " (10 March).

In spite of all their efforts and a splendid speech by Fox

[1] R. B. Barlow: *Citizenship and Conscience*, p. 23.

appealing "not merely for General Toleration, but for that system" which ensures "the Universal Rights of Human Nature", the Bill was rejected. The House being what it then was, Pitt's appeal to prejudice carried the day; Fox's conclusions, he declared, "throw open a door for the entrance of some individuals who might consider it a point of *conscience* to shake our Establishment to its foundations."[1]

Burke had followed on with an attack on "abstract principles", and had done his best to prove that the Church was in actual danger. He had quoted "inflammatory" passages from Priestley and Price's writings, and also produced a printed catechism written by the Reverend Robinson, which he said would be given to Dissenters' children "to teach them to lisp out censures in condemnation of the Church Established, while, possibly, the Dissenting teachers were preaching up robbery and plunder as in France."[2]

Wilberforce and Sir William Dolben had equally played on the fear of the French Revolution, supposedly beloved by most Dissenters. The government majority was 189 (105 for, 294 against the Bill) and the Church-and-King men could sleep soundly in their beds.

A week after the debate, Lindsey wrote to Frend saying that "the Dissenters are not at all disheartened by the insolent and injurious usage they met with from the house..." One of the principal ones among them told Lindsey "that William Pitt had deceived him once but should never do it again. That he did think he had some principles, but he was persuaded that he had none at all."

Lindsey adds that "This is the growing opinion of the Dissenters who certainly contributed mainly to bring him in; and how has he rewarded them?"

On 22 April he comments bitterly, "Every one I know here is elated by our late repulse and the triumph of the Xch. As Dr P & I were walking the streets today we met Bp

[1] Barlow: *op. cit.*, p. 267.
[2] *Ibid.*, p. 269.

Horsley[1] in the lightest purple coat (with a street cassock) I ever beheld, wh cd not but attract notice."

The Ministry must have considered Theophilus Lindsey a particularly dangerous man, for besides his keen interest in religious liberty he was one of the staunchest supporters of the French Revolution at this time. He had written to Frend, in August 1789, that "abroad, great and important changes are coming on, which I trust will have the best effect on the moral state not of one country only but of the whole world" (10.8.89); and on the first anniversary of the Revolution he wrote "I congratulate you upon the most glorious and grandest and I hope happiest event in human things on Wednesday last at Paris" (19.7.90).

There are enough well-informed comments on the news of the day to show that Lindsey had a sharp political eye; he remarks, in the spring, that "the quiet and stability of the proceedings at Paris is said to be very offensive here"; and in the autumn, expresses his alarm "at the reports of the National Assembly that they are in danger of soon coming to nothing", but trusts "that they will be able to support themselves, and that their work will remain." He had nothing but contempt for eminent British figures who should have known better than to malign the French Republic: of the poet H. J. Pye's Toryism and his anti-Jacobin speeches he says, "the Laureat doubtless speaks not barely his own mind, though there are some political fears of others in declaring themselves openly . . . "

On 2 November 1790 he writes to Frend angrily about Burke's *Reflections on the French Revolution*, just published in reply to Dr Price's sermon in favour of the Revolution: "It is a curious accusation which Mr Burke formally and with all seriousness brings against . . . the French Republic of a design to overthrow the Christian religion. His declamation

[1] Charles Horsley, then Bishop of St David's, later of Rochester and in 1802 of St Asaph, and Dean of Westminster. A bitter opponent of Priestley (whom he attacked in 1783 and thereafter in *Seventeen Letters*), he was a supporter of the Evangelicals.

on this topic, his assertion from his own imagination of a similar design in our revolution society [a respectable Whig club] and its abettors at home, his pathetic paintings of the horrors of such an event and declarations that the english will never indure it etc. etc. will tend to inflame and excite the zeal of churchmen and set us at a greater distance from Reformation. I am afraid it may cool the earnestness and stop the efforts of some who but now were very forward. But let me not make bad omens. Nous verrons." Lindsey goes on, with more bitterness than usual, to accuse Burke of being "wholly ignorant of what true religion and the gospel is and requires: with all his self-boasting and pretensions to knowledge in general and knowledge of men, knowledge of books, he knows not the first principles of a just government.

"His book, like all his speeches of late . . . overwhelm with verbiage and a desultory imagination; and little sound sense upon any subjects. In some parts he is quite frantic, and talks just like one that had the strait waistcoat upon him—especially when certain ideas come across him. A friend of mine . . . said at the time, that if the Riots of 1780 had continued three days longer Burke would have gone out of his senses. I think his imagination has been heated with these ideas ever since, so that he does not possess himself at all when burdening upon some things."

Lindsey wonders how "I have come to write so much to you on this book wh is only just this very day come out. I was very far from intending it when I began. You will judge when somebody lends it you. For it is not worth laying out 5 shillings upon it . . . "

And on 10 November (1790) he is attacking the *Reflections* again: "Mr Burke who has no more knowledge than a horse of what [the Gospel] really is, imagines that it can only subsist and be supported by the splendour of riches and great secular power." In this, however, "he has many on his side: and you have scarce an idea of the triumphant air with which many of the two learned professions as well as the church speak of the service he has done to religion by his book."

But in spite of Burke and his bogeys there was all through 1790 widespread support for the French Republic among people of all classes in England. Various societies which had always been dedicated to Parliamentary Reform welcomed the Revolution, if cautiously; and the London Society for Constitutional Information of 1782 which had for some years been quiescent, became active again, with the participation of many new members of varying social background, though predominantly "respectable". Groups modelled on the S.C.I. sprang up in most of the larger provincial towns, aspiring to promote ideas of reform, social justice and to enlist support for the French Revolution.

William Frend, stimulated by his travels and encouraged by his new friendships, was anxious to join in all this activity. It was not enough for him to distribute books for Essex Street, nor to join the Society of Friends to Religious Liberty, which Capell Lofft organized in March 1790. Robert Robinson's Constitutional Society in Cambridge was fulfilling a useful function, and Frend decided that what was needed to combat ignorance and spread the truth about France, while creating support for Reform in England, was a chain of such societies across the country. In the summer of 1790 we find him corresponding with his friend John Hobhouse in Bristol about the possibility of forming groups like the S.C.I. in the provinces.

Frend says he is going to Town and will make it his business to inquire whether there is anything in existence similar to what is proposed. Hobhouse in the meantime writes to Thomas Cooper, the Bolton chemist, a very active Reformer, friend of Dr Priestley, Thomas Walker and other prominent Radicals; Cooper had recently been "refused admission into ye orthodox Royal Society on account of his heretical principles & junction with ye dissenters in their late application."[1] Later, when the Royal Society refused to

[1] R. E. Garnham to W.F., 28.3.1790.

accept a paper by Cooper on obtaining chlorine from sea water salt, Priestley offered his resignation.[1]

On 10 July 1790, Hobhouse told Frend that he "had consulted Cowper assuring him that I relyed upon his concurrence and activity in promoting so beneficial a plan", and that he had received an answer on 9 July: "He heartily approves and informs me that with much pains and perseverance such institutions may be formed in Lancashire and Cheshire." Hobhouse asks, "Have you through the means of other friends felt the pulse of other Counties? Many societies throughout England, founded upon so liberal a basis, united for so glorious a purpose and endeavouring to attain it by means so well adapted to the end, must necessarily succeed better than one fixed in the Metropolis. You have I trust been making exertions to accomplish this excellent design."[2]

Frend had certainly been making exertions; but—perhaps conjecturing that Theophilus Lindsey might not altogether approve—had not publicized them. However Lindsey had got wind of them, for he wrote to Frend on 26 July: "I forgot to mention that Mr Cooper of Manchester lately asked me about a plan that you and Mr Hobhouse had projected; & young Mr Toulmin told me that it was for the dispersion of religious tracts, but I answered that I believed he was mistaken, as if it were so, I should have heard of it."

There are no letters to tell us whether the "excellent design" was carried out by Frend and Hobhouse, but we may be fairly sure they played their part in the proliferation of radical ideas and literature throughout the country during the following months.

Lindsey might not have cared to be associated with such a directly political campaign, but many ministers joined actively in promoting the ideas of the "constitutional Society"; the Central London Society included among its members Unitarians, and some clergy—John Bonney,

[1] Gillam: *op. cit.*, p. 223.

[2] Hobhouse to W.F., 10.7.1790.

Jeremiah Joyce, and Horne Tooke (Church of England) being the most prominent. Whether or not the provincial ministers of radical sympathies would publicly play a political role varied according to the locality; in big towns such as Birmingham, Manchester and Bristol, a minister was less exposed, and might be more active than in small places. Yet there were exceptions, such as Rev. William Winterbotham, a Baptist, of Plymouth, and Thomas Fyshe Palmer, Unitarian, of Dundee—later to suffer harsh punishment as a result.

Robert Robinson would no doubt have spoken out; but Cambridge was to lose this staunch radical supporter in the summer of 1790. To Frend's deep sorrow, Robinson died, on 8 June, in Birmingham during a visit to Dr Priestley. He had been unwell and it had been hoped "that an interview with Dr Priestley which he had long desired, would have proved beneficial to his health and spirits", so Dyer tells us. "But a few days after his arrival, and the delivery of two sermons at Birmingham meeting houses, he died in his sleep —according to his wish, 'softly, suddenly and alone'." The following Sunday Dr Priestley preached a funeral sermon in which he said that the impression left both by Robinson's conversation and his preaching was that "he was of the Unitarian faith and had received considerable light from his [Priestley's] own theological writings." [1]

This, to the Evangelicals with whom Robinson had originally been associated, was "a tale of horror". His heart, they said, was "removed from under the influence of evangelical truth and fully prepared to drink the cup of Socinianism to the dregs . . . There is a thrilling horror in recording the event . . . the day after he had been permitted to utter such awful sentiments he was found dead in his bed!" [2]

George Dyer, who at the time "was unbending his mind at a friend's seat in Huntingdonshire" (John Hammond's home), wrote an ode referring to the funeral:

[1] Dyer: *op. cit.*, pp. 399–403.

[2] A. C. H. Seymour: *Life of Selina, Countess of Huntingdon*, p. 340

The sons of freedom o'er his bier
Hung in attentive silence lost
Dropt o'er his grave the generous tear
And precious held his dust.

Whatever the Countess of Huntingdon thought, even his former Baptist colleagues, many of them, admitted that he had moved from the Tabernacle to the Meeting House through sincere conviction and belief in religious freedom. In this Robinson followed the same trend as many liberal Baptists and Presbyterians during the previous half-century.

More exceptional was his public defence of the French Revolution; he was an active campaigner and one of his last acts was to translate an Advertisement in the Paris Revolutionary Magazine, beginning, "The revolution itself is a truly wonderful work. Reason exerts her most and best ... Such events teach the purest morality, by exposing the horrors of vice, and by displaying virtues ... especially that virtue which is never cherished without producing a harvest of happiness to whole nations at a time."[1]

Frend's grief for Robinson's death did not lessen his enthusiasm for the cause of the French Republic. He must have been encouraged in his efforts to promote Franco-British understanding, by a letter some weeks later from his friend Felix Vaughan. This young graduate of Jesus College (later to become a distinguished barrister, known for his able defence of many of Pitt's victims) had gone to spend a few months in France, and had arrived in time for the Bastille Day anniversary celebrations in Paris; on 26 July he wrote expressing his approval of what he saw: "The disposition of the people was particularly well calculated for such a purpose for I never saw any set of men ... who better understood the advantages of their present government or of the happy manner in which it was obtained ... they knew well how to distinguish between liberty and licence."

As to the celebrations, "M. Bailly the Mayor and M.

[1] Dyer: *op. cit.*, pp. 427, 428.

de La Fayette took the wisest precautions conceivable for the peace and good order of the city.—No person was allowed to enter the Champ de Mars with sticks or anything that looked like a weapon.

"No Carts or Carriages were allowed to pass the streets on that day. The National Guard patrolled the streets & were at every avenue of the Champ de Mars advising every body in the handsomest manner what they were to do . . .

"A committee sat in each district of Paris to prevent mischief in each quarter so that it might be immediately quelled there without spreading any farther. The event proved that these measures were either unnecessary or else very effectual.

"The concourse of strangers in Paris was immense: . . . many of them took their places in the Champ de Mars by three o'clock. For myself I did not get there till six. At that time it was nearly filled."

After a detailed description of the proceedings, Vaughan remarks that "I know it was said by the Aristocrates of London & was hoped by the Aristocrates here that this assemblage of so many thousands of people would be attended with ill consequences.—To them it has been fatal indeed: for at this moment I believe no nation upon earth was ever more firmly united for the destruction of despotism and the preservation of the public good . . . "

Commenting on the provincial Deputies, "everything has contributed to affect the judgement & the imagination of those men. The Bourgeoisie of Paris have this day given a dinner in each district to these provincial deputies, who dine under tents in the open streets. The town has been illuminated for the last five nights. Places at the theatres are reserved wholly for Mssrs les Deputes des provinces & tonight Le Siege de Calais is bespoke at the theatre de la nation by those of that division.

"In short, everything has contributed to affect the judgement & the imagination of these men, who will no doubt carry with them into their several countries an impression which can never be removed but by the universal corruption of the people. Add to this that in every principal town throughout France this same ceremony of federation was performed at the same hour and I hope with the same success." He says Frend "may judge . . . how little credit is to be given to those vile libels in the London newspapers & especially in the Morning Herald on the subject of French politics . . . The French speak of us with great respect, & wish much for an alliance with England & peace with all the world."

Vaughan's second letter, if less eulogistic, is an interesting account of provincial attitudes to the Republic. At Nantes, he says, "My Lord the Bishop is at present so discontented with the regulations of the national assembly that he sees nobody & revenges upon himself what there is now perhaps little hope of resisting or revenging upon their authors." On the other hand, when he asked the girl of the inn "What she thought of what had taken place in the last twelvemonth", she answered, "that although she & her father lost money by the few travellers who came amongst them since that time, they both knew that all would go well by and by." To the question what did she think of the queen, "she exclaimed ah! c'est une vilaine gueuse que celle-la."

He is persuaded that "the revolution is no where so well assured as in this province & particularly in the town of Nantes.—The gentlemen Merchants & common people are all of the most spirited kind. Their conduct with their bishop who resisted the decrees of the Assembly has set an example to the rest of the nation & will probably break the neck of the episcopal coalition . . . I need not tell you of the attachment of the Mssrs Nantais to the English, as you must have heard of their mission to the Revolution Society in London . . . "

Vaughan finishes however on an anxious note—very different from his cheerful conclusion in July ("every man seems to wear a face of content, & the king seems to be the idol of his people. I think they are an example for mankind in general & I trust such a one as will not remain without imitation"); for such an ardent supporter of the Revolution it is odd to read (6 December) the words "I can only tell you that the *Republicans* are now more in my opinion more to be feared than the *Aristocrates*." He promises "to enlarge on that matter on a future occasion"; as no letter on it survives, it is probable that he enlarged to Frend viva voce during a convivial evening in Jesus College, with a bottle of port to counteract pessimism.

Felix Vaughan was not the only one to have forebodings; Lindsey, at the end of December 1790, was equally apprehensive:

"... If public and private accounts may be credited, the storm is thickening now more than ever to burst upon the new Government in France: but I trust that divine Providence will continue to protect and support it. Insurrections in different parts of the kingdom: the king refusing his consent to the change of ecclesiastical property. The emperor having already a great force, and in six weeks time will have an army of upwards of a hundred thousand men in Flanders. The king of Sardinia and Spain also declared to be ready to co-operate. This comes from an officer lately in the Belgic army; who says that it is believed the catholics in general, and the officers and a great part of the soldiers will repair to the standard in favour of the French king, which the emperor is to erect."

* * *

When he was not engaged in correspondence about politics and Unitarian publications, Frend was busy working on his share of the translation of the Old Testament, which he had promised, as far back as the spring of 1789, to do for Dr Joseph Priestley.

"The Doctor", as he was known to his friends, had written (on 12 May 1789) to the Rev. J. Bretland "the plan of a translation of the scriptures." He had mentioned that "my part is the Hagiographa, Mr Dodson engages for the prophecies, Mr Lindsey for the New Testament, & Mr Frend for the historical books."[1]

He noted on 25 November (1789) that "Mr Garnham is a valuable part of our corps, as I hope Mr Frend will also be."[2]

There seems to have been a good deal of discussion as to whether to press Gilbert Wakefield into the "corps" of translators; but in the end it was generally felt that Wakefield was a difficult man to work with, and it was obvious that he preferred to plough his own furrow.

Lindsey had told Frend in January that Wakefield "was about to publish a translation of the New Testament . . . I am sure it will be the most improved version that is extant. I should not be surprised if he also publish a translation of the Old, as soon as some other persons who are about it." He thought it unlikely Wakefield would want to co-operate, but "I am sure he is a scholar & an ingenious, well principled, bold and ardent lover of truth and the gospel, and I honour him particularly for some of his late exertions."

Wakefield, who later achieved renown by his editions of Lucretius, was already recognized as a distinguished scholar through his *Georgics* and the first part of *Silva Critica.* He was living at Nottingham at the beginning of 1790, after a restless career (classical tutor at Warrington till 1783, then a series of teaching jobs, till he was appointed to Hackney College). Crabb Robinson's description of Wakefield is no doubt a fair one—"He was a most gentle creature in domestic life, and a very amiable man; but when he took part in political or religious controversy his pen was dipped in gall." Even when discussing small points of scholarship or doctrine he seems to have used acid instead of ink, as we can guess from the opening lines of a letter William Frend wrote to him on the matter of translating the New Testament:

"Jan. 15 [1790] I thank you for the frank and open manner in which you have expressed your surprise that I did

[1] Rutt: *op. cit.*, p. 24.

[2] *Ibid.*, p. 45.

not benefit by the remarks you have made on the disputed text in Romans."

Frend explains that he had not yet seen Wakefield's "very valuable work"; "you will pardon me if in the instance to which you allude I do not think myself reprehensible." He does his best to smooth the ruffled scholar down: "I shall make further use of your name not that you can receive anything from me but if in my little way I can encourage our young students to study the sacred writings that the classic manner in which you treat the subject may render the way smoother & more agreeable to them". He finishes his letter with a compliment to Wakefield, and an interesting allusion to Cambridge bookshops:

"I understand that you have removed your Books from Johnsons to Deightons. What think you of Johnson.[1] Is he not rather out of the way? We have an Heretical Shelf or two at a Bookseller here by means of Johnson & I was surprised at not seeing any of your Books among them. The plan was first formed with no other design than to put Books in the way of Students & it was the intention of a couple of us to be at the expence of a certain number & run the risque of their sale.

"If your works are your own property & not that of the Booksellers & you think it advisable to send me a Cargo it would be of use both to us Heretics & the Academick Students."

In the event, the bulk of the Old Testament was left to Frend and R. E. Garnham. The latter was an energetic Unitarian who lived at Bury St Edmunds where he had established "a public Library which though yet in its infancy will soon boast ye works of Dr Jebb, several of Dr Priestley's, Micaiah Towgood's Dissent fully justified . . . etc. etc." as he wrote in 1789. "This is ye way we mean to pay ye Hierarchy for ye

[1] Joseph Johnson (1738–1809), "father of the book trade" of his day (*D.N.B.*), earliest publisher of Cowper and Erasmus Darwin, Mrs Barbauld and Dr Priestley. 1789 Johnson's bookshop was in St Paul's Churchyard where he printed and sold radical literature.

trouble they have taken in persecuting our friend. We set off with fourscore subscribers & have gotten a most abominable committee of Whigs and Heretics."

Garnham had welcomed Frend home from the continent as warmly as Lindsey had, in a letter dated 13 January 1790, congratulating "not only you but all ye brethren of ye reformed religion upon ye happy event of your return to Cambridge: where I hear you are now getting your books about you again & pursuing ye path in which you have been & I hope will without interruption continue to be most eminently useful," and excusing himself for not writing "ye moment I heard of yr arrival . . . I am closely engaged in a private work in which I am exceedingly happy to understand you take a share."

This of course is the translation, which he seems to find a slightly unnerving task. "My portion is all ye Epistles; an undertaking which I own is greater yn I at first conceived it to be; but I hope to get through tolerably well in time & with application." Rather conspiratorially he adds that "I am fully convinced of ye necessity of Secrecy in ye business & shd by no means have alluded to it on this occasion had it not been to a gentleman whom I am happy & proud to call fellow-labourer."

Heretics, he says "have not been quite idle—they have pretty well tamed that portentous monster of orthodoxy, St Lewis."

He concludes his letter hoping that "yr present Master will find some other way to bishopric than persecuting you", and wishing William "health & quiet & uninterrupted pursuit of your studies."

All through 1790 there are references in Frend's correspondence to the great task of translation. Lindsey wrote in July "Dr P will ask concerning the Pentateuch & following histories & I shall tell him how you have buckled to the work for the summer . . . " (26.7.90).

A long letter from the Doctor himself, on 11 August, discusses the problems they are both tackling. After some remarks on Cambridge University ("certainly the advantages of the University, whatever they are, ought to be open to all the country, and not confined to the members of the church of England. You must excuse our railing a little at what we cannot come at") he goes on "I am sticking pretty closely to our translation, as I hope you do. Besides my proper part, *Psalms, Proverbs,* and *Ecclesiastes*, I fancy I shall have something to do with the prophets except *Isaiah* which Mr Dodson will take care of. He thinks it will be sufficient if we take the versions of *Blayney* and *Murciani* for the rest; but I am of a different opinion. We must not depart as far as they do from the present translation. It must not, according to our rules, be altered, except for the sake of some *real improvement.*

"I hope you will find time to divide this task with me, so as to take Jeremiah, Ezekiel or the *minor prophets with Daniel.* If you can, take your choice, and I will take some of the other parts. Perhaps Mr Garnham or some other of your friends, will not object to a part. Please to consult him, and let me know in time. We must have all the parts ready before the next April, and this I hope will not be very difficult."

An eight-page letter (undated) from Garnham to Frend shows that they were both deeply involved in the work, and exchanged ideas about their respective labours. Garnham endeavours "to propose some better rendering" of the sentence "In ye day yt thou eatest thereof", but finally agrees to Frend's version. "It must I think be left to ye acuteness of ye English reader to find out . . . I apprehend any man who has no more learning yn what every man of good understanding brings with him to ye reading of ye English Bible, will be able to make out the true signification." He then consults Frend, in his turn, "for a good translation of 'Christ's abiding in us & we in him'. My idea of ye signification of it is that of a friendly connection, as between members of ye same family, which figurative language seems to be used even with respect to the Deity, John xiv, 2,3. 'We will take up our abode with him.' . . . I shall be obliged to you for a good rendering."

Frend worked away industriously at the Prophets all through the late summer and autumn of 1790, and found it hard going, as Dr Priestley's letter of 2 November shows:

"I cannot help smiling at all you say, of the difficulties in your province of the translation. I would very thankfully exchange with you. I am sure I might complain with as much eloquence, and as much truth as you do, on the subject of my insufficiencies, but consider, that all we profess is an improved and improvable version. And with the helps that we all have, or may procure, a little plain good sense, with a general knowledge of the subject, is of more consequence than all the rest . . ."

So Frend soldiered on; when his nose was not to the grindstone of his "improved version" he was working hard to spread what he believed to be religious and political truth. Lindsey's letter of 2 November referred to the Cambridge Unitarian Society: "twenty or so are no contemptible church"; and Priestley wrote to encourage him in his good works—whether proselytizing, translating or teaching—declaring his conviction that "Now is the time to bring forward the evidence of Christianity in every point of view; and I wish it to appear that the greatest enemies of the Corruption of Christianity stand forth the most strenuous and the noblest defenders of Christianity itself, that the objection to us as Deists, or lukewarm Christians, may be no longer made."[1]

Dr Priestley himself was extremely busy and besieged on every side by requests for discourses, sermons, replies to attacks. Lindsey told Frend that he had advised the Doctor "not to let the preparation for a certain Translation, being ready in the next spring, hinder him from attending to any present demands: because it seems to me that it will be judged proper to delay it still another year: for probably within that space, Mr Wakefield's N.T. will be out, which it may be of gt use and benefit to see."

If Theophilus Lindsey could have looked into the future

[1] Rutt: *op. cit.*, p. 94.

and foreseen the fate of the MSS he would certainly not have advised the Doctor to postpone publishing the results of so many months' work by so many devoted people. But in December of 1790, things did not look so dark as all that, and he ended the year on an optimistic note, telling William Frend that "on Friday we are to dine at the King's Head in the Poultry, and make the first opening and settlement of our new Unitarian Society.

"I have no doubt of it producing beneficial effects in favour of true inquiry into the Scripture beyond the expectation of almost any of us. Such a phalanx of Unitarians, whose names it will exhibit in a few years, will give such countenance to their cause, as will make it even creditable."

7

ALLIES AND OPPONENTS (1791–92)

While Theophilus Lindsey was organizing the new Society in London Frend was finding plenty to do in Cambridge. Although no longer Tutor he had many college duties, for he was elected Steward from 1791 to Michaelmas 1792, and thus found himself involved in college affairs, from the passing of accounts, to the controversy over William Otter's election to a fellowship. Early in 1791 he was working hard on the translations for Dr Priestley, reading extensively, and indefatigably distributing books throughout the University. As he said later: "During the agitation of the questions on the Slave Trade and the Repeal of the Test Act, I distributed a vast number of books in this place, and carried, in person, to every head of a house, a valuable work of Bishop Horsley on the liberty of conscience." He reckoned that "ten thousand books of various sizes have been dispersed" by him or by Bowtell, the bookseller, under his direction.[1]

Frend was thus well known in Cambridge as a leading radical, possibly the most active in the area now that Robert Robinson was no longer alive. There were many who shared his views (though few so energetic in promoting them) and in later years he congratulated himself on the number and quality of his friends. Besides Tyrwhitt and Jones and Lambert there was a brilliant set of undergraduates—S. T. Coleridge, who came up in 1791, Charles Legrice (also from Christ's Hospital, the son of the vicar of Bury St Edmunds who had been persecuted for his liberal opinions a few years earlier) and Basil Montagu of Trinity (William Wordsworth's friend). And there was John Tweddell, the very gifted classical scholar, also of Trinity College, who graduated in

[1] W.F.: *Account of the Proceedings*, p. 110.

1790, but was living in Cambridge during these years, then in London studying law till his untimely death in Athens in 1799. And there was Henry Gunning, author of the *Reminiscences of Cambridge*, who was twenty-three in 1791, and in 1792 held the post of "Bedell". Gunning's sympathies were with the Reformers, though he never belonged to any Radical society, and he later suffered some petty persecution probably because of his "Jacobin" associates.

A mutual acquaintance of his and Frend's, was Henry Musgrave, a resident of Cambridge whom Gunning describes as "most consistent in his political principles, an ardent friend of civil and religious liberty, he would have died at the stake sooner than he would have abandoned them."

Musgrave was a keen Abolitionist during the Slave Trade agitation. "With Clarkson, Wrangham, and John Owen", Gunning tells us, "Musgrave was particularly intimate. Committees used to meet at his house, where their resolutions were formed and their plan of action decided on", and associations "entered into pledging the members not to use those articles that were produced by slavery." William Frend must have been present at some of these meetings, and later he always kept in touch with Musgrave, who (although he bought a plot of land in Middlesex in order to be able to vote for Sir Francis Burdett) continued to reside in Cambridge in later life.

Outside the University Frend's staunchest allies were George Dyer and Benjamin Flower the printer, a firm Unitarian from Harlow.

Two families who lived in the country some miles out of Cambridge were consistently kind and hospitable as their many long letters show. One was the Hammond family at Fen Stanton. John Hammond was an intelligent and cultured man who adored music and philosophical discussions; he had been a Fellow of Queens' until Milner's Methodist broom swept out suspected Nonconformists, and after that he became an open Unitarian, resigning his living and vicarage at Stanton but staying in the village as a small farmer. His main regrets were that he had had to abandon his books ("when you recollect how ardent we both were in quests of science ... you will be apt to exclaim: what a falling-off! what a dereliction is here!" he wrote) and his music: "Even Music itself has fallen a sacrifice to my propensity for wallowing in the mire and daubing myself with clay ... "

Hammond had seen a good deal of Frend while they were both young Fellows of their respective colleges, and he wrote nostalgically in 1797: "I cannot say how much I wish to converse with you on the subject of German literature & to enjoy once more those philosophical disquisitions with which we formerly diverted ourselves, & which I can never reflect upon but with satisfaction & delight."

The second country house where Frend was always welcome was the Reynolds' at Little Paxton, near St Neots. Richard Reynolds was that rare specimen, a country gentleman with radical views. He was described by a contemporary as supporting "almost single-handed the cause of civil and religious liberty in his county" and being known "as the Abdiel of Huntingdonshire".[1]

Reynolds' grandfather was Bishop of Lincoln, and his father also a cathedral dignitary. Richard had been a student at St John's College where he had been a "chum" (i.e. shared rooms with) Theophilus Lindsey; and their friendship lasted till the latter's death, sustained by numerous letters and visits.

Reynolds had had an interesting life before he retired to Paxton, having, among other trips abroad, accompanied Lord Sandwich as private secretary to Aix-la-Chapelle at the time of the signing of the treaty. But he "preferred being a country gentleman, a magistrate, and a champion of liberty and independence". He had a very nice property at Paxton Hall, with a farm, and a flower garden which Mrs Reynolds, a lively talkative lady, looked after, among her many domestic and social activities.

[1] *D.N.B.*

The orthodox county gentry looked on the Reynolds' with some suspicion, just as the orthodox members of Cambridge University suspected Frend and his liberal-minded colleagues—for from 1791 onwards, anyone professedly in favour of Reform and Change was considered highly unreliable. There was talk of some members of the university carrying on a treasonable correspondence with the National Convention in France; it was said that five persons were concerned in it, and that Pitt knew their names and had possession of their correspondence. Frend's name was one, and Lawrence Reynolds (the squire's nephew, a B.A. of St John's) another. Dr Edwards was said to be the third, and the fourth, Martin Naylor of Queens' (Third Wrangler in 1787) "a man of coarse and rough manners, but much esteemed by those who knew him intimately, for the kindness of his heart and the benevolence of his disposition". The fifth was unknown. Whatever their opinions, the conspirators only once in their lives met together, at dinner, quite by accident, so the conspiracy was obviously a complete myth.

There was a good reason however for building up the legend; and the man responsible for it was Isaac Milner, whom we have already seen was probably the most ambitious, as well as the most dynamic and colourful person in Cambridge. Milner had recently been elected Master of Queens', and with one foot on the rung of the ladder to fame he was eager to climb as high and as fast as possible. At this time, what better way was there of catching the eye of those who were in power, and could give promotion, than to be discovering plots, and destroying nests of republicans and levellers (as dissenters and radicals were now named)?

Milner himself could certainly be guaranteed true blue. He was still a close friend of William Wilberforce, with whom he had toured in Europe in 1784 (converting the latter to Evangelical Methodism), and through Wilberforce Milner had, or imagined he had, access to Pitt's ear.

As previously mentioned, Milner was an outstandingly

clever man, a brilliant chemist and logician; his arrogance and autocratic ways were legendary from the time when, as a young sizar at Queens' College he was "reproved for upsetting a tureen of soup" and exclaimed "When I get into power I will abolish this nuisance!"—which he did. He was also famous for his eccentric behaviour; he ate and drank to excess, did card tricks, dosed himself with morphia, walked about naked in the rain in the Master's garden, forgetting or not caring that he could be seen from neighbouring windows.

After his appointment as Master we learn that "the College entirely changed its character, and the society which . . . had been distinguished for its attachment to Civil and Religious Liberty, became afterwards as remarkable for its opposition to liberal opinions. The number of students increased but the majority of them were . . . Methodists, Calvinists and Serious Christians." Before Milner became president "these Low-Church doctrines had been entirely confined to Magdalene College." (Dr Gretton, Master of Magdalene for sixteen years, had previously declared that "there must be something in the air of Magdalene that makes men Methodists", for, said he, "we have elected Fellows from Clare Hall, from Trinity, and other Colleges, whom we have considered to be most anti-Methodistical, but in a short time they all became Methodists.")

In view of promoting Methodism in Queens', Milner gradually ousted members of nonconformist views, and replaced them by safe Church-and-King men, even when the radical was far the best qualified for a Fellowship—as in the case of Wrangham, of whom Gunning says: "The more effectually to injure Wrangham reports were circulated that he was a friend to the French revolution . . . to the falsehood of these charges everyone who knew Wrangham could testify."

As Milner himself said, "I was positively determined to have nothing to do with Jacobins or infidels and custom has placed in my power the appointment of the tutors provided they be Fellows of our own College. Our own being very unfit, we went out of college sorely against the wish of several; however by determining to make no jobs of such things, but to take the very best men I could find, I carried the matter through, in no less than three instances." Had Milner not been Master, it is likely that Thomas Fyshe Palmer would instead of removing to Dundee in 1789 have been elected a Fellow of Queens', and saved from the Scottish judge's sentence of transportation and death in Botany Bay.

Milner was a curious combination of ambition and laziness, spiritually reactionary yet mentally energetic. He was one of the few professors who gave lectures, and his "experiments in optics—very little more than exhibitions of the Magic Lantern on a gigantic scale—" drew crowds of students. He had been pleased at being elected president of Queens' in 1786—a post which combined dignity and power with comfort and very little work—but he did not care for the idea of being Vice-Chancellor, for which he was the obvious candidate, and during 1790 he had rumours circulated about the wretched state of his health—surprising Cambridge which had always looked on him "as one of the most robust and healthy of our members." The portrait of him in Queens' College dining-hall certainly does not represent a weakling, and his favourite armchair rivals Henry VIII's seat in King's Chapel in cubic capacity. He was said to weigh over 20 stone, and though fatness does not necessarily signify health he seemed solid enough in other ways: "Whenever he entered the Senate House his voice might be heard from one end to the other"—and yet it was reported that "his symptoms threatened pulmonary diseases, and his most intimate friends represented him as being in considerable danger."

When he appeared in public nobody could see any difference in him or "believe he could be in that delicate health that was represented"; at official dinners "he ate and drank more, talked louder and laughed more heartily than anyone present." The truth was what was generally guessed—that he did not wish to be Vice-Chancellor as that office "was a very troublesome one; and it was also attended by much expense. No remuneration was attached to the office except that arising from a share of money paid by compounders, and from the interest of the balance in the bankers' hands."

When in the summer of 1792, in spite of his objections, the Heads of the other colleges determined he should take the office of Vice-Chancellor, "he began to procure a medical certificate which might induce them to discharge for him some of the most troublesome duties."

He wrote a long letter setting out his ailments to his doctor, who obliged as requested with a certificate. "The heads agreed to divide among themselves almost all that part of the Vice-Chancellor's duties which required him to leave his room." Relieved of any onerous tasks, Milner took on the job and thoroughly enjoyed it; he entertained lavishly and jovially at official functions: "He was always in high spirits on these occasions and the bottle circulated very freely. The public dinners were followed by private ones, which were quite uproarious", according to Henry Gunning who was, as Bedell, a frequent guest.[1]

Milner must have been a splendid host, to judge by another contemporary description of his conversation; he had "dipped into innumerable books, and talked with shrewdness, animation and intrepidity on them all. Whatever the conversation and whatever the theme, his sonourous voice predominated over all other voices, even as his lofty stature, vast girth and superincumbent wit defied all competitors."[2]

Such a man was, or could be, a formidable enemy; among the many he had got the better of, was Dr Paley himself. In the words of Gunning, "in the early part of 1792 he was appointed Dean of Carlisle; it had been generally thought that Paley (who had been Chancellor of Carlisle for some time) would have had this particular preferment; but many

[1] Gunning: *op. cit.*, i, pp. 238–241.

[2] J. Stephen: *Ecclesiastical Studies*, ii, p. 358 seq.

of his friends suspected with reason, that Paley had been misrepresented to Wilberforce and had little chance of getting preferment from the Crown."

If even Paley, who after all was well known not to be averse to reversing a position if circumstances required, was to be injured (through Pitt, via Wilberforce) by Milner, what chance had William Frend, who would never budge from his opinions, against so formidable an opponent?

* * *

Frend knew, through all the political gossip in Cambridge, the kind of risks he was running by sticking to his guns, but it seemed to him that to do so was his best safeguard, and that he and his friends must advance as far as was legally possible, so as to be in a strong position when things became more difficult.

At the beginning of 1791 he welcomed Lindsey's new Unitarian organization, and sent its founder suggestions for it. Lindsey wrote on 14 February, "I presume that Dr Disney may have written to you and told you of our respectable commencement of the New Society"; there had been a respectable number present, respectable names, and a respectable sum of 100 guineas contributed by Mr Tayleur of Shrewsbury.

Mr Tyrwhitt had emended the name from Society "for religious knowledge" to "christian knowledge", which Lindsey thought "very proper, as we are already called a Society of Deists." The full name suggested was "the Unitarian Society for promoting Christian knowledge on the principle of the Unity of God"; Lindsey adds "however I have no idea of differing from him or you if we were a quarter of an hour together."

Frend had suggested having "correspondents" attached to the Society, and this had been taken up: "a worthy person present added that he hoped we should have not only correspondents but members in America, and also upon the

Continent of Europe, where our language is very wide spread . . . So you perceive we already see big expectations."

Lindsey was at this time (spring 1791) active on the national Standing Committee of Dissenters which was supporting the Catholics in their petition to Parliament (somewhat to the surprise of the Catholics "who had rather expected opposition from that quarter").[1] Although in favour of the proposed Bill, Lindsey wrote to Frend expressing annoyance at the proviso "that the act shall not extend to Persons writing against the Trinity." He asks "What business have Catholics with this? They are known Trinitarians and never supposed to write against it. The truth is, this article did not come from the Catholics themselves but was imposed upon them as necessary to make their bill pass . . . How curious and cunning to bring in thus by a side word a confirmation by Parliament of an Act of a century past & known to be of so shocking a nature that they dare not act upon it!"

The bill was passed, repealing old statutes against "popish recusants", and Lindsey praised Fox for his speech announcing "his intention of bringing in a bill on better and more extensive principles for the relief of Protestant as well as Catholic Dissenters if the Minister would not undertake it".[2]

But even though Fox was on their side, the Unitarians were over-optimistic. The Ministry linked all this Dissenting activity with the agitation for reform, the many meetings of new societies and clubs, the wide sales of Paine's *Rights of Man* and radical pamphlets, all over England, and the increasingly radical happenings in France. Dissenters were accused by the Tory alarmists of being republicans and levellers, and were closely watched.

It became known that good money was available for spying, and free drinks for those who would join a mob to hound down the Reformers; and with the growth of organized persecution, the general public began to be a little wary;

[1] McLachlan: *op. cit.*, p. 66.

[2] *Ibid.*, p. 67.

Dr Priestley, the most celebrated of the victims of mob violence, that very year, wrote: "in spite of all we can write or do . . . the love of liberty is on the decline."

Lindsey continued to write hopefully, however, saying on 23 April that Dr Priestley is well, and busy on the translation: "but they do not expect to be in readiness to go to the Press before next Spring . . . I trust all will be in such forwardness so as to have time to look over each other's work before any part be handed to the press."

His trust, alas, was not to be justified. On 14 July 1791, the Birmingham Church-and-King mob, with the tacit approval of authority, attacked and destroyed Priestley's house and laboratory. Along with his most treasured possessions, scientific writings and the results of a life-time of work, the manuscripts of his devoted group of translators all went up in smoke.

It was impossible to compensate Priestley for the loss of irreplaceable papers; but the amount offered him for damages was absurdly small. Lindsey wrote to Frend, that "Dr Priestley is come back from the Warwick Assizes. Indeed he never meets with any insult but from one low Person of Warwick. And I think he is better for the excursion though the Jury have not sent him home with heavy pockets. There is however a talk of the sufferers in general applying to Government for indemnifications as the Judges, who both behaved very handsomely, were not at all satisfied with the verdicts given."

Priestley had a great many friends and admirers, known and unknown, who were highly indignant, and promised him support when he left Birmingham, hoping he would stay in London. When he packed up and left with his family and Thomas Cooper for America in 1794, Frend was one of four Cambridge graduates who presented him with a handsome silver inkstand inscribed "To Joseph Priestley LL.D. on his departure into exile from a few Members of the University of Cambridge who regret that this expression of their esteem should be occasioned by the ingratitude of their country."

The signatories were William Frend, James Losh, John Tweddell and Godfrey Higgins.

Early in 1792 the idea of a society for encouraging radical and pro-Reform groups all over the country, which Frend had advocated in 1790, materialized when the London Corresponding Society was formed in London. Its members were mainly working men, and it seemed to the authorities to be much less "respectable" than the Society for Constitutional Information, and potentially far more dangerous. Thanks to the energetic secretary, Thomas Hardy, a shoemaker in Piccadilly, there was a multitude of meetings, demonstrations, new groups springing up, sales of *The Rights of Man* and other "revolutionary" literature. The government took fright. In June a Royal Proclamation was published, warning the King's "faithful and loving subjects" against the "subversion of regular government", and letting it be known that riots, tumults, wicked and seditious writings would not be tolerated, and that the authorities would take strong measures to suppress such goings-on.

Although the immediate effect of this was to increase the sales of *The Rights of Man* through the unsolicited advertisement, and the L.C.S. and provincial societies continued to meet, the King's Proclamation marked the beginning of an authorized witch-hunt. The Radicals had still a certain amount of nominal freedom, but it diminished fast as the months went by. Dissenters met to worship and members of "Constitution" Societies met for discussion, but it required considerable faith and courage to do so, as the meeting-houses and even private homes, such as Thomas Walker's in Manchester, were attacked by rioters. Almost every sizeable town had its Church-and-King mob; it became difficult to find premises, as the publicans often refused their rooms; booksellers displayed radical publications but found themselves threatened if not actually arrested. In the autumn of 1792, the Government increased the pressure, making the most of the popular revulsion to the "terror" in France (but not explaining the reasons for this—the threat to the

Republic by the French emigrés and their allies) and seizing writers, printers and even preachers of radical views. On 5 and 18 November Rev. William Winterbotham, a Baptist minister of Plymouth, preached two mildly "republican" sermons and was arrested. On 20 November, Mr John Reeves, ex-governor of Newfoundland provided an instrument to make it even easier for Pitt to suppress his opponents. He formed an Association for Preserving Liberty and Property against Republicans and Levellers, which was to be a focus for the activity of the Anti-Jacobins. It had branches in all sizeable towns, pledged to suppress sedition and to aid the magistracy to round up the suspects.[1]

Cambridge was not behind other places, either in its "jacobinism" or its "loyalty". Gunning tells us that "an attempt was made in the University and town to represent those who differed from Mr Pitt as enemies to the Constitution, and as elsewhere, Associations were formed, and resolutions circulated against Republicans and Levellers in very offensive language ... All those who declined signing [the Association's statement] were stigmatized as enemies to their King", including the Dissenters en masse. "Sir Busick Harwood led the band with the remark 'every Dissenter should be considered a rogue until he had proved himself to be an honest man'."

Although popular newspapers such as *The Herald* of Leicester and the *Manchester Herald* had been forced to close down, in Cambridge Benjamin Flower started, soon after, defiantly to print and publish *The Intelligencer*. The reason that he escaped the jackals may be that Cambridge town was small and he was protected to a certain degree by the patronage of a number of influential university men. But Flower was lucky, for Cambridge, which one might, if innocent, expect to be more enlightened than other centres, did have its riots and its Church-and-King mob—which included young rowdies from the university of the type who had in former years annoyed Mr Robinson by their antics

[1] cf. F. Knight: *The Strange Case of Thomas Walker*, Chaps. 9 and 10.

in his church. They attacked unfortunate individuals on the merest hearsay: "The word went round that a grocer named Gazam had uttered seditious expressions. The mob constructed a figure to represent him: a halter was put about his neck and was affixed to a gallows; this was carried to the door of all good subjects, and those who did not subscribe were considered deficient in loyalty." Gunning was standing at the gate of Emmanuel College "when the effigy was exhibited."—"We were joined by the Master, who laughed heartily; he gave the men who carried it five shillings and desired them to shake it well 'opposite Master Gazam's house'."

Poor Gazam—he packed up and left Cambridge for America the following year, when mob violence threatened to increase; and he was probably wise, for according to Gunning "in Cambridge, almost every evening during the latter part of this winter [1792] there were riotous assemblies and the windows of many of the Dissenters were broken. A very numerous mob collected one evening, who, after breaking several windows, did great injury to the Meeting-house. They were headed by two chimney sweepers, under whose direction they proceeded to the Market-place and attacked several houses, endeavouring to burst open the doors; this was prevented by the interference of some M.A.s, several of them Fellows of St John's."[1] Together with the magistrates they dispersed the crowd, after reading the Riot Act. Not all the St John's Fellows were so public-spirited: "One of them later addressing his pupils, expressed the opinion that the riot was a laudable ebullition of justifiable zeal."[2]

Things were going from bad to worse for the radicals, and it was perhaps natural for the publicans of the town of

[1] According to the *Cambridge Chronicle*, "a number of people paraded the streets with music and meeting with Mr Musgrave insisted on singing God Save the King . . . [Then] proceeded to the New Meeting House where they broke upward of 120 squares of glass and committed other outrages." 22.12.1793.

[2] Gunning: *op. cit.*, pp. 251–252.

Cambridge to be nervous of having their property destroyed should they be suspected of "jacobin" sympathies. In Manchester and elsewhere the use of rooms in public houses had been refused to the "Painite" clubs. But the Cambridge publicans were surely going unnecessarily far in meeting and issuing their Declaration:

"If with our knowledge any person or persons, either by public conversation, or by public reading, or circulation of any books, pamphlets or papers of a treasonable or seditious tendency, do endeavour to inflame or unsettle the minds of his Majesty's subjects, thereby promoting and encouraging riots and tumults, we will immediately give notice thereof to the magistrates, and do our utmost to bring to justice all those, who by the above or another means, may endeavour to disturb the public peace"—which was signed by one hundred and twelve public house keepers.[1]

On New Year's Eve, as if to mark the desired end of republicanism along with the end of the troubled year 1792, and to forewarn "jacobins" of what was coming in 1793, Thomas Paine was burnt in effigy by "the populace" on the Market Place. Half a mile from the scene Isaac Milner and William Frend respectively in their quiet college rooms may have looked out and seen the glow of the flames—and wondered what would ensue.

[1] Gunning: *op. cit.*, pp. 253–254.

8

PEACE AND UNION
(Spring 1793)

AT THE BEGINNING of 1793 Frend, though he was disapproved of and disliked by the more reactionary of his colleagues, had considerable standing among the staff, and a good deal of influence among undergraduates both in his own college and in the University. He was no longer a tutor but, as steward (till Michaelmas 1792) had held a highly responsible post, and still carried his share of staff duties. He saw a good deal of the students, who admired him as a strong colourful personality and as a rebel.

Coleridge recalled how he was brought to Unitarianism by Frend and how he was reproved by his guardian George Caldwell for associating with a person of Frend's tendencies; to which he replied that Frend's company was "by no means invidious".—"He is intimate with Dr Pearce himself." Moreover, "though I am not an Alderman I have yet prudence enough to respect that gluttony of faith yclept orthodoxy."[1]

Frend was evidently influential in college elections, for E. D. Clarke, who had by then left Jesus College (where he had spent much of his time constructing an air balloon, launched with a small kitten as cargo from the central court of the college in June 1790) and had been travelling about the continent, wrote to him on 10 February from Naples: "It is doubtful whether this will ever reach you considering the troubled countries through which it has to pass . . . If it should be so fortunate I hope you will excuse the Motive which induced me to send it. I know it is not usually approved of, when anyone who offers himself as a Candidate for a Fellowship attempts to biass those who have the dis-

[1] E. K. Chambers: *Coleridge: A Biographical Study*, pp. 18–19.

posal of such preferment, previous to the period appointed for the Election ..." but he hopes that his "peculiar situation" will have some weight "with you whose friendship I have experienced in such an essential manner upon many a former occasion." As "I am getting my Bread in the best manner I can" it is impossible to appear at college for the approaching Election for Fellows. He hopes "the Fellows will dispense with my returning to England", and he has sent "several copies of a Latin Epistle to the Fellows" entrusted to the care of Mr Plampin. He asks Frend for "your friendly support" and adds "I am not enabled to show (my gratitude) by any return of the favours I have received so often from you ... I hope for a time when I may have the power to repay them."

Coleridge, as we have already seen, was influenced by Frend who was certainly one of the gownsmen who met at evening parties in the poet's rooms. These, "on the right hand ground floor of the staircase facing the gate, were a centre of conversation, largely on politics", Charles Legrice reported, and "at these parties Aeschylus and Plato and Thucydides were pushed aside with a pile of lexicons etc. to discuss the pamphlets of the day ... There was no need of having the book before us," says Legrice; "Coleridge had read it in the morning, and in the evening he would repeat whole pages verbatim." As a learned biographer has said, "Coleridge was an admirer of Burke ... but his politics of 1793 if not strictly democratic were certainly anti-war and anti-Pitt. This was the general tone of undergraduate Cambridge, and in Coleridge's case we may once more suspect the influence of William Frend."[1]

Frend clearly was doing all he could to encourage and stimulate the enthusiasm of the young generous spirits of this circle, not only for Unitarianism and against Pitt's régime, but for a positive political philosophy, and for social and parliamentary reform. He had for some time past been studying these questions, and had come to the conclusion that

[1] E. K. Chambers: *op. cit.*, p. 20.

in order to achieve any measure of social welfare it was essential to reform the electoral system. There had since 1789 been a great revival, in all sections of society, of the movement for Parliamentary Reform, started by Major Cartwright twenty years before, and Frend had been caught up in the campaign. In his own words, "For nearly these two years my attention has been carried to other pursuits [than his academic studies] ... The perusal of various popular writings, and the conversation of all around me, led me to reflect seriously on the state of the nation."

He was not employed in any particular work just then, since he had finished his translation for Dr Priestley—which, as he says, "was lost in the flames enlightened by the blind zeal of the church at Birmingham." So he decided to put his ideas on Reform together, for his own benefit and for anyone else who would read them. "I was not connected with any party," he writes. "I had been a witness to the miseries of the French, but saw no reason for adopting all their principles, or their conduct in government. There were many defects and abuses in our own government: yet the lenient hand of reform seemed sufficient for their removal; and to encourage this spirit in the governors and the governed, I wrote my pamphlet entitled Peace and Union." [1]

He summarized the pamphlet in a later publication, and, as it was soon to cause such a storm, we should perhaps quote him here:

"The reforms recommended were classed under three heads, representation, law, and religion. Under the first, the shortening of the duration of parliaments, increase of votes in boroughs, extension of the rights of suffrage to copy holders as well as freeholders, and the antient system of government introduced by . . . the king, were recommended. Under the second head, some evils in the modern system of law were enumerated ... Under the third head, some changes in the religious establishment were desired."

The writer set out "to explode the foolish ideas enter-

[1] Frend: *Sequel to an Account of the Proceedings*, p. 9.

tained of uniformity of opinion; to recommend what had prevailed even in popish times, a diversity of liturgies . . . He considered it too as absurd, that any person should be subjected to the rites of a church of which he disapproves, and that to enjoy a civil office a religious test should be thought necessary."

These ideas, widely canvassed at the time by many very respectable Whigs, would, one might have thought, hardly have caused such a tidal wave. Nor would they have, probably, had it not been for a last-minute addition to the pamphlet, which was quite unpremeditated and which proved unexpectedly volcanic.

Frend had almost completed *Peace and Union* and was going to send it off to be printed when, on 23 January 1793, Louis XVI was executed in Paris, and a few days later war was declared against France. Frend was furious at the country being plunged into war on this pretext: "With respect to the late king of France," he wrote, "I cannot conceive what right an englishman has to cut a frenchman's throat on that account, any more than he has to assassinate a ruffian for the deposition of the late czar. Till some more convincing reason appear . . . I must say as before, that, if all the kings on the continent were put to death by their subjects, it is not our business to punish their conduct. We should be indignant at their presuming to change our government; & what pretext can we have, from a change in theirs, to interfere in their internal concerns?"

He decided that he must add an appendix to what he had written in his pamphlet, and sat down to compose a diatribe against war, and against this war in particular: "I am convinced", he wrote, "that as rich men are the great gainers by war, either by contracts, loans, commissions in the army and navy, titles, commissaryships, or other similar gratifications, the whole expence of war should be confined to the rich." The poor "are enticed or taken away by force from their families, are subjected to hardships, the chance of wounds or death; and the honour if honour is to be gained by murder and bloodshed, falls not to their lot, but to an indolent spectator it may be of the bloody conflict."[1]

He broke off the development of this theme, to ride out into the country and visit his friend Hammond at Fen Stanton. They talked for a while, then Frend set out on foot to St Ives, to "inspect the printing of these few sheets". On the way, he says, "I joined company with two men of the village, who, being employed by the woolstaplers to let out spinning to the poor, had lately received orders to lower the value of labour. We were talking on this subject, when the exclamations of a group of poor women going to market, overhearing our conversation, made an impression on my mind which all the eloquence of the House of Lords and Commons cannot efface."

"We are to be scotched three pence in the shilling!" cried one, "We are to be scotched a fourth part of our labour!" Another called out "Let others work for me, I'll not."—"What is all this for?" they clamoured, crowding round Frend and his companion.

Frend "did not dare to tell them what it was for, nor to add insult to misery", for, "What is the beheading of a monarch to them? What is the navigation of the Scheldt to them? What is the freedom of a great nation to them but reason for joy? . . . What must be their fate when we suffer under the most odious scourge of the human race, and the accumulation of taxes takes away half of that daily bread, which is scarce sufficient at present for their support?"[2]

With the villagers' lamentations in his ears, Frend rode back to Jesus College, where he started re-writing the Appendix to his pamphlet. He quoted the women's words, and went on:

"Oh! that I had the warning voice of an ancient prophet, that I might penetrate into the innermost recesses of palaces, and appal the haranguers of senates! I would use no other language than that of these poor market-women. I would

[1] *Sequel*, p. 113.

[2] *Appendix, Peace and Union.*

cry aloud in the ears of the first magistrates: 'We are scotched three pence in the shilling, the fourth part of our labour—for what?' Is there a man who could stand out against this eloquence? Yes! Thousands . . . They know not what a cottage is, they know not how the poor live, how they make up their scanty meal." He asks any sympathetic person in the House of Commons to tell the House "what the deduction of 3d in the shilling occasions among the myriads of England."

He suggested "an easy method" to relieve them: "Let . . . the rich men of the nation, all who are for war, be scotched one fourth part of their annual income to defray the expence of it. Let them be the first sufferers, let the burden fall on them, not on the poor. Alas! my poor countrymen, how many years' calamity await you before a single dish or glass of wine will be withdrawn from the tables of opulence.

"At this moment, perhaps, the decree is gone forth of war. Let others talk of glory, let others celebrate the heroes who are to deluge the world with blood, the words of the poor market-women will still resound in my ears: 'We are scotched three pence in the shilling, one-fourth of our labour, for what?' "

Frend checked up on the truth of the women's remarks by going to visit one of the main wool dealers in Cambridge, who showed him a printed bill confirming the drop in payment for spinning, owing to the war scare. Then he rode over with the manuscript of the Appendix to St Ives and left it with the printer. Two weeks later the pamphlet was ready, and being delivered in bundles to the Cambridge booksellers.

Its author tells us that the pamphlet "occasioned on its first appearance no small ferment in the university. The fellows of St John's College were particularly clamorous, and they were joined by that set of men, who, from particular pretensions to particular sanctity of manners and zeal for orthodoxy, have gained among us the appellation of saints." The chorus against him was also joined by others who, Frend suggests, "not being capable of acquiring distinction by any laudible pursuits in the paths of literature, were anxious to intrude themselves by noise and intrigue on the publick notice." They disparaged the book, and spread abroad "very unfavourable reports of its author", accusing him of "a falsehood on a matter of fact which is known to thousands within an hour's ride of Cambridge."[1] He is referring to the "studious endeavours" of the Rev. Mr Watson, fellow of Sidney Sussex College, to blacken his character. When he heard that Watson was asserting that the facts reported were pure invention, Frend wrote off angrily to tell him where he had found them:

"Mr Frend gained his knowledge ... from the poor employed in spinning; from the persons employed by the wool-dealers to deliver out wool to the poor; and from the printed papers sent round by the wool-dealers ... Mr Audley, a wool-dealer in this town is willing to corroborate this account ... Jesus College, March 4, 1793."

Mr Watson wrote back: "Whenever the oppression of the poor of Fenstanton has been the subject of conversation ... he asserted that he wished to believe that Mr Frend thro' ignorance had misrepresented the fact."[2]

Frend informed him on 14 March, that in consequence of his last note, "Mr Frend called this evening on Mr Audley, who has given him a printed paper just made for Cambridgeshire, parts of Hertfordshire, Bedfordshire and Huntingdonshire, and shown him letters from Yorkshire, and other parts, informing him of the progress in the lowering of the price of spinning. At a meeting in Suffolk, spinning was lowered again 2d per pound, from 9d to 7d."

On 15 March Watson tried to extricate himself by saying that he had realized all along that the price of spinning had fallen, and sarcastically suggested that it was hardly a subject of interest to a Cambridge don. "You may probably be better skilled in the mysteries of woollen manufactories than I can pretend to be; my trifling knowledge of the trade

[1] *Account*, p. ix.
[2] *Ibid.*, pp. 55–56.

does not attempt to account for the reason for paying what is term'd a shilling's worth of labour with 9d or 10d but I believe it to be a notorious fact that in proportion to the fluctuating value of the manufactur'd commodity the price of spinning a certain quantity of wool has varied in different degrees downwards from one shilling . . . " This information he "received from some of the most respectable inhabitants of each of my parishes" he says adding: "I did not think myself so interested about any part of your pamphlet as to be studiously earnest in having it discussed in various companies."

Frend would not let him wriggle out, but pinned him down firmly, the very same day: "Mr Frend did not write to Mr Watson to enter into any controversy on the mysteries of woollen manufactories, which, like the pretended mysteries of religion, are only such to those who do not give themselves the trouble of gaining knowledge from the proper sources. It is of a misrepresentation of a matter of fact to the injury of Mr Frend's character that he complains, and however light the subject may appear in Mr Watson's eyes, as long as truth is violated, it becomes Mr Watson to acquire just information, & having done that, either to convict Mr Frend of a falsehood or to retract his former assertions: . . . it appears strange that Mr Watson should delay to call on Mr Audley, from whom he will gain more information on this subject than from the most respectable inhabitants of his parish, who are not immediately concerned in letting out spinning to the poor. March 15."

Mr Watson riposted with a longish note, beginning: "You assert that I deny what you positively affirm I do not," continuing "I am not conversant in the knowledge of . . . woollen manufactories. I cannot from myself presume to contradict what you from your professed extensive investigation of the subject positively affirm . . . ", and begging leave "to decline any future correspondence with you on the subject of the fall of the price of spinning at Fenstanton."[1]

[1] *Account*, pp. 57–62.

It was, clearly, the anti-war Appendix which was the real thorn in the flesh of the orthodox, rather than the anti-clericalism of the rest of the pamphlet. It was the first time that Frend had come out with a damaging *political* shaft, revealing him as a "jacobin" as well as a nonconformist.

Soon after it was discovered how explosive they were, the two pages of dynamite were removed from many copies of the pamphlet—in some cases by shocked anti-jacobins, in others by the booksellers who, for their own sakes or for Frend's, advised him to cancel the Appendix in future editions of his pamphlet for fear he (or they) should run into a prison sentence or worse.

Frend agreed, though unwillingly, to withdraw the "most offending parts" of what he had written from the printed copies. He stood by every word, and indeed the hard economic fact that he had observed and registered in his appendix, with the human consequence, was probably the starting point of his subsequent interest in political economy and of his understanding of the connection between peace and social reform; it sparked off, also, his hatred of war, now based on reason as well as on emotion, which developed and found constant and eloquent expression during the twenty-two years of hostilities which followed.

But there was no doubt that Frend's printer and booksellers would be at risk. As we have seen, in the autumn of 1792, magistrates all over the country, with the backing of Mr White the Treasury Solicitor, were tracking down anyone suspected of sedition, particularly anyone known to be writing, selling or distributing subversive literature; dozens of booksellers had been arrested and heavily fined. Thomas Muir was arrested at his home near Glasgow, in early January 1793, for seditious utterances (and was later to be transported, with Rev. Thomas Fyshe Palmer, to Botany Bay for this "crime"). Rev. William Winterbotham had been arrested after preaching two mildly critical sermons in a Plymouth chapel, at the end of November '92. In Cambridge jail a few minutes' walk from Frend's study, a young man was held on the word of a drunken highway robber, for having exclaimed "Damn the monarchy, I want none", and having "wished to see King's Chapel turned into a stable."[1]

Knowing all this, as Frend undoubtedly did, why was he determined to have his pamphlet published, and to push it so vigorously? conveying, and getting messengers to convey, parcels of copies all over Cambridge and the country round? Because he was proud of his handiwork and was unwilling to see his efforts wasted, owing to the prejudices of men he despised? Because he was so firmly convinced of the rightness of his case and the wrongness of the other side? Because he looked forward to a battle of wills, if it should come, with Isaac Milner, heavyweight champion of the Right?

With all his good qualities, Frend had a strong streak of obstinacy and of intolerance; a little tact and flexibility would have saved him endless trouble. But he was not made that way.

His Dissenting friends wrote to him with good advice and what encouragement they could offer—for it must have seemed to them dreadfully rash on Frend's part to have rushed his pamphlet into print at this precise moment.

An old acquaintance, Matthew Robinson (who later took the family title of Lord Rokeby) former member of Parliament for Kent, and a progressive public-spirited person, wrote back from his Weald village indicating that he recommended prudence to his young friend and preferred to practise it himself in these difficult times:

"I beg leave for certain reasons to excuse myself at this time from entering in a letter into our present Politics. I have however neither signed nor associated, and I concur very much with you and the market women concerning the war. It is my earnest desire, if any fatal catastrophe shall . . . happen during my days in this Country, that I may be able to say within myself, that I have directly or indirectly had no hand in it nor contributed to it; which, it is through the changing shifting and shuffling of our parties to be feared,

[1] *Cambridge Chronicle*, 4.12.1792.

very few persons will be well warranted to do." He stresses the uncertainties of the postal service, obviously referring to the authorities' way of opening mail:

"The passage of letters may at the present moment be somewhat doubtful", and "I shall be very happy to see you at Horton where we may fully and freely talk over religious, political and other subjects."[1]

Frend was unable to go to Horton just then and he did not really care whether the police spies read his letters or not; but although convinced that he had done nothing illegal he was rather concerned about his future prospects. He knew that on 22 February five Fellows of Jesus College had sent a protest against his pamphlet to the Vice-Chancellor (Isaac Milner) and to the Visitor (the Bishop of Ely) asking them to take measures for the "effectual suppression of its dangerous tendencies." This action had been followed by a meeting presided over by Milner, at Queens' Master's Lodge, where twenty-seven Fellows of the University, headed by Dr Kipling, formulated resolutions in favour of prosecuting the author of *Peace and Union.*[2]

Frend, on hearing of the meeting, wrote three notes to Kipling and two to Milner asking for a copy of the resolutions, but this was denied him. In the Radical London newspapers, according to Frend, "some very severe censures were passed on the twenty-seven, which put the authour under the necessity of writing" to the *Morning Chronicle* "to give the Publick . . . a clear statement of this extraordinary business without an appearance of biass on either side."

This "statement" concludes: "I shall not renounce any positions in my book unless some valid arguments . . . are adduced in confutation of them. The book will probably be published in London, when the publick at large may have an opportunity of commenting on the danger of those

[1] M. Robinson to W.F., 7.3.1793.

[2] Bishop of Ely: *Correspondence.* Ely Diocesan Records. (E.D.R.). C. U. Library, C5/3 and 4.

truths which have excited so great a ferment in the university."[1]

A little uneasy in spite of himself about the possibility that he might lose his Fellowship should Jesus College follow the lead of Dr Kipling, he asked Matthew Robinson's opinion of the risk.

The old gentleman replied, "I was much hurt at reading your account of the attack made upon you. The A.M. [*sic*] removed from your name will certainly be facilis factura; but the loss of a Fellowship might be a more serious matter." Robinson recalled a Fellow of Trinity Hall deprived of his degree by the Vice-Chancellor for some trivial offence: "There was with us no conception or imagination that this circumstance affected in any manner his Fellowship. He troubled himself little or not at all about it & lived for several years and died thus deprived of or suspended from his degree but Fellow of the College . . . It appears to be nearly a case in point with yours . . . It is therefore to be hoped that the consequence (hinted at by you) respecting your Fellowship will not and cannot follow; although the immediate event should happen which you suppose."

Knowing William to be impulsive and outspoken, Robinson recommends "in these times a cautious & circumspect conduct on certain subjects.

"It is certainly unfit & unbecoming an honest man to prevaricate, to deny or disavow his true sentiments; but Silence is a shield & guard which nature gives & allows us for nice or difficult cases.

"When a person is surrounded with a crowd who believe, or pretend to believe on any subject very differently from what he is himself known to do, there is a sort of dignity in absolute silence & in an apparent indifference concerning the systems or doctrines of others.

"Our heads of the Church & Champions of Orthodoxy do certainly at the bottom not believe more, but much less than you.

[1] *Account*, p. xiii.

"They consider in consequence Articles & Creeds, as Rectories, Prebends, Deaneries & Bishopricks & swallow them accordingly & the more the better.

"You have without scruple declared your Ideas to the Public: they will sooner or later have their effect, if they are well founded. May not an example of difficulties rather discourage others from the same steps, who may be of the same sentiments?"[1]

Knowing William, Matthew Robinson must have realized that such advice would not be heeded; for the author had not gone to the trouble of writing his pamphlet just to stand silent when it was being attacked. He was in fact preparing to defend himself to the last.

[1] M. Robinson to W.F., 19.3.1793.

9
COLLEGE DISCIPLINE

All through March "I expected every moment to be cited into the vice-chancellor's court", Frend wrote in his *Account of the Proceedings*, but he did not receive his summons till 24 April. However some colleagues at Jesus College were impatient to mete out punishment on their side, and after the Master had consulted several of the Fellows, and made a special journey to London to obtain Sir William Scott's advice, Frend was called to a college meeting on 3 April at 11 in the morning.

"The attention of the university was now turned to this meeting . . . and the opinion which the master had brought down with him from town was thought by the faction a sufficient ground for expulsion from college. This [opinion] the master would not permit the authour to have a sight of, though it was shown by him to his friends out of college" who spread the report that the college would co-operate with the twenty-seven Fellows (known as "the cubicks") in the execution of their designs.

"The friends of the authour were alarmed", Frend tells us. "They came round him and intreated him to be no longer passive." Separately and together they visited him and urged him to send to a lawyer for a professional opinion.

"Does it require the astuteness of a lawyer to understand a plain college statute?" objected Frend. But finally he agreed to lay his case "before a civilian in town". This was Dr Harris, who answered on 31 March from Doctors' Commons, that the College statute which Frend was accused of contravening applied to such heinous offences as perjury, sacrilege, rapine, theft, homicide, adultery, incest, or any gross misbehaviour or violence towards the Master or any of the Fellows, or "other crimes which may stamp infamy on the offender."

Frend could not be accused of any of the afore-mentioned crimes, and Harris, "on a very attentive perusal of the pamphlet", could not find any doctrine or opinion in it "which can be said to fix a stain on the maintainer." He added, "I am strongly led to think that Mr Frend can have no reason to be apprehensive of any sort of censure from a majority of literary, well-informed and candid men, such as his college is reputed to be composed of."[1]

Frend took these comments straight to the Master on 2 April and "desired him to lay them before the Fellows". Dr Pearce had himself been busy seeking advice, and had written several letters to the Visitor bewailing "the difficulties" of the case: "There is a doubt whether the Statutes give us the power of rusticating a Fellow without expelling him; rather than Mr Frend should continue in the College I was ready to go to expulsion"—but Plampin and Costobadie had told him on 24 March that neither they nor others of the Fellows would agree. He tells the Bishop on 27 March that he has been researching into cases of Fellows' expulsions from different colleges. "I can find no case where the College proceeded first [to expel] and the University followed . . . however, as the College has a right to act independently & of itself, & as its credit requires it to act on this occasion, we are justified in beginning before the University." This letter showed that the University was definitely considering strong measures.

* * *

On 3 April the college meeting took place. The encounters between the Fellows and Frend resembled a prolonged tennis match, questions being bandied back and forth, Frend refusing to make any statement until he was accused *in writing*, and the Master refusing to produce any written accusation.

[1] *Account*, pp. xv–xvii.

At last Dr Pearce announced that he and the majority of the Fellows present had previously passed several resolutions, viz: that certain passages in the pamphlet tended "to prejudice the clergy in the eyes of the laity"; "to degrade the doctrines and rites of the Church of England"; "to disturb the harmony and interests of the college." Mr Frend was guilty of an offence against the college laws by publishing the pamphlet.[1]

"What have you, to say in your defence, Sir?" asked Dr Pearce.

"I request that I might be given a written copy of the accusation," repeated Frend.

"Be so good as to withdraw then, Mr Frend, that the matter may be put to the vote."

The accused kicked his heels in an ante-room for about half an hour, and was called in again to hear the Master read the meeting's decision *not* to deliver any charge to him in writing. "And now, Mr Frend, what have you to say in your defence?"

Politely, Frend asked again for a written accusation, and again was asked to retire. At 9.15 p.m. he was called in once more, and told that the meeting would proceed without hearing him.

"Very well," said Frend; "I must consider the resolutions as an accusation." He asked them to tell him *which* passages offend against *which* statutes; "I will then proceed on my defence."

"Be so good as to retire, Mr Frend," Dr Pearce said, for the third time. Frend bowed ironically and went into his room where he sat and read, and finally went to bed without hearing any more of the meeting—though the wrangling went on for another full two hours.

Next morning he was "summoned into the parlour between 9 and 10. The master was going to read something to me, but I requested to see first the proceedings of yesterday." This was refused, and Dr Pearce said he should have

[1] *Account*, p. xviii.

spoken in his defence the previous night, to which Frend replied that he had been asked to retire and not called back to defend himself. The Master waved this aside, and produced a paper, which he proceeded to read aloud.

"Is it the opinion of this meeting, that Mr Frend be removed from the college ... and from residence in it, till he shall produce such proofs of good behaviour, as shall be satisfactory to the Master and major part of the Fellows?" In the affirmative: the Master, and six fellows, including Mr Plampin and Dr Costobadie, as expected; in the negative, Mr Newton, Mr Warren, Mr Whitehead and Mr Otter. All agreed "that he may be allowed a month from this time to settle his affairs in college."[1]

Dr Pearce wrote to the Bishop on 8 April, describing the college meeting as satisfactory, on the whole, though "Mr Newton started some difficulties ... Not one of the Fellows would go as far as expulsion, and it was hinted to me that not all the five who signed the petition to your Lordship could be depended upon even so far as rustication ... We had a great many difficulties to encounter, not for any asperities of language (for everything met with perfect decorum without any personal rancour) but for the art in which Mr Newton and Mr Warren demonstrated their cause ..."

The Master insists that Frend could have defended himself: "If he did not it was his own fault—it was not becoming the meeting to call him any oftener, especially as by adding to his requisitions there was no knowing where they would end." One can almost hear his sigh of relief at the thought that "we have secured (if your Lordship confirms) the main point, of freeing the College from the infection of his principles and a variety of Evils which attended his residence here ..."[2]

Frend then drafted an appeal to the Visitor, no doubt recalling the fact that it was the same Bishop of Ely who had

[1] *Account*, pp. xviii–xx.
[2] Bishop of Ely. E.D.R.

ordained him and written a sympathetic note on his resignation from the Church in 1787.

He asked the Visitor to intervene "to prevent the execution of this sentence, passed in so irregular and unstatutable a manner."

The Master and five Fellows (Stockdale withdrawing this time) sent a counter-appeal; the two documents lay on the Bishop's table for several weeks, joined by two more long letters from the injured Frend.

The Bishop did not answer them officially; but he was not neglecting his duties as Visitor: a number of letters from Dr Pearce between 3 April and the middle of May show that the Bishop had asked the Master to obtain further legal advice for him before making up his mind about Frend.

On 25 April Pearce told His Grace that he "had consulted Sir Wm Scott how the College ought to act at the expiry of the month, and Sir Wm thought the appeal while pending was of the nature of an inhibition . . ." On 29 April he wrote, "I saw Sir Wm Scott yesterday who says that Dr Harris would have given the same opinion of Tom Paine's book as he has given of Mr Frend's."

The Bishop's personal adviser, Mr Willis of Boswell Court, when consulted recommended caution and no hasty decision by the Visitor.

"No great inconvenience can happen from a little delay", he said, "because if, as will probably be the case, he shou'd be removed by the University the College will be rid of him without the aid of your Lordship. But be that as it may, I would much rather that the College shou'd be plagued with him for some time longer than that it should be open in the *least* degree to anyone to criticize your Lordship's handling of the affair."[1]

So the month which had been allowed by the Fellows' Resolution to Frend for settling his affairs in college, passed by, and in May he was still one of the senior members—disliked by some, respected by others of his colleagues, and with

[1] Bishop of Ely. E.D.R.

an admiring following among the young radical undergraduates who looked on a rebellious don as something of a hero.

On the other hand, one or two of the Fellows who had sided against Frend were correspondingly unpopular, not only with the students but also with some of the graduates. Frend, though not always easy to get on with, had always carried out his academic and college duties meticulously; while some of those who had opposed him and now supplanted him were disgracefully irresponsible and slack.

One member of the college went so far as to write anonymously to the Visitor telling him of the lack of discipline and the low level of teaching, particularly in classics: "no lectures in that branch had been given in Jesus College for some years past." His Lordship should intervene "to prevent that small spark of learning and discipline which yet remain from being intirely extinguished."

The Bishop asked the Master who the anonymous writer was, and what truth there was in his accusations. Dr Pearce did not know the handwriting but said "I have no doubt in my own mind of its coming from the party of Mr Newton and Mr Frend.

"As to the general state of the College, there have been some irregularities," he admits, "both in regard to the College accounts and Lectures. These I have been endeavouring to correct ever since I have belonged to the College by such means as I thought most prudent." As to lectures, "it is but justice to say that Mr Newton is a very diligent and excellent Lecturer and has correct ideas of College discipline in every respect but lately in regard to Mr Frend in which either personal pique or personal favour must have overpowered a man otherwise very conscientious."

It was evidently Plampin who was the main offender; Frend had already notified Dr Pearce in April that the new Steward was very unsatisfactory: "The Master should order Mr Plampin to settle the Steward's accounts immediately. It is now half a year since Mr Frend quitted the office and there remain two bills unpaid. Repeated applications to Mr

Plampin have been treated only with contempt. Mr Frend must repeat in writing what he has urged frequently in Conversation with the Master: that the criminal neglect of Mr Plampin to do his duty as Classical Tutor and his extreme remissness in discharging the College bills do very particularly hurt the Credit and Interests of this College." (Far more, he might have added, than any pamphlets of William Frend.)[1]

* * *

Frend put a brave front on his uncertainties, but he had, from the start of the college proceedings, begun to wonder what lay in store for him, and he revealed his growing anxiety in letters to sympathizers.

Dr Disney[2] answered one of these in a reassuring note, written on 5 April; he had been seeing Dr Harris, the legal adviser, who "much approved your conduct. Reserve, taciturnity, are the only weapons for inquisitors." Frend had evidently written him an account of the meeting in the parlour. "I could not have persuaded myself that the Master and Fellows could have conducted themselves with as much intolerance & malignity. Take down the names of all present when any general meeting is held . . . Keep a regular journal of all original papers, opinions, proceedings, in a fair transcript as they arise."

Disney then asks, "What is the University doing, or what proceeding is intended from that quarter?" Frend did not know the answer to that one; he had not faced the possibility. But he now began to make enquiries, and discovered some disturbing facts. It was said that Dr Kipling, that much maligned composer of bad Latin verse, had set his heart on having Frend tried for breaking the University statute *De Concionibus*.

[1] Bishop of Ely. E.D.R.

[2] Dr John Disney, brother-in-law and colleague of Lindsey at Essex Hall.

Frend wrote off to the learned Matthew Robinson, to ask whether in his opinion he (Frend) could justly be accused of contravening the statute; to which Mr Robinson replied (2 May): "I don't know that I ever heard before of the Statute De Concionibus etc. It should seem . . . as if it applied only to Sermons and Academical Discourses deliver'd or publish'd within the pale of the University; but your publication is totally of a different kind. It . . . was printed at a distance, is address'd to the whole world, concerns all mankind and not in particular the University . . . It seems therefore intirely out of the jurisdiction of that body and the Vice-Chancellor . . . I must stick to my old text, that your adversaries are adding persecution to hypocrisy; that it is their disbelief which renders easy all subscriptions of Articles & professions of faith."

He recalls how Cambridge deprived the mathematics Professor, Whiston, of his post "because he declared that he did not believe the Trinity" and appointed Mr Saunderson, the blind mathematician, "whom everybody perfectly well understood to believe no more in the divinity of the Bible than of the Alcoran." He wishes Frend "health and likewise security against bigotry and hypocrisy."

Frend set to work to prepare his "defence" although as he was in the dark as to what was being charged against him it was not easy to plan ahead. He decided to take the offensive, as far as possible, and to use the great men of the Church to confound the small Church-and-King men who were persecuting him.

He wrote to his friend E. Evanson, of Blakenham, asking where and when it was that Archbishop Tillotson expressed the opinion "the account given of Athanasius's Creed seems to me in no wise satisfactory; I wish we were well rid of it." Evanson replied (29 April) that this "well-known wish" was to be found in a letter to Bishop Barnet and gave chapter and verse. He went on to declare, "I am exceedingly provoked by the shamefully illiberal usage you meet with both from your own College and from such contemptible time-serving reptiles as the Vice-Chancellor and Dr Kipling; but I was glad to see your appeal to the Visitor; which, if he does not do you justice, I hope you will carry to a higher court. For according to the words of yr statute, your persecutors, not you, ought to be rusticated."

Evanson, who had been tried himself in the ecclesiastical courts, says the prosecution against him "was on such different grounds . . . that it cannot furnish one suggestion that cou'd be of use to you whose appeal, I understand, must be made to Chancery not to Doctors Commons." He wishes "that you triumph over all your enemies & that our Alma Mater may soon be cleared of all despicable Plampins, Kiplings, Watsons, etc."

The above letter "missed the diligence by a few minutes", so Evanson added a note to the effect that in the meantime he had realized "a circumstance of seeming importance in your business" which he thinks will enable Frend to turn the table on his persecutors.

"Your announced prosecutor, Dr Kipling, assisted at a meeting at the Vice-Chancellor's Lodge to plan and resolve upon this prosecution & the resolutions respecting it were formally drawn up and deposited with the V.C. who refused you a copy of them. The V.C. has therefore most iniquitously previously consulted & combined or conspired with Kipling in the plan & process & made himself a party in a prosecution to be brought before himself.

"I am confident no judge in any other criminal court, civil or ecclesiastical, wou'd have been guilty of such partiality & injustice and had a jury in the common courts done the same thing the whole panel would be challenged and immediately set aside."

If Frend found that Milner was at the meeting he should "instantly appeal against the authority of a court where he who was to try me was both prosecutor and judge."

Dr Disney also offered counsel and help, with a quotation from King James' Declaration in the General Assembly at Edinburgh in 1590: "And for our neighbour Kirk of England their service is an evil said Mass in English. They want nothing of the Mass but the liftings."

Disney adds that "when I contemplate on ye state of your business at Cam I cannot devise what measures the inquisitors meditate."

If friends can be found "to bear ye expense" application must be made "to the KB (King's Bench), in which case I think Erskine should be retained for I would in such case develop both Jesuits and inquisitors to public scrutiny."

Evidence remains today of at least one friend (and there were no doubt many more) who stepped forward to help "bear ye expense" of securing justice. Richard Reynolds enclosed a note for £20—a very considerable sum for a private individual at that time—in a letter as rich in sympathy as in guineas.

And sympathy from another quarter was equally warming. At the beginning of May, when it was announced that Frend was to appear before the Vice-Chancellor's court, there were spontaneous demonstrations in his favour by the undergraduates. They chalked slogans on the college walls and traced the words LIBERTY and EQUALITY in a train of gunpowder on the smooth green lawns of Trinity and St John's.[1] Coleridge, Copeley (afterwards Lord Chancellor Lyndhurst, one of Frend's pupils), William Rough of Trinity and a future bishop whose name has not been passed down, were chased by the Proctors at night through the streets for chalking up on the wall *Frend for Ever! ! !*—the future bishop alone being caught.[2]

The generous and impulsive gestures of the Cambridge students—risking punishment and possible rustication—must have been a considerable comfort and encouragement to Frend and those who supported him on the eve of his unequal struggle with the establishment.

[1] Chambers: *op. cit.*, p. 20.

[2] H. Crabb Robinson: *Diary*, Vol. iii, p. 401.

10

THE VICE-CHANCELLOR'S COURT I

On Friday 3 May 1793, the Vice-Chancellor, Isaac Milner, flanked by nine Fellows, his "Assessors", the Bedells (Gunning and Beverley), George Borlase (the Registrary) and other officials and dignitaries, assembled in the law schools of the university.

John Beverley, Esquire Bedell, announced pontifically that a summons had been personally served on William Frend. Dramatically, a door was flung open and Mr Frend appeared; at which, says the report of the proceedings, it was announced that the court was adjourned to the Senate House.

With due solemnity, the participants processed across the courtyard to the adjoining elegant new Palladian building, shining white in the May morning sun, and entered the room which was already half filled; the gallery was humming and stirring with undergraduates (among them young Coleridge, sitting next to Charnock, a friend with one arm), most of them keen radicals unaffected by "Association" propaganda, and ardent supporters of Fox, if not of Paine, and hence on Frend's side.

Soon everybody had settled into their places. One can imagine the scene—sober but not without touches of colour, the fashionable crimson, green and russet of the eighteenth-century clothes not quite hidden by the black gowns of the senior members, and glowing against the dark oaken seats. We know that there were one or two professors not in academic dress—Dr Kipling, the "promoter", in his light breeches, and Mr Mansell in fustian coat and white stockings—striking a note out of harmony with the warm deep tones of the scene.

Frend himself under his college gown wore a blue coat with brass buttons, which he had adopted since he had left the Church. He sat at a table on the north side of the Senate House, facing his accusers across the room. Beside him, in academic dress, sat his staunch friends Tyrwhitt, Jones and Lambert (the latter two Head Tutor and Bursar of Trinity College, respectively).

The defendant showed from the start what a tough customer he was going to be. Just as the Vice-Chancellor, in stentorian tones, was calling upon Dr Kipling to open the case, Frend stood up—cool, collected and contemptuous—and before the promoter had time to object, he read out a long statement firmly refusing to accept the jurisdiction of this court. He objected to the mode of trial adopted, and declared that he was only present here "out of civility and respect, not from duty or obligation." The violation of university laws, particularly the statute *De Concionibus*, should be tried not in the Vice-Chancellor's court (which existed for the purpose of receiving complaints and hearing causes) but by a tribune consisting of the Vice-Chancellor and a majority of heads of colleges.

Dr Milner, on hearing this, consulted hurriedly with the Commissary, and they both left the room accompanied by others of the prosecutors, for half an hour. On coming back Milner pronounced in favour of the jurisdiction of the court.

Frend refused to be hurried. He wanted at least the semblance of a legal hearing, and he desired that a grace (of 1609) "on the order to be observed in the university courts" might be read. The Vice-Chancellor, impatient to get on to the main business, waved the request aside and asked Dr Kipling to proceed.

In Frend's words, "the promoter rose, and Mr Frend, rising at the same time, addressed the vice-chancellor and desired that the accuser might not be permitted to speak until he had put on his proper academical habit. At this, a violent burst of laughter and clapping from the audience ensued. The vice-chancellor seemed vehemently moved and looked up to the gallery as if going to reprimand the young men; but the burst was over, and the noise had ceased before the vice-chancellor could speak to order."[1]

Some of the most vigorous clapping had come from where young Coleridge was sitting. A proctor hurried up the stairs to apprehend the offender—but by the time he reached the spot Coleridge had changed places with Charnock, who could not possibly be accused of clapping, as he only had one hand.[2]

There was nothing for Dr Milner to do but to glare at the gallery and to proceed with the business.

Dr Kipling was heard to say with heavy sarcasm that "the vice-chancellor, he supposed, would be required next to put on his robes too." Dr Milner boomed "Mr Frend's requisition is frivolous. Proceed, Dr Kipling."

The promoter read out the eight articles of accusation, which had perhaps better be catalogued here for future reference. Each day the court dealt with one or two of them.

First: The University of Cambridge was founded and endowed . . . "for the maintenance of godly literature, and the virtuous education of youth within the said university."
Second: Frend "did publish and cause to be dispersed within this university, a scandalous book or pamphlet" of which he was the author.
Third: In the 29th page Frend had defamed the public liturgy of the established church.
Fourth: In certain pages Frend affirmed "that the publick worship of the great body of Christians is idolatrous; including in this charge the members of the church of England . . . "
Fifth: Frend asserted that "ecclesiastical courts . . . ranks and titles are all repugnant to the spirit of Christianity."
Sixth: He had "profanely reviled and ridiculed the most sacred offices of religion . . . "
Seventh: At the time of publishing, Frend was a master of

[1] *Account*, pp. 7–8.
[2] Gunning: *Reminiscences*, i, p. 274.

arts and member of this university and still is, "and therefore notoriously subject to the jurisdiction of this court." *Eighth:* The laws of this university, particularly by the statute De Concionibus and a decree passed in the senate in June 1603 provide that anyone "impugning religion, as by law established, may and ought to be proceeded against and punished by suspension from academical degrees, *by expulsion or by banishment.*" [1]

The articles having been read (Frend objecting to the first) Dr Kipling proposed to call witnesses. To this the defendant objected that witnesses should not be called before the *secundus dies juridicus*; he asked for time to answer, according to the statutes.

The Vice-Chancellor acceded with a not very good grace to this, and "accordingly adjourned the court to be holden at the senate-house" one week later, warning Dr Kipling and Mr Frend then and there to appear.

The proceedings on 10 May proved notable mainly for Frend's stone-walling and delaying tactics. His contention was that this court was irregular, that there was no case to be tried; he considered the whole thing was a farce and should be treated as such.

He had however realized that this was an exceptional opportunity for presenting his case, and was determined that the young men in the gallery should learn something from the hours spent "in court", about defending personal and academic freedom.

He began by protesting against the formation of the court; refused to be tried under the statute *De Concionibus*; and denied all the "articles", asserting them "to be false, wicked and malicious."

Nevertheless the case went forward. Witness after witness was called by Dr Kipling to prove that *Peace and Union* had been distributed by, or on behalf of, William Frend. College servants, booksellers and their assistants had been summoned

[1] *Account*, pp. 9–12.

for the purpose of identifying Frend as the man who had ordered or sent or paid for the distribution of the offending pamphlet. The next day much the same business continued. One fact that emerged from the wearisome cross-questioning was that the sales of the booklet had been considerable. Copies had been sold by the dozen, and had been bought by professors, students, owners of coffee-houses. Several booksellers testified that they had received parcels of a hundred, and almost all had been sold, and more re-ordered and sold.

All this evidence was received with satisfaction by Dr Kipling though it must have seemed to those present a glimpse of the obvious.

Having thus ascertained who had "published and dispersed" the pamphlet, the promoter set about proving Frend the author.

Specimens of his handwriting were produced; mention was made of notes he had written to pupils, and the correspondence with Rev. Mr Watson about wool was cited as evidence that Frend's handwriting was indeed his. Addressing the curate, Kipling asked, "Did you make some inquiries concerning the price of spinning wool?"

The Vice-Chancellor barked out: "What! What! Spinning wool! What has this to do with the business?" Dr Kipling hurried over to him and whispered in his ear, at which Milner grunted, "Ay, ay—go on."[1]

Mr Watson's examination went on interminably. All the correspondence about the Fen Stanton spinning industry was read out, to very little effect. This part of the proceedings mystified some of the audience (which was not an entirely academic one) and Frend later quoted an amusing comment overheard in the court-room, with the words "on the whole, the remark of the two countrymen seems to me the best that can be made on this wool-spinning business: Seeing Mr Watson standing so considerable a time in a very forlorn situation, examined by the promoter, confronted with other witnesses, questioned by the bench, again examined, again

[1] *Account*, pp. 50–51.

confronted, reading letters about wool, and answering interrogatories on the same subject, 'Alas! Poor gentleman!' says one to the other, 'he is guilty, he certainly stole the wool!' "

Kipling next called Edward Kilvington, a former pupil of Frend's to prove his tutor's writing; this gentleman was one of "the twenty-seven" (accusers) and a peculiarly slimy character. He rather nastily alluded to talks he and Frend had had, as "Mr Frend's studied attentions shown to me, as I believe they were shown to all those whom he was desirous of proselytising to his own opinions"; these were "such as to have impressed very deeply upon my mind the recollection not only of his handwriting but of a thousand other circumstances much more minute."

Dr Plampin, Frend's successor as tutor of Jesus College, was also cross-examined about handwriting. Frend asked him, "Do any of your pupils have an opportunity of knowing your handwriting at lectures?" to which Plampin retorted, "Certainly not. It is not my duty to write in their presence." Frend, referring to Plampin's notoriously desultory ways, then asked, "*Does* Mr Plampin give any lectures in college?" —a point over-ruled by the Vice-Chancellor, but no doubt taken by the students of Jesus College in the audience.

A rather pathetic note was introduced at this point by the appearance in court of Herbert Marsh,[1] an old school-fellow and a cousin of Frend's, whom Kipling wanted as a witness; Marsh had taken an advertisement of *Peace and Union*, at the author's request, to the *Cambridge Chronicle* for insertion on 9 February, and could therefore testify that Frend was indeed the writer of the pamphlet. When called as a witness, Marsh demurred, and "frequently expostulated with the promoter on the cruelty of forcing him to attend"; nonetheless, he was sent for, and in the court again protested against being asked to give evidence against "a near relation, and a

[1] Herbert Marsh (1757–1839), German scholar, translator of Michaelis; later (1812) involved in controversy with Milner over the Evangelical Bible Society.

confidential friend."—"I think it hard, nay, even the prosecutors themselves, if it was their own case, would think it hard, extremely hard, to be dragged forward in this public manner, to act against a man with whom they were connected by the bonds of friendship, and united by the ties of blood."

The Vice-Chancellor then retired with the commissary and heads, but returned in about a minute and announced that Mr Marsh "ought not to be examined, unless Dr Kipling particularly insists upon it."

The promoter "with some reluctance then gave up the point: and Mr Marsh retired."[1]

More questions and answers about handwriting; more cross-examining on the matter of parcels of books; at long last Dr Kipling declared that he was satisfied that publication and authorship were proven, and he would now proceed to Article 3—(that Frend had defamed the public liturgy of the established church).

He read out a passage as evidence, and was promptly met by an objection from Frend that the passages as quoted were not in the book; Dr Kipling hummed and hawed and finally admitted he had left a phrase out "because he did not understand what it meant". He proposed now to read a passage out of a different pamphlet of Frend's published in 1789, also defaming the liturgy.

Dr Milner, however, objected strongly—probably the thought of having to go through the business again, of proving that another pamphlet was published, dispersed and written by Frend, was too much for him to stomach.

Dr Kipling therefore proceeded to the fourth Article, accusing Frend of "charging us directly with idolatry". His mumbling and confused remarks annoyed Dr Milner, who said sarcastically, "I should be glad, Dr Kipling, to hear how you make out that the Church of England is included". Kipling muttered that he "could have produced better evidence if I had been allowed."

[1] *Account*, pp. 63–67.

Coming to the fifth Article, Dr Kipling quoted a passage from page 39, so he said. "Mr Frend looked up and down the page, but declared he could not find it."

Dr Kipling said, "It is there." Mr Frend repeated, "I cannot find it." Dr Kipling turned to Milner: "Mr Vice-chancellor, it is exactly the same, 'tis all there except an omission." This brought "a loud laugh on all sides."[1]

At the end of the afternoon there remained only the ninth Article to read, which prayed "that right and justice be done", and the court adjourned for a week.

When it reassembled on 17 May, Dr Kipling submitted his evidence, reading from notes made by the Commissary to the court.

As it transpired that Kipling had been in possession of these notes ever since the previous court sitting, Frend protested vigorously, suggesting that alterations might have been made in the evidence, and claiming the right of a week's time to prepare the defence, instead of making it the same day. And so the court was again adjourned; and again assembled a week later, to hear Frend's defence, to which the students, if nobody else, had been looking forward for three weeks as the climax of a most unusual encounter between academics and heretics.

[1] *Account*, pp. 75–77.

11

THE VICE-CHANCELLOR'S COURT II

FREND BEGAN BY asking if "such a very extraordinary cause" had ever before been recorded in Cambridge University. When had "a number of masters of arts and doctors combined together to attack the rights of a member of the senate"? When was it thought necessary to create "an inquisitorial office" for this? When had the publication of a pamphlet given rise to a similar persecution? Which, "from the malignity and base arts of the conductors and the total violation of law and justice ... exceeds anything in history."

Dr Kipling had asked Frend to avoid everything personal and offensive, but he could hardly have expected his victim to refrain from hitting out at his prosecutors:

"Doubtless," said Frend, "he had a right to make this request, as there is no personality in declaring a member of the senate the authour of a scandalous book! It is not at all personal to assert that Mr Frend is unfit to breathe the air of this place! It is by no means personal to endeavour to deprive him of his degrees, and to expell him from the university!"

With withering scorn he turned on Kipling's notorious lack of scholarship: "Had I indeed, Sir, taken notice of a late publication of the learned promoter, had I asserted that the work which he has given to the publick under the sanction of the university is a disgrace to a man of letters, that ... it abounded with so many and such gross blunders ... had I asserted such things of the learned doctour, I should have been called a dealer in personalities; but when he accuses me of writing a scandalous book, then, Sir, it ceases to be a personality!"

After a good deal of sarcasm at Dr Kipling's expense (we may suppose, for the entertainment of the gallery), Frend set to work disposing of the evidence collected against him; this he did by discrediting the way in which the witnesses had been assembled. Mr Lloyd, for instance, one of the "cubicks" sitting in judgement, had given evidence; Mr Plampin, and Kilvington, though amongst his accusers, had also witnessed against him;—Kilvington's case was particularly disgraceful in view of the fact that this young man had a few years previously written him effusive letters protesting his respect and affection for him ("it will give me the greatest pleasure to render you any service in my power, either in this or in any other part of the world") and describing his curacy ("I am persuaded you will be happy to hear of my success . . . ").

Frend dismisses the evidence about distribution of books—"ten thousand books . . . written by various authours, have been dispersed in this place, either by myself or by Bowtell, under my direction" (as mentioned earlier, at the time of the campaigns against the Slave Trade and against the Test Acts).[1] This therefore was "no proof of my being author of this work." He protested again very strongly against Kipling's witnesses, and against the removal of evidence in writing; then he demolished the accusations one by one—he had said nothing defamatory about the liturgy; he had never called the worship by the Church of England idolatrous; he emphatically denied Kipling's charge "of comparing the orgies of Bacchus with the rites of the eucharist . . . No such comparison is drawn . . . nor could it be drawn . . . Let the promoter continue his daily sacrifices to Bacchus [an allusion to Dr Kipling's weakness for the bottle] but let him not impute to me any approbation of them . . . "

The fifth Article gave Frend another opportunity of entertaining the gallery. He was, he said, accused of asserting that "ecclesiastical court . . . ranks and titles are all repugnant to the spirit of Christianity." He noticed that the accusation omitted "a certain particular":

[1] *Account*, p. 110.

"Ecclesiastical *dress* is as much objected to in the pamphlet as . . . courts and titles." With an air of mystery, he went on: "There must be something, I said within myself, extraordinary in this: the promoter has certainly his fears that all is not right about his dress, and that any remarks on this subject must be injurious to his cause."

Frend now produced a fat volume, saying that he had consulted the canons of the Church, "and I shall now read to you the 74th, in which decency of apparel is enjoyned to ministers." He solemnly began to intone from the book: " . . . hoping that in time new fanglenesses of apparell in some factious persons will die of itself"—"that all church dignitaries, including doctors of divinitie, shall usually weare gownes with standing collars and sleeves streight at the hands, or wide sleeves, as is used in the universities, with hoods or tippets of silk or sarcenet and square caps."

Here the Vice-Chancellor interrupted Frend with, "Surely, Mr Frend, you do not think that this will be of use to you in your defence?"

"Certainly not," replied Frend, with the utmost blandness, and went on reading: " . . . all the said ecclesiasticall persons above-mentioned shall usually weare in their journies, cloakes with sleeves . . . without gards, welts, long buttons or cuts. And no ecclesiasticall person shall weare any coife or wrought night-cap, but only plain night caps of black satten or velvet."

Here Dr Milner, unable to contain himself, broke in again: "What is all this to the purpose, it cannot do you any good."

"Certainly not, certainly not, Mr Vice-chancellor," replied Frend, unperturbed, and continued reading. (As he said later, he "was very well persuaded from his knowledge of the Vice-chancellor that nothing but a thunderstorm could have done him any good; but he read this canon to show the fallacy of enforcing an old statute, when one of so much later date was so openly violated with impunity in the university.") " . . . In private houses and in their studies the sayd persons ecclesiasticall may use any comely and schollerlike apparell. Provided it be not cut or prickt, and that in publick they goe not in their doublet and hose without coats or cassocks, and also that they weare not any light coloured stockings . . . "

Addressing the Vice-Chancellor, with a wave of his hand towards Dr Kipling, Frend remarked, "Such, Sir, is the law of the church with regard to dress; how well it is observed by the promoter is too apparent. So far from obeying the law is he not frequently on horseback in contempt of all ecclesiastical discipline, without the priest's cloak to cover his nakedness? nay, have we not seen him here exposing himself in defiance of all decency, in his doublet and hose?"

Turning towards the group of "cubicks" and peering at their clothes, Frend castigated them too: "Are the sub-promoters more attentive to their priestly apparell? At this very moment I discover among them the indecorous phenomenon of white stockings!" (We are told later in the account that "Mr Mansell, the new disciplinarian, was as usual in light-coloured fustians and white stockings.")[1]

"If, Sir, the promoter can thus despise the laws of the church," said Frend in an exceedingly solemn tone of voice, "it is no wonder that he should be fearful of any mention of ecclesiastical dress . . . he must be held up as a fit object for derision and ridicule."

Becoming serious, the defendant put down the book of canons, and asserted that his remarks had been distorted and that the charge was false. Kipling had "taken an unwarrantable liberty in misquoting and misrepresenting a passage . . . " He had said "the words quoted were exactly the same as a sentence in the book, excepting only an omission and an insertion." Frend added with savage irony, "to be sure it is perfectly justifiable to omit and insert at pleasure, but such liberties, though they may suit the promoter's purposes, totally destroy the meaning of a writer. Sir, by the same mode of garbling and mutilating sentences, the sacred scriptures might be quoted as containing the most

[1] *Account*, p. 129.

horrid blasphemies, and it would be easy to convict the bible of atheism."

Frend then repeated the sixth Article, in which he was accused of having profanely reviled and ridiculed the most sacred offices of religion. This he strongly denied; his remarks were directed at the "popish priests", he said, and not the Church of England, whose priests should be respected as teachers of Christianity.

The last article accused Frend of having contravened the University statute *De Concionibus*, by "impugning religion" and "impugning ecclesiastical ranks and dignities", for which he could be punished by "suspension from academical degrees, by expulsion or by banishment."

The defendant demanded that this Grace be read to him out of the original grace book of 1603. The Registrary said the book was in his office. Dr Milner boomed, "I suppose, Mr Frend, it is not very material—you do not wish to give the registrary the trouble of going out of court for it?"

"Sir, I must," said Frend. "I have reasons why I conceive the production of the original very material. The office is not far off." He added, "as I feel myself rather fatigued, this little delay will be some relief to me." (His fatigue was not surprising, as he had been on his feet several hours and faced a couple more.)

To quote the *Account*, "the registrary went out of court, and returned in about ten minutes with the original grace book. Mr Frend then desired that the grace of 1603 might be read, and after some pause the vice-chancellor replied that it was not to be found.

"Mr Frend rose and spoke with some degree of warmth:

"No, Sir, it is not to be found. The grace of 1603 is not in those books. It is not in the place which could alone give it a statutable existence. This grace, on which so much has been said, which is to be held out in terrorem to academicks, appears to be a non entity, a phantom. When brought to the test it vanishes into air."

Frend was hammering away at the fact that the grace was

non-existent and "no proof can be brought of any one suffering under its penalties" when Milner interrupted, to say that even if it were not in the Grace book it was in the Vice-Chancellor's book. But Frend pointed out that in the latter it was un-signed by the Registrary who had copied it in, and therefore had no validity.

Referring to the university rule that offences against statutes can only be tried by a court consisting of the Vice-Chancellor and the heads of colleges, Frend then declared that this tribunal of the "twenty-seven" could not legally judge him. "I do maintain that every right of englishmen and academicks has been violated in this trial."

Frend's one-man marathon was drawing to an end. Three things remained for him to do: to sum up his objections to the *De Concionibus* statute; to ask Dr Kipling a few questions on Mr Charke of Peterhouse who was deprived of his Fellowship in 1572 ("was Mr Charke cited in to the Vice-chancellor's court?—was any near relation or intimate friend cited to appear against him?—were any private letters ... betrayed for that purpose?"); and to deal a final blow on behalf of freedom of speech while he had the opportunity. The conduct of his accusers is disgraceful, he declares. "These men misconceive entirely the nature and character of this university." Frend proclaims to the world, whose eyes are on him, and to posterity, his own conception of what the university's role should be:

"By our studies to investigate truth, it is our ambition to lay it open to the world; and should any one of us in the course of his reading see reason to alter his former opinions, or should he explore any latent truth, we will not on that account hold him up to public censure.

"We applaud his researches, we approve of his zeal, we rectify our own notions by his discoveries, or if he errs his errours teaches us to guard against some fallacy, and paves the way for future enquiries." What would have become of Locke, or Newton, "had the university been always of the same mind with the twenty-seven?"—"We must have been doomed to one beaten round of dry metaphysicks, we must have plodded in the same dull course, and no one would have dared to follow the best of his genius, lest the discovery of truth should banish him from the seats of literature."

Frend went on to defend the freedom of the press, and attack the suppression of truth: "In a well constituted government, no danger can possibly ensue from the publication of any sentiments religious or political; and that state of religion and government must be bad indeed, which can be overset by a shilling pamphlet." A trial such as this may be looked on as a public benefit, like an experiment in natural philosophy, "and serve to show what progress the public mind has made in the investigation . . . of truth." He concluded his long defence by exclaiming: "In future times it will be thought an extraordinary phenomenon, that in the eighteenth century, in a place dedicate to the pursuit of literature, a man should have been thus summoned, thus tried, and thus persecuted for the publication of opinions, which no one of his accusers attempted to refute."

"Free inquiry cannot be injurious, except to wicked and depraved minds. Society may be meliorated but can never suffer by it . . . let us recollect that the errors of genius are momentary and pardonable: how shall we dispel that horrid gloom of intellectual darkness, which the promoter and his cabal are endeavouring to spread over this university!"[1]

A sense of anti-climax must have come over the court, when Frend sat down, and Dr Kipling rose to reply. Regretfully, he said he would be brief: "When he considered the number of hours which had already been wasted on this trial, the precarious state of the Vice-chancellor's health, and the various duties annexed to his office, he felt the necessity of confining himself, in his reply, entirely to the merits of the cause."

In spite of this, Dr Kipling proceeded to repeat some of the accusations previously made, and refuted by Frend; he also described at some length negotiations between himself

[1] *Account*, p. 162.

and Herbert Marsh, Frend's cousin, over the case, mentioning that "He told Mr Marsh that in his private opinion, if Mr Frend recant and make a proper confession, he would not be brought before the vice-chancellor" but Mr Marsh had not been authorized to say anything to Frend, and there the matter had dropped.

As to Frend's charge that he was being tried under an obsolete law, Kipling thought that "it did not follow that a law which had been long disused was therefore never to be enforced . . . the times might be such as to demand every exertion, and to call on all the authority which the laws had given. The very times in which the pamphlet had been published were full of alarm, the press teemed with publications calculated to spread disaffection and discontent over the whole kingdom . . . If in this place we had suffered such a daring attack on the establishment to go unnoticed, we should have proved ourselves ungrateful to the best of sovereigns."

Dr Kipling defended his witnesses as acting for the good of the community in deciding "to stand forth and endeavour . . . to repress an evil of such a dangerous nature."

Frend made a few final remarks, replying to those of Dr Kipling, handed in a written statement to Dr Milner, and a protest against the validity of the minutes of the evidence (removed by Dr Kipling), and retired to await the Vice-Chancellor's verdict, to be given the following Tuesday, 28 May.

Tuesday came, and the court assembled. Dr Milner, standing enormous and imposing in the middle of the room, intoned his decision (for it seems that he had sole authority to give an opinion!) that Frend, being proved the author and publisher of the pamphlet, had offended against the latter part of the statute *De Concionibus*; he directed Frend to retract and publicly confess his error and temerity.

A paper containing the unanimous opinion of the Vice-Chancellor and nine heads of colleges as to Frend's "error", and a copy of the recantation, was handed to the defendant.

Frend began reading it, half aloud; " . . . am required to retract my errour and temerity—what does that mean?" Milner interrupted him, but Frend went on: "requires me to retract my error—that error must first be pointed out." The Vice-Chancellor (to quote *The Account*) "here again interrupted; and Mr Frend was again proceeding in his remarks, when the vice-chancellor called out with much vehemence —order! order! the court must not be trifled with any longer." Frend said he must consider whether he could subscribe the document or not. The Vice-Chancellor, clearly exasperated, announced that he was adjourning the court till Thursday: "and I warn you to appear and to retract in the manner in which you have been directed," said he. "If you neglect to appear or refuse to retract, you must take the consequences."

Frend did not neglect to appear. As to retracting, he was prepared to take the consequences of refusal. But he was determined to fight to the last, and when Milner read out a declaration that Frend had incurred the penalty for offending against the statute, he rose to protest against what he was asked to subscribe, "Mr Vice-chancellor, the form, directed to be subscribed by me . . ." but was refused a hearing. The Vice-Chancellor interrupted him with "Order! Mr Frend, I have already heard you five hours in your defence, and would willingly have heard you for five hours more if you had chosen to speak upon the statute de concionibus. You must not read or speak anything now, but say whether you will or will not sign that recantation."

Once more to quote the *Account*:

> Mr Frend attempting to read again from the paper, the Vice-chancellor again called out with vehemence— Order, Sir, Order! Order!
>
> Frend: Aye, Order! Mr Vice-chancellor, I am for order; if you are a court of inquisitors, you may silence me; but here I must be heard.
>
> Vice-chancellor: You cannot; it is too late, if you do not

read this form, we shall consider it as a refusal to retract and proceed accordingly.

Frend, abandoning any hope of reading his protest as he had intended, passed it to Dr Milner, who took it, consulted with the heads and the commissary, and decreed that, as they all adhered to the form prescribed, and considered Frend's protest as void, "you must now only answer, whether you will or will not submit."

Frend: I expected the errours which I am to recant would be pointed out.
Vice-chancellor: The errour is, that you have offended the statute.
Frend: I declare, upon the honour of a gentleman, and the credit of a scholar, that neither I nor my friends can understand the form.
Vice-chancellor: I will hear no more.
Frend: Am I then to subscribe this as my recantation?
Vice-chancellor: You are.
Frend: Then I would rather cut off this hand than sign the paper.

There was a general stir in the court at this dramatic declaration. Dr Milner ignored the reactions of the gallery and busied himself with the heads of colleges, getting them one and all to sign the sentence, which had been prepared and brought into court. He then cleared his throat preparatory to making his big speech summing up the case. But Frend had one more delaying tactic—a written plea for absolution, under a recently granted end-of-term dispensation for minor offences. Milner was not allowed to start his speech until he had at least perused the paper—which he did "slightly", then "threw it again on the table." There was then nothing more that even the inventive Frend could do to stave off the final blow.

Milner's speech is worth quoting for the light it throws on

his personality and attitudes. He started off by reminding the audience how very frail he was: "the ill state of his health" had made him acquiesce in his election as Vice-Chancellor "with much diffidence and anxiety. He foresaw that the remains of his health might be injured by the office, and his mind was agitated by this painful reflection . . . He was in hopes, however, that the peace of the university would not be disturbed."

As this event had nevertheless taken place, he was forced to investigate, he told them. "He entered on this unpleasant business, conceiving that, as a bold and indecent attack had been made upon the religious institutions of the country, and the statutes of the university openly violated, the very existence of the university might soon be endangered . . ."

Dr Milner's speech consisted mainly of a tirade against "the profane and licentious spirit of infidelity and irreligion", and against republicans and levellers; a defence of Dr Kipling's Latin was included, along with a rebuke to Frend for his frivolous attitude ("he had not shown the slightest vestige of contrition", nor "treated the cause with . . . seriousness but expected to make an impression on his judges by legal quibbles, strokes of wit, and allusions to novels.")

Towards the end, the Vice-Chancellor "addressed the junior part of the university. He would not, he said, animadvert on the noisy and tumultuous irregularities of conduct by which the proceedings on some days had been interrupted." (Frend says, in a footnote to the *Account*, "it is absolutely false that the proceedings were ever interrupted; but men without large wigs have risible muscles.") "He informed them that their passions and affections had been founded upon some vague idea that the accused person had been persecuted." He assured them that there had never been a fairer trial; and the only cause for doubt was "whether the judge . . . did not carry his patience and forebearance to an almost unwarrantable length". He expressed his satisfaction that in these times when the church was in danger "there were to be found in these seminaries, respectable characters who could accuse with liberality, and judges who could condemn with firmness and moderation." (Frend comments, "the moderation of the judge was evident, when he vociferated Order! Order! to prove the strength of his lungs and made more noise than the president of a bear garden".)

Dr Milner concluded with some advice, "short but important", to the students in the audience: "Beware of entering into religious controversies at this period of your lives," he blared: "Improve your understandings by the diligent pursuit of academical studies; obey your tutors; frequent the service of God according to the established forms, both in your private colleges and the university church . . . take it for granted that our forefathers had some good reason for steadily adhering to . . . these venerable institutions. Take it for granted, at present, I repeat it." He speaks, he says, as "one who addresses you thus from the purest motives of good will . . . whose pride and ambition have ever been able to obtain in the various branches of useful science, solid information for himself and others, and whose health has been almost exhausted with academical labours."

He lamented the necessity of the enquiry, but thought it his duty to go through it with energy, "and found it impossible to acquit Mr Frend of having offended against the statute, without sacrificing every principle of truth, justice and honour." [1]

In stentorian tones the Vice-Chancellor then read the sentence, decreeing, declaring and pronouncing, that William Frend, by writing a pamphlet, and by publishing the same within the University of Cambridge, "and having refused to retract, and confess his error and temerity, in the manner prescribed to him by me, . . . with the assent of the major part of the heads of colleges, has incurred the penalty of the statute, and that he is therefore banished from this university."

"Thus ended the proceedings in the Vice-chancellor's court," wrote Frend—proceedings which read now like a

[1] *Account*, pp. 178–187.

comic opera, and which, even if one feels that the juvenile lead overplayed his part, throw a discreditable and farcical light on the dons and Doctors of the university establishment. But the outcome was more melancholy than comic, for Cambridge was to lose a good mathematician and a much needed champion of civil rights, and Frend was to lose his post and all the good things of university life. However, even at this stage we shall see that he had not given up hope of salvaging something besides his reputation (that, at least, he was convinced he had saved).

And he wasted no time in setting about salvage operations.

12

APPEAL AND AFTERMATH
(Summer 1793)

FREND "WAITED ON the Vice-chancellor on 1 June," to declare his intentions of appealing to the senate against the sentence of the court; and on the following day, the proctor "inhibited" the Vice-Chancellor in the usual form from putting his sentence into execution.

It was nearly a month before the case came before the court, but at last, on 28 June, Frend was called to the Law Schools, where Sir William Wynne, John Hey, Rev. John Seale, and two other M.A.s were gathered to hear the appeal. All were well-known Church-and-King men, Seale in particular being a boon companion of Milner, who had done him various favours not strictly within the letter of the law.

Robert Tyrwhitt was supporting Frend, and started the ball rolling by protesting against the illegality of the Grace which permitted a court consisting of the accusers' close friends. Naturally the protest was rejected, but Tyrwhitt had made his point, and drawn public attention to the fact that "he had not been allowed to speak in the senate when the Grace was passed proposing the delegates [to the court]". His objections, he said, "were opposed in the Senate House by some persons there, with a degree of petulance and violence extremely unworthy of any member of the university."[1]

The proceedings consisted of the reading of the minutes of the trial, by the registrar; Frend then said the evidence was invalid, owing to Dr Kipling's having taken it out of court.

(Registrar: "I cannot speak to that."

Frend: "This is another incidence of the irregularities of this business.")

Later there was a long discussion on procedure, Frend

[1] *Account*, p. 195 *seq.*

claiming the right to several days' adjournment, and the judges insisting on hearing the defence the next day.

Frend: "I must maintain my objection to the appointment of tomorrow for hearing my gravamina as informal and irregular."

Wynne: "We take that irregularity upon ourselves."

It was one of the many that they took upon themselves in their effort to destroy Frend.

The next day, therefore, the accused stated his grievances: the first was "the malice of the Vice-chancellor's court, which had driven them on to prosecute him (even when there was no clear law or statute against which he had offended) and which produced as evidence passages of the book, misquoted and mutilated . . . by leaving out whole propositions."[1]

Another grievance was that the cabal met at the Vice-Chancellor's lodge: "Yes, gentlemen, incredible as it may seem, my prosecutors were suffered, nay encouraged, to meet in the house of the judge himself." The sixth grievance on his list was that evidence "was taken out of court and put into the hands of the promoter, the very man from whose wicked and malicious designs I had most to fear . . . an act which any court of justice ought to invalidate the whole."[2]

Frend protested vigorously against the manner of investigation—"in a place devoted to the purposes of literary improvement, how utterly inconsistent with the very end and design of our institution", where "false or dangerous opinions should be answered by reason and argument." He declared the whole trial illegal and asked for a reversal of the sentence "as totally unfounded in law."

"I would rather submit my cause to any jury of twelve men . . . from whatever ranks impanelled, than to a set of judges, however qualified by learning or abilities, who can . . . act in the unprecedented and unwarrantable manner of the Vice-chancellor's court. Much as I value the distinction of a master of arts at this university I feel myself

[1] *Account*, p. 216. [2] Frend: *Sequel to the Account*, p 8.

infinitely more happy as an Englishman, that I cannot be punished but by law . . . "

In ringing tones he went on to proclaim that "I have all along considered myself as acting in behalf of every member of the university; that we may none of us hereafter be exposed to the inconvenience and obloquy that I have laboured under for many months . . . or be in ruin from a factious cabal, composed for the greater part of men intriguing for preferment or led away by bigotry and fanaticism."

It was of no avail. The sentence was affirmed: "the judge had acted rightly, justly and lawfully", in the opinion of Sir William Wynne and his colleagues. Frend, now officially "banished" from the university, announced, before the delegates dispersed, his intention to appeal "from this unjust sentence to the court of King's Bench, where I hope every Englishman will meet with justice." [1]

However sincerely Frend believed his trial was unjust, he could not have expected any other result under the circumstances; he had brought out his pamphlet at a moment "when the public mind was filled with the strongest apprehensions of dangerous plots against the peace of this kingdom, and insurrections were supposed ready to break out in every quarter", as he wrote himself. Many years later he was to remark that "were it now published for the first time, it would fall stillborn from the press . . . " [2]

Some of the old gentlemen among the twenty-seven were no doubt genuinely alarmed and acted as they thought wise; on the other hand, Dr Farmer commented, in a letter to Dr Parr, (28 June 1793) "the pamphlet is a poor business and certainly would not have been noticed at any other time, but the damned iteration of appendix upon appendix, to call up the mob, is intolerable . . . " [3] and Milner no doubt preened himself on having dealt with the rascally jacobin in a manner which would recommend itself to

[1] *Sequel*, pp. 95–98.
[2] W.F. to A.B., 5.4.1831.
[3] Dr Parr: *Works*, i, pp. 447–448.

the highest authorities (Wilberforce would see that it was noticed).

* * *

When the dust had settled and Frend was able to take a long cool look at his situation, he found that it was not so disastrous as he feared. It was true that his academic career was shattered; banishment signified that he could not teach nor study in the university, and rustication meant that he could not live in Jesus College till he gave impossible guarantees of future orthodox behaviour. But he still had his Fellowship, and would draw a Fellow's income till he married; he was still a Member of the College, and of the University Senate, and would be all his life. As he said, many years later, his opponents meant "to deprive me of my degrees and to take away my fellowship: in neither did they succeed, but in such a conflict and in such times the wonder is not that I did not lose every thing but that I did retain any thing." [1]

He would have to leave Cambridge. But he loved the place (if not all its inhabitants) and lingered on enjoying the academic surroundings, the library, the conversation of Tyrwhitt, Malthus, Otter and others who were not too hostile, in the Combination Room.

He stayed through June and July in college, much to the Master's annoyance, but nothing could be done to oust him until the Bishop's decision came.

Dr Pearce was heartily thankful when the letter with its episcopal seal arrived, towards the end of July, confirming the sentence of rustication.

He gathered the Fellows together, and read the Visitor's decision. This was no doubt what everyone had expected, and there is no suggestion of protest or objection being raised. But the Master's troubles were by no means over; instead of packing up and leaving at once, Frend was in no hurry to go; on the contrary, he wanted to show that he considered the

[1] W.F. to A.B., 5.4.1831.

College decision illegal, null and void, by staying as long as possible.

The Master wrote on 31 July in a tone of great vexation, telling the Bishop all about it: "I informed your lordship in my last letter that I had read the confirmation of Mr Frend's sentence to the Fellows & to Mr Frend. The morning following, I told Mr Frend that it was my duty to inforce the sentence, & hoped that he would go away without giving me any trouble. To this he said nothing but asked whether that was all I had to say to him. I waited to see what he wd do from that day, Wednesday, to the Saturday morning, when I asked him when he meant to leave College, to this he replied that this was an extraordinary question to come from me, & said that we had not answered his reply, in which was a very heavy charge against us of falsehood . . . He added that he was going out of College that morning, & should return the Saturday following, to pack up his Papers. This was the only expression that looked like an intention of removing—not choosing to rely on this expression, I took the opportunity of going up to Town and consulting Sir Wm Scott what measures were best to be taken to enforce the sentence."

Sir William came up with the following opinion:

"If Mr Frend persists in staying . . . then the Master may direct the servants of the College to forbear attending upon him and supplying him with necessaries.

"I see no reason why furniture may not be removed to a secure Place thence to be delivered to him on his order, notice being given him, and a Padlock put on his Chamber Door." The Master "may order the Porter to refuse him admittance into the College . . . and wd be justified in using force to turn him out, no more force being used than was absolutely necessary for that Purpose . . . " (signed Wm Scott, 24 July 1793).

The Master acted on this on Tuesday 30 July: "I thought it not right to wait any longer" he tells the Bishop, "and sent a letter to him by a Messenger who found him at the

Hammonds in Fen Stanton," to the effect that his furniture and effects must be taken away, and admittance to college refused. "On Friday next . . . I shall order all the College servants to forbear supplying him with anything or attending upon him in College, & the Porter to shut the Gate against him.

"It is extremely inconvenient to me to have staid here so long, being in Cornwall on very interesting business, but I could not well delegate the affair of Mr Frend to another, especially as it appeared every day to be coming to a crisis."

On 4 August the College Porter received a note with the order: "when ever Mr Frend should be in the town of Cambridge to keep the gates shut against him. If Mr F. should enter the College by surprise the Porter is ordered to shut the gates as soon as Mr Frend goes out—but if Mr Frend should persist in staying in College and should not go out the Porter is ordered to shut the gates and to prevent any person from having access to Mr Frend till the College shall take other means to oblige Mr Frend to leave."

The Master, in a letter (dated 4 August) to the Bishop describes Frend's comings and goings during that day, when Dr Pearce had hoped he would have left for good: "About 11 on Friday morning he returned hither and went to his rooms. He seemed to make his preparations for departing . . . He then came to my house, accompanied by Mr Reynolds, desiring to see Sir Wm Scott's opinion under which we acted. This being refused to him, he inveighed against the illegality of our proceedings and the stretches of arbitrary power which were made against him. In the afternoon he walked into the Town & when he came back the Porter had shut the gate."

Frend himself in a note of protest to the Master expressed astonishment at the gates being closed against him at 7 p.m. and said "the Porter gave a very confused account of this unusual proceeding"—this hardly tallies with the Master's version: "When the Porter opened [the gate] to see who was there, Mr Frend rushed in by force and went to his room."

Dr Pearce tells the Bishop that Frend had later gone out again. "He did not return that night, and the next morning we heard that he had left the Town." The Master, heaving a sigh of relief, hoped "now to be at liberty to go into Cornwall, & to set out from Cambridge tomorrow." He left for his holiday on Monday 5 August, having given orders to the College servants "how to act if Mr Frend should return again. The Fellows also promised to pursue the plan laid down by Sir William Scott."

Two days later he tells the Bishop that "I have heard nothing of Mr Frend since my last letter. I found Mr Plampin in Town & have prevailed upon him to agree with Mr Mathew that one or the other of these shall be at Cambridge all the summer and to manage their excursions accordingly. With respect to the removal of Mr Frend's effects from the College, I have consulted Mr Graham in addition to Sir Wm Scott, & with these opinions, Mr Mathew and Mr Plampin will be sufficiently instructed how to act." [1]

The Master need not have worried; Frend had no intention of returning to the college—he recognized that he had lost the battle in Cambridge and he now decided to carry on his activities elsewhere.

First however he was going to appeal to the highest possible court and though—in the present worsening political climate, with the war consolidating the anti-republican opinions of all but the extreme radicals—it was too much to hope for restitution, it would at least give him a platform for several pleas which he had been unable to make at his university trial.

He based his appeal to the House of Commons on the absurdity of the sentence passed on him, on the absurdity of a man of letters and scholar being forbidden to write and publish opinions; he called for urgent reform in the university where abuses existed through which progressively-minded men were penalized for their ideas.

"Remove at once . . . all your penal laws respecting

[1] Bishop of Ely. E.D.R.

religion," he wrote to those responsible for the national education. "Put it on the same footing with philosophy." As to the "set of propositions drawn up by quarrelsome divines above two hundred years ago, let the subscription be confined to those who are to teach them."

He asked "supposing non-Christians to be admitted, where would be the harm? may not an infidel be a very good classical scholar, an excellent mathematician, a good logician? . . . I should be very willing to exchange a few of our most orthodox men, with long faces and empty skulls for the learning, talents & integrity of infidels . . . There is nothing so well calculated for the happiness of mankind as religion; but, when it becomes an instrument of policy and is made a discriminating mark in society," it proves "a source of infinite vexation." [1]

Complaining that "the education of our young men is confined . . . to the clergy", he asked "cannot the same discipline be kept up by well-bred men of letters, as by the starch manners of cloistered life? And are a large wig, a long band, and a black dress, better qualifications for a lecture room or a college lodge, than the plain dress of an english gentleman?"

He touched on "the absurdity of requiring celibacy from fellows of colleges", and said the universities should be made "proper to qualify men for the situations which they are hereafter to occupy in life", with the removal of "those ridiculous statutes which, in the present days, no one can obey."

The university may be made a great national benefit, said Frend. "The magnificence of its structure, and the extent of its revenues occasion envy only in little minds . . . " and he declared that there was not "a more sincere friend to the university than myself."

"I wish to see it flourish; and I lament that such men bear sway in it, as are qualified only to indulge in the repose of a prebendal stall or an episcopal throne . . . and when the

[1] *Sequel*, pp. iv–v.

church receives no more encouragement than any other profession, our Alma Mater will become eminently useful to her country, and cease to exhibit such scenes as have lately tempted her sons to believe her in her dotage." [1]

The curtain falls here on the Cambridge scene; but an echo sounds in a letter written, nearly fifty years later, by Augustus De Morgan, Frend's mathematician son-in-law, to the then Master of Jesus, when returning books belonging to the College found among William Frend's possessions after his death.

"After the proceedings against Mr Frend in 1793, which ended in his banishment, the sentence was enforced without any allowance of time for the arrangement of his affairs at Cambridge. His papers were accordingly left in his rooms to the care of the solicitors, who took possession of everything found there."

The solicitor packed up all papers, and the packages were eventually returned to Frend, says Dc Morgan. He also reveals that Frend cared much more for Cambridge than would appear in his stiff obdurate attitude. Though he had through his pride and obstinacy largely brought about the breach and refused to yield an inch to what he considered obscurantism and chicanery, it must have caused him real grief to give up all that the University meant to him and offered him. This is very evident from De Morgan's closing words in his letter to the college, speaking of "the affectionate regard" with which Frend had looked back upon his connection with the University and in particular with Jesus College. "Nothing could show the bent of his mind in this respect as well as the vivid manner in which he could always remember the most trifling minutiae of College habits or discipline, which was accompanied by the most frequent recurrence to the subject whenever he was in company with a Cambridge man." [2]

[1] *Sequel*, p. vii.
[2] Letter. Jesus College Library.

PART II

BANISHMENT

13
FREE LANCE IN LONDON

On leaving Cambridge Frend decided to settle in London and live on whatever work he could pick up as an economist, writer, teacher.

He had to find somewhere to live, and we learn from a letter written in the autumn of 1794 that he was "at present in the Chambers of a Friend" in the Inner Temple, with "a decent shew of books around me." [1]

He visited the Lindseys and Dyer frequently and made occasional journeys into the country to stay with the Reynolds' or to see his family at Canterbury; he saw Dr Priestley shortly before the Doctor's departure to America, and, as already mentioned, joined with three Cambridge colleagues in presenting him with "a handsome silver inkstand" on that sorrowful occasion.

One of Frend's self-imposed tasks was to write up an account of his trial, which was published towards the end of 1793. That done he devoted several months to his book *Principles of Algebra* which appeared in the autumn of 1795, earning him praise from Tyrwhitt—as rare as it was welcome—approval from Baron Maseres, and indirect compliments from his good friend Jones of Trinity College; the latter wrote that owing to eye trouble, he could neither read nor write by candle light, and had not been able "carefully to peruse your Algebra", but he had "heard very handsome things said of your Algebra ... and never a syllable of an opposite tendency." [2]

Although banished from Cambridge Frend was keeping in touch with scholars there and receiving chatty or learned letters from Higgins (later to become a distinguished

[1] A. F. Wedd: *Love Letters of Mary Hays*, p. 228.
[2] W. Jones to W.F., 18.12.1795.

Egyptologist), Musgrave, and Thomas Manning (Lamb's friend, mathematician and Sinologist) who was teaching privately in Cambridge; having refused to subscribe to the Thirty-nine Articles, Manning was debarred from taking his B.A. and from any university posts.

Letters from former pupils show that Frend was in demand as a teacher. One of them asks for a recommendation to the celebrated classicist Richard Porson, Frend's exact contemporary at Cambridge:

"I thought that your being so kind as to mention it might have some weight . . . If Mr Porson would be so good as to take me in hand I shou'd not despair of the First Honour here, with the assistance of your mathematics . . . Do you think it wd be better to come up to London to read Mathematics (if you will take the trouble of teaching me again) this vacation, or to wait till the Easter Vacation?" A postscript informs Frend that "I am just going to get a piece of Brawn to send up for yr breakfast, if you will do me the favour of accepting it". [1]

Frend liked teaching, and he doubtless took on this pupil; but his strongest urge at this time was to throw himself into political battles. Having so recently tasted persecution he was determined to fight for the right of the individual to act and speak freely about what concerned every citizen so closely—the war, the heavy taxes, the soaring cost of living—and for political rights which, he was now aware, could only be won by organized action for parliamentary reform.

He therefore joined the only body still in existence which could be said to represent the popular movement—the London Corresponding Society. The Society (L.C.S.) had suffered severe setbacks during the persecution of the last two years, and had taken particularly hard knocks in the twelve months following Frend's trial.

The story has been fully told elsewhere;[2] but as it was the

[1] R. Smith to W.F., 1794.

[2] cf. E. P. Thompson: *The Making of the English Working Class*, chaps. 1 and 5.

back-cloth to Frend's life at this time, we have to recall its outlines and its highlights and dwell briefly on the happenings which Frend witnessed or joined in during these critical years.

A National Convention organized by the L.C.S. in Edinburgh during the autumn of 1793 was followed, to the dismay of democrats, by the arrest and trials of several leading radicals (some of them later transported to Botany Bay). More trials followed in the spring of 1794, including that of Thomas Walker, former Borough reeve of Manchester; and then came the arrest of over a dozen L.C.S. leaders, the trial of Thomas Hardy in October, followed by that of Horne Tooke in November.

The shocking sentences imposed by the Scottish Court, and the impressive defence of the radicals in London (acquitted by fair-minded juries) brought the L.C.S. support and prestige. When the verdict "not guilty", so humiliating to the prosecution, was given at Tooke's trial, huge crowds were waiting to hear it. "The burst of excitement inside the court was the signal of acquittal to the multitudes without", said Rev. Jeremiah Joyce, one of the accused: "A separate shout broke from the mass of the people and was caught and echoed to every part of the metropolis in an instant. No telegraphe could convey the news with the electrical velocity of their enthusiasm. It was known at the remotest corners of the town in a minute after the event." [1] Such was the popular enthusiasm for the L.C.S. and the indignation at its treatment at the hands of the government.

By early 1795 the L.C.S. was reorganizing itself. The former leaders retired, or became less active, but new figures—Francis Place, John Gale Jones, a surgeon, John Binns, a plumber from Dublin—stepped in. Frend, a newcomer, got to know them well, particularly Place, the ambitious energetic journeyman tailor and trade union organizer. We know from Place's journal that Frend used to call upon him in his Holborn workshop, "where he would

[1] Joyce: Appendix to sermon, 1795 (*Cambridge Intelligencer*, 4.5.95).

gossip with me for an hour while I worked." Place was not a man to miss a chance of improving his mind and Frend, we know, was always ready to improve another's. "I had", said Place, "always some questions to ask relative to language or science and he was always desirous to give information, and thus he became to me a most valuable instructor. As I knew a little of mathematics and something of astronomy, Mr Frend took pains to teach me as much as he could of these two sciences, he also put me forward in Algebra, and had I remained in Holborn (or had leisure) to receive his instructions I should have become a tolerably expert mathematician."[1]

Frend threw himself into the work of writing, organizing and advising the L.C.S. He made himself useful on the Committee chaired by William Clarkson (the anti-slave trade champion) which was set up at Essex Hall on 12 March to collect funds "for defraying the expenses of the Defendants in the Trials for High Treason." These costs were heavy as it had been necessary to summon about 500 witnesses from outside London and keep them during the duration of the trials.

In two weeks £313 9s. 0d. was collected, the Dowager Lady Stanhope heading the list with £20. Frend's name and Dyer's are mentioned as collecting subscriptions. By the middle of May 1795 the Committee had raised £1,090 8s. 0d.—a proof of the support and sympathy prevalent in the country for the cause.[2]

We have little detailed information about Frend and his doings, but his name often appears in the columns of the *Cambridge Intelligencer*, to which he was also an anonymous contributor. This radical weekly continued to come out under the direction of his old friend Benjamin Flower, and today it provides a lively picture of radical activity during this period. We see reflected in its pages the gathering popularity and momentum of the L.C.S., the only move-

[1] Place. B.M. Fn Fol. 75. Add. Mss. 35. 142/3/4.
[2] *Cambridge Intelligencer* (*C.I.*), 11 April, 23 May 1795.

ment unequivocally opposing the war, at a time when the desire for peace was intense.

Its policy was supported by many sections of society. As early as January 1795 the *Intelligencer* reports that "a London Corporation headed by the Lord Mayor and attended by upwards of 5000 of the Livery met to consider a petition to the House of Commons to promote the object of a speedy peace . . . Against were not one to fifty."

The city of Norwich and others followed London's example and petitions poured in, as rates and prices rose, and taxes weighed every month more heavily on the people. A typical letter to the newspaper complaining of "the increase of Rates already barely supportable", condemns "ill placed confidence in the Ministry and support of the present miserably disastrous War", and advises "not to expect better times but rather to prepare for greater evils except the blessings of Peace were speedily restored."[1]

There was money about—Oxford, in full convocation, "decided to make a present to the French refugee clergy of 2000 copies of the Latin Testament of the Vulgate translation now printing at the Clarendon Press"—but most people felt the pinch of the taxes imposed on such essentials as bread, cheese and beer. A suffering maltster wrote, "Why not a tax on tea, coffee, cocoa?"

In fact, these particular luxuries were already heavily taxed and were left at the current high price, while in its search for new revenue the government put a tax of £2 2s. on hair powder; this inspired much ribald comment such as the verse in the *Intelligencer* on 23 May:

> You must be blind to all my deeds, Our worthy Billy cries—
> So takes the dust from off our heads, to throw it in our eyes.

And someone suggested that by abolishing hair powder

[1] *C.I.*, 7.2.1795.

altogether the bread problem could be solved: "16,350 sacks of flour will be gained weekly from the disuse of powder by 50,000 wearers."[1]

Far more drastic measures however were needed, and by the summer, nothing effective having been done about it, flour was in very short supply. It appeared that this was partly due to hoarding and profiteering, and hungry consumers now often decided to take the distribution of flour and of meat into their own hands. Typical incidents occurred towards the end of July at Cambridge, where, the *Intelligencer* tells us "a mob seized a lighter laden with flour going down the river to Ely and were preparing to divide it", only giving it up on the intervention of the Lord Lieutenant, the Earl of Hardwick, who promised the price of loaves would be reduced.

Next day "the croud crowded the market at an early hour and seized meat. The Mayor caused the meat to be brought out and publicly sold. The same was done by many other parcels till at length the mob increased both in numbers and demands for 4d a pound. They assembled in very large numbers as night approached and were prevailed on to disperse only after the publication of a handbill."

This was addressed "to the Poor Inhabitants of the Town of Cambridge: Suffer us to entreat you to depart to your respective homes . . . and we will take every legal measure to reduce the price of meat by preventing Butchers buying and selling in the same market, and all Forestalling, Ingrossing and Regrating."[2]

In Huntingdon, the authorities had to make the same promises: Richard Reynolds wrote to Frend, on 31 July, that "tho' it is said our county is better provided with wheat than neighbouring counties, yet it sold yesterday at St Neot's at the rate of 16/– a bushel . . . and if any attempt is now made to send any out of town a mob rises and forces it back again; this case happened this morning at St Neot's—

[1] *C.I.*, 23.5.1795.
[2] *Ibid.*, 25.7.1795.

a waggon containing 20 loads going to Stamford was stopped by the mob near our turnpike last night, came back . . . was guarded all night on the Market Place and then the owner sold the wheat to the miller at St Neot's mills, which contented the people who are now dispersed."[1]

As a result of such popular demonstrations, speculation was curbed and fairer distribution ensured by the authorities in most localities; but this did not measure up to the central inefficiency and waste: fuel was added to popular anger by such news as that "12000 quarters of wheat had been spoiled while waiting to make a landing in France and sold at a shilling a bushel to feed hogs."

The *Intelligencer* remarked on 4 July, "the plain truth is—no government were ever more criminal in not endeavouring to prevent a scarcity, than the present one."

Individuals also incurred public wrath. In 25 July's *Intelligencer* we learn that "Lord Hardwick attended two meetings at the Rose . . . to vote the disposal of upwards of a thousand pounds on the Purchase of Uniform Jackets for our gentlemen of the Yeomanry Cavalry and Bridles for their Horses." Ben Flower comments that "instead, his Lordship ought to call a Meeting to consider of a Petition to put an end to this accursed war. It would do more for the relief of the poor than any or all of the measures yet proposed."

Against this seething background, William Frend wrote a long letter headed "The Scarcity of Bread, a Plan for reducing the high Price of this Article", addressed to William Devaynes Esq. at the London Tavern (in the Chair at a "respectable" meeting to consider the food situation). The letter was reprinted as a short pamphlet and it shows how deeply involved Frend was. He reproached the Chairman and the meeting "for not speaking out boldly the whole truth"—mentioning short produce and unfavourable weather, but leaving out "the material article from which scarcity arises—the War."

Frend asks "whether you omitted this article from the fear

[1] Reynolds to W.F., 31.7.1795.

of offending members? . . . or from fear of telling people the truth lest they should join with one heart in demanding a speedy end to . . . the horrors of the war . . . " The shortage was due to the fact that "France was competing for American grain, and Poland too distracted to supply both us and the immense armies . . . " The price, Frend insisted, must be lowered and the poor subsidized by assistance voted in Parliament, or by the better-off members of society.

Fifteen hundred merchants had, at the outbreak of war, volunteered their lives and fortunes (worth £2,000 each at least); why should not the twentieth part of these fortunes be contributed if necessary in loans, or in instalments, to relieve distress caused by the war and "unfair taxes"? At present, said Frend, "we pay a high proportion of taxes in the price of cheese, bread, beer, shoes, candles. The reverse ought to take place." He asked the Chairman "to rccommend it to the meeting to petition for sufficient supplies for relief and the lowering of the prices of necessaries."

To a summary of the above, printed in the *Intelligencer* of 25 July, Frend added: "Those who have encouraged the war . . . are now bound to come forward and alleviate with the fortunes they offered, that distress which they have partly occasioned." He sent a copy of the letter to his friend Richard Reynolds who replied thanking him for this and "the little History of yourself, the soldiers and justices" which accompanied it.

Frend was evidently sticking out his neck, and Reynolds was concerned: "You seem to me determined to defy all danger and to let no occasion slip of manifesting your determined zeal for the welfare of your country. For my part I would not have good patriots engage themselves too hastily in promoting the very best designs—they may suffer and bring inconvenience on themselves, and I see no chance of their turning our Ministers from their pernicious and destructive measures." Reynolds himself was a valiant fighter and patriot, but faced with "the blindness and infatuation

[of] the mass of the gentry and yeomanry who no distresses can cure at present of their approbation of this infernal war" thought it useless to try to raise the anti-war banner in Huntingdon: "You should see our Council Meeting and the resolutions for relieving the poor", he tells Frend. "The Bishop, Gentry and Justices, seem extremely satisfied with themselves for voting a little subscription. There was a little subscription. There was a silence as to Peace, the word not mentioned in the Shire hall. I felt the great propriety of calling the attention of the county to petition for peace, but standing single and unsupported, I had not the courage to make the motion."[1]

The "patriotic" merchants of course kept their fortunes to themselves. The government did nothing. "A little subscription" was the palliative offered by county councils in some areas; others followed the Speenhamland magistrates' decision to regulate the relief of wages in relation to the price of bread. But hunger increased and agitation spread. On 31 October the *Intelligencer* reported that "machinery of a Mill for trimming Flour was burned down . . . in Barnard Castle, Yorkshire, by the Populace . . . At Darlington . . . a rise of corn having been occasioned by the farmers selling large quantities of it to a Miller at a distance the Populace also rose and prevented it from leaving the town."

The Editor appealed "to Friends of Tranquillity and Good Order who cannot but be aware that the War is the chief cause of the present scarcity and that such tumults may not often be suppressed without dreadful consequences to the lives and limbs of their Fellow Creatures", to do their duty "by imploring Parliament to address his Majesty for Peace without considering any form of Government existing in a Foreign Country as an obstacle to it."

In fact, in spite of continued "tumults", the authorities' use of suppression rarely resulted in "dreadful consequences", because the militia was often on the side of the demonstrators, and the protests against speculating and against the

[1] Reynolds to W.F., 31.7.1795.

adulteration of food seemed right and justifiable.[1] That it did happen on occasion is evident from the L.C.S. report: "The argument of the rioters to the Magistrates now was, You did not shoot us when we was rioting for Church and King, and pulling down the Presbyterians' meetings and dwelling-houses, but gave us plenty of good ale and spirits to urge us on; now we are rioting for a big loaf we must be shot at and cut up like bacon pigs!!!"[2]

The general discontent and the anti-war feeling brought massive support for the L.C.S. and from a state of disruption in late 1794 it grew steadily in numbers and influence throughout 1795. In May that year it boasted a membership of several thousands; its seventy London divisions had an overall weekly attendance of some two thousand people.

To anyone in the centre of things as William Frend was, London must have been an exciting place at this time. There was constant activity and huge meetings, such as that in St George's Fields in June, when 100,000 turned out to hear Gale Jones call for Parliamentary Reform. In July the secretary noted in the L.C.S. minute book that "our numbers increase with a rapidity unequalled at any former period—near 800 within this last month."[3]

There were of course differences within the society, as in any not very homogeneous body aiming to co-ordinate other groups.

Persons belonging to other societies "left us because they could not agree with each other" (these were the Reforming Society and the Friends of Liberty). "We are on amiable terms with them both and wish they were with each other." And in the leadership there were clashes of personality and points of view: John Binns, a fiery young Irishman, and Gale Jones were for reform by revolution and urged the holding of mass meetings to force through the Society's demands.

Francis Place on the other hand was for proceeding "as

[1] cf. Thompson: *op. cit.*, pp. 70–72, 156.

[2] L.C.S. Records, Nuffield College Library, Oxford.

[3] *Ibid.*

quietly and privately as possible." William Frend was somewhere between the two: he saw the need for mass protest and direct action, but was against violence. Thus he represented a bridge between the two parties which was valuable to the society now that Horne Tooke and other middle-class supporters had withdrawn from activity.

Frend worked hard for the L.C.S. and as he had many "respectable" friends, one of his tasks was to obtain their support and invite them to L.C.S. functions. A letter from Lord Stanhope survives, "declining the honor you kindly intended me of being one of the Stewards for your Dinner", but assuring him "wherever I am you know that I am unalterable in all my Civic Principles", and signing himself "Your faithful Fellow Citizen".[1]

Meanwhile discontent grew in the country as nothing happened to improve the condition of the people. The war itself was going badly and Flower jeered in his newspaper of 31 October: "The loss of St Lucia, the devastation of St Vincent's and Grenada, the disasters of the Jamaica and Mediterranean fleets, the slaughter of Quiberon and the failure of the Comte d'Artois will be triumphantly displayed by the government as 'negative successes'."

On 26 October there was another great demonstration, in Copenhagen Fields, again 100,000 strong, addressed by John Thelwall, Jones and Binns. Resolutions were passed, protesting against "the present awful and alarming state of the British Empire", "the exorbitant prices occasioned by the present ruinous war", and "that pernicious system of monopoly due to Parliamentary representation." And a "Remonstrance" addressed to King George asked "Whencefore in the midst of apparent plenty are we thus compelled to starve? Why when we incessantly toil and labour must we pine in misery and want? . . . Parliamentary Corruption . . . like a foaming Whirlpool swallows the fruit of all our labours."[2]

[1] Stanhope to W.F., Letter. University of London Library.

[2] Thompson: *op. cit.*, p. 158. L.C.S.: *Account of the Proceedings of a Meeting.*

These massive demonstrations, though as "peaceful and harmonious" as their organizers claimed, were very alarming to the government.

Even more so was a spontaneous protest at the beginning of November which showed that even the Throne itself was not sacrosanct. When the King went in state to open Parliament on 29 October "the concourse of people", according to the Cambridge newspaper's correspondent, "almost exceeded belief ... Expressions of loyalty were but faintly heard through the numerous acclamations of No War! No War! Peace and Bread!" The tumult increased as the King drove along till "opposite the Ordnance Office, some person had the audacity to throw a stone which broke the coach windows." The King was not touched, but is said to have gasped out in terror, "My Lord, I, I, I've been shot at!"[1]

His carriage was pelted all the way along Pall Mall, and on entering St James' Palace "the hissings and hootings were more violent than ever.

"Later the King went out in his private coach and the Mob completely surrounded it and prevented it from proceeding, crying out 'Bread! Bread! Peace! Peace!' The guards were brought and his Majesty returned safely to Buckingham House."[2] The next day when the King went to the theatre the streets were cleared and he was attended by 100 foot, 200 horse and 500 constables.[3]

Although his Majesty had come to no harm the authorities reacted to the demonstration immediately and harshly. A King's Proclamation ordered the discovery and punishment of "the Authors Actors and Abettors concerned in such outrages" and offered a reward of One Thousand Pounds for every offender caught. The sort of punishment meted out is shown by the report some months later that "Kidd Wake was convicted of a Misdemenor in hooting and making wry faces at His Majesty and crying out No War, Down with

[1] Thompson: *op. cit.*, p. 158.
[2] *C.I.*, 31.10.1795.
[3] Thompson: *op. cit.*, p. 158.

George", and was to be "confined to hard labour in the House of Correction in Gloucester for five years and stand once in the Pillory and at the expiration of his sentence give security for good behaviour for ten years in the sum of £1000. To stay in gaol till he found such security."

Poor Wake—the security he found was that of the grave, for he died in prison before his release.[1]

The government's panic infected its supporters: on 7 November 240 M.P.s voted in Parliament for continuing the war, and Pitt felt it safe to introduce two Acts clamping down on public meetings, and making it a treasonable offence to incite to hatred or contempt of King, Constitution or Government. As Flower put it in the *Intelligencer* of 14 November, "All complaints which have a tendency to excite or stir up the people to a dislike of his Majesty's Ministers are to be punished with Fine, Imprisonment and Transportation."

But there was an immediate reaction from Fox and his followers in the House, and from the public outside. As a gesture of defiance, on 12 November 800 gentlemen drank the healths of Thelwall, Hardy and others at an anniversary dinner to commemorate their acquittal.

One toast was "The L.C.S. for its exertions in the cause of freedom and parliamentary reform", which Horne Tooke amended to "the last effort of expiring Liberty."[2] His pessimism was premature: the L.C.S. was still full of fight and organizing widespread protests against the Acts.

Petitions began to pour in to Parliament, from Sheffield ("several thousand persons"), from York, Canterbury, Bristol (4,000), Norwich (many thousands), from Reading ("at one of the most numerous meetings ever known there"), against the bills, for negotiations with France, for ending the war. An L.C.S.-sponsored petition "was signed in the City of London, with Westminster and their environs, amounting to 10,131, chiefly respectable trades people and mechanics."

[1] *C.I.*, 14.5.1796.
[2] *Ibid.*, 14.11.1795.

And on 5 December, "the shipwrights in His Majesty's dockyards, though immediately dependent on government for bread, have in general . . . publicly protested against the two bills."

Pitt's friends presented their own petitions: one was signed at Huntingdon by "evangelical priests and cavalry officers", but "so few that it was thought proper to sign for others by proxy . . . the petition was rejected."[1] The *Intelligencer* noted on 7 November that "at Norwich one Alderman showed his loyalty by making an Elephant drink the King's health", and recorded with disgust that "the corporation of Cambridge had a snug private meeting on Thursday last . . . and voted a very dutiful address to His Majesty. Not a word in it about peace or the present attempts now going forward against our liberties." The editor fulminated on 14 November: "Is there a spark of Freedom left in the breasts of the Inhabitants of this Town and County and of the members of an illustrious University? Illustrious not merely for its learning but for the honorable distinction it has acquired—that of the WHIG UNIVERSITY?"[2]

A few weeks later Flower got his answer and his "spark of Freedom", when Pitt visited Cambridge. After attending service at St Mary's the Prime Minister "was much hissed as he got into his carriage . . . On which after giving one of his scornful looks at the populace he remarked to the Bishop of Lincoln, 'Half of them do not know what they are hissing about.'—We beg to differ", retorts Flower: "Not the poorest or most uninformed but well knew whom he was hissing and what he was hissing about: the war, the extravagant price of provisions, the loss of some of our most valuable liberties . . . fully justified the people in showing their indignation."[3] This number of the *Intelligencer* was sold out, as it often was at this time, because it voiced the feelings of the man in the street "whose opposition to the abominable

[1] *C.I.*, 7.11.1795.
[2] *Ibid.*, 14.11.1795.
[3] *Ibid.*, 23.1.1796.

Bills dooming us to slavery continues with unabated vigour."

Threatened with Pitt's punitive measures, the spirit of the people was indeed remarkable: "They almost everywhere assemble in large numbers", says Flower, "and their behaviour is as fair, manly and peaceable as spirited." The weeks between the introduction of the Acts and the Royal Assent (18 December) were the last and greatest period of popular agitation, with Fox and his fifty-odd supporters in the House fighting every stage of the Bill's passage, and campaigning alongside the popular societies.

Two hundred thousand men, women and children (a guarantee of peaceful intent) turned up at an L.C.S. emergency demonstration on 12 November; and a final great meeting was held on 7 December in Marylebone Fields, in the thick of which we find William Frend.

Joseph Farington the painter went along "at one o'clock when great numbers of people were passing to and fro" and noted in his diary: "Three Hustings were erected in different parts and before each one a crowd of people was assembled." The speakers were "Citizen" Jones, Thelwall and Frend. Farington was not complimentary about Thelwall—"A little and very mean looking man with a sickly yellow complexion and black lank hair"[1]—nor about Jones, who was afflicted with "an almost constant convulsive twitching of his hands, shoulders and arms" and clad in a green coat and half boots "presented a figure such as is usually called shabby genteel." Frend, according to the diary, "is a gentlemanlike looking man; of good stature and bulk; apparently about 30 or 35 years of age; dark hair without powder."

The speeches were not dreadfully inflammatory; Frend reassured his listeners as to the dangers of Pitt's Acts, saying "that the Bill of rights limited even the power of Parliaments"; and even if Citizen Jones did speak "with great inveteracy against Pitt and of his being brought to publick execution", the audience were mostly "respectable people"

[1] This description is not borne out by Thelwall's portrait in the National Portrait Gallery.

and "no tumult took place nor was any offence given to such as did not hold up hands or join in the plaudit."[1]

The authorities were not yet prepared to suppress "respectable people" such as these—the memory of their discomfiture at the 1794 acquittals was still raw. The speakers went temporarily free and the Corresponding Society did not close down. But the Acts were passed and, once law, began to stifle the radical movement.

By March 1796 membership had dropped considerably, and meetings became difficult as spies eavesdropped and reported back.

Farington wrote in his diary for 24 January that "Mr Pitt was informed (by Lancashire supporters) of a society . . . established by the Jacobins, since the Sedition Bills passed, where the members at their meetings sit with a kind of muzzle over their mouths and converse only by signs and writing . . ."

In London, people showed their anti-Pitt feelings by celebrating Fox's birthday with unusual ritual; the *Intelligencer* advertised on 23 January a birthday party at the Rose Tavern: "Dinner on the Table at 4 o'clock and to consist of only Potatoes and Barley Dumplings. Tickets 1/–. After Dinner, Political Conversation"—to include a discussion on "the Propriety of singing the Ballad of God Save the King on one Knee or both." At the London Tavern and at the Crown and Anchor, Fox's health was drunk with "enthusiasm and rapture" as a reward for his endeavours to foil the two Acts.

The L.C.S. struggled on, but after the arrest of some of its leaders (including Jones and Binns, taken when addressing a meeting in Birmingham) things became very difficult. Francis Place for a while stuck to the committee, and wrote that "the business of the Society increased after its members fell off. It was necessary, to keep it from absolute ruin, to appoint deputations from the general committee to the divisions whose delegates ceased to attend the

[1] Farington Diary, 1795, p. 133.

district committee, as well as to those which were sluggish or met in small numbers . . . This was an arduous undertaking."

Place had to run around, often to several meetings on one evening, urging them "to a state of greater activity"; he also had to organize a fund for the defence of those arrested. But gradually he withdrew from committee work, and by March 1797 he had ceased to be delegate even of his own division, no doubt seeing trouble ahead.

Place had always been a prudent person, and as Chairman of the L.C.S. had "advocated the political tactics which he continued to believe throughout the rest of his life." He advised against large public meetings and in 1795 was proved wrong; but his caution was justified in 1797 when mass support had dwindled. In April, a meeting organized by the Society near St Pancras Church was dispersed by the constables, all the platform arrested, and the L.C.S. left "in a very low state." Following this came a raid on a committee meeting, and the arrest of 28 leading members—they were to be held without trial for three years. The prisons were beginning to fill up again.

We do not know what part Frend had played in the Society during the previous months, but he emerges again as an active supporter in '97, when the Reformers' immediate task was to raise money for Pitt's victims and their families. Francis Place, by his own account, "was left almost alone in the work of collecting and distributing subscriptions and pressing for payment of an allowance to the wives and families of the prisoners, which was at last granted by the Government." He turned to William Frend for help: "I applied to him to assist in procuring money for the families of the persons in prison. He readily undertook to do so and said he would assemble some of his friends the following Saturday for the purpose."[1]

A large, rather tattered sheet of paper covered with notes and numbers has survived, showing how Frend kept his

[1] Place: *Autobiography*, Ms. Vol. ii (Add. 35,143). B.M.

accounts on behalf of those "now detained in the different prisons of this Metropolis on a suspicion of treasonable practices." We read the note, in Frend's tidy scholarly handwriting, "that about 30 of them are confined in Clerkenwell Bridewell on Bread & Water only", and that "the greatest part of these persons are in very distressed circumstances & their Wives and Children destitute of the Support of their Industry are literally starving."

Below this is a list of subscribers which includes Lord Oxford, Sir Francis Burdett, Mr Whitbread and Mr Grey—all of whom gave five guineas; Mr Rutt (Priestley's biographer), Horne Tooke, Mr Bonham, Prince Hoare (the painter)—a guinea each; "seventeen workmen"—fifteen shillings and sixpence; and there are many more names and initials, showing that Frend had worked hard, and that he had many good and sympathetic supporters.

He probably felt that he himself was fortunate to be on the "outside". Even being respectable was now no guarantee against arrest. Friends of well-known democrats were concerned about them: Jones, the Bursar of Trinity College, wrote to Frend on 18 December 1796, "I am afraid lest Ben Flower's fiery indignation against the present measures should expose him to the penalties of one of the late bills. A hint will be of use to him . . . "

Flower escaped for the time being and continued to publish the *Intelligencer*, which in spite of "hints" never ceased to criticize whatever the editor disliked. Some years later the authorities pounced, on account of an unflattering reference to Pitt, and sued Flower for libel—but for some strange reason he survived at a time when heads were falling all around. Frend no doubt rejoiced, as he passed on a hint, that the Bills did not strike at Flower; and grieved in equal measure at the arrest and imprisonment of Johnson, the brave bookseller and publisher, and of Gilbert Wakefield who had had the temerity to deliver a broadside against the Bishop of Llandaff and defend it in the High Court. His was one of the last and most heroic personal protests in the story of the radical 1790's; after this, people wondered what was the use of protest?

More than ten years were to pass before such political drama was witnessed again in England.

* * *

Although Frend had escaped arrest and with the demise of the London Corresponding Society virtually given up radical activity, he was closely watched as a politically suspect character. He was several times mentioned disparagingly in *The Anti-Jacobin*, the rabidly reactionary journal which was launched in 1798 to promote "loyalty" to the government and destroy the characters of Reformers and Radicals.

In one article devoted to proving that Dissenters were traitors, Frend is attacked ("expelled the University of Cambridge ... now associates with Dissenters") and in another, his Trinity College friends are reproved for having supported him: "Ought not every sentiment towards such an individual ... to have been sacrificed without a murmur to the danger of injuring their college in the opinion of the world?"

Even the College itself is criticized because only three of its members joined in prosecuting Frend, and is stigmatized with the epithet of "jacobinical".[1]

George Frend, William's elder brother, a regular reader of the journal, was greatly shocked, and wrote, "I am very sorry to see your name in the Anti-Jacobin ... As a follower & at the command of H.T. [Horne Tooke] & as a member of the corresponding society, take care that some new act of parliament does not involve you in the disgrace of your patron, for something seems to be preparing for him."

William had evidently offered to send him his latest pamphlet, for George declines "any of your political publications; as to the principles of Taxation [William's latest title] I have no concern about the necessity of it. I am convinced

[1] *The Anti-Jacobin*, 1799, p. 261.

of & will chearfully pay my proportion to the support of that government which so well protects me; when our domestic & foreign enemies exert their utmost strength to work our destruction, great exertions must be made & I still hope we shall gloriously vanquish our foreign foes & crush domestic traytors."

George finished this letter regretfully: "Our partys my dear brother are too opposite for us ever to agree—I wou'd die for the support of my King . . . & for the government which I admire, therefore let us never speak or write a word on the subject of politics." [1] He was probably wise, for his younger brother would not willingly give up trying to convert one of his family—even the true blue George.

William Frend was used to petty persecution and he did not mind the disapproving looks cast in his direction by loyal tories; but he had to earn a living, and he was beginning to realize how hard this was for someone as unorthodox as himself. He had hitherto managed to exist on a few lessons and the proceeds of his pamphlets, and he hoped that the second volume of his *Algebra* (published in 1799) would bring in something.

We know that at least it brought him praise, if nothing more substantial, from a letter which must have pleased him from the difficult Tyrwhitt: "The copy of your Principles of Algebra did not reach me so soon as you expected. It found me under confinement by the Gout in my feet, which lasted some time longer. You authorize me to say *our* Principles of Algebra, as Midwives are allowed, I Suppose, to call those whom they assist in bringing into the world *their* children. I acknowledge the relation upon your own terms . . . I hope it will prove healthy & strong & do you no little credit by its reputation in the Algebraical World . . ." [2]

Frend must have hoped that this book would bring him pupils, and perhaps an audience for lectures. He wrote to Lindsey for advice on organizing a course, but his old friend

[1] George Frend to W.F., 18.11.1799.
[2] Tyrwhitt to W.F., 1799.

was discouraging: "No lectures but medical ones are well attended. The first course of the Aikins did pretty well, as many of their young friends . . . made a point of it; but at the last course there was a great falling-off. Still less may be expected from so dry a subject as Mathematics in these days . . . " Nor did Lindsey think advertising would help Frend much: "Private recommendation would seem the least objectionable and most effective way." Then out comes the hard, bitter truth: "It is not merely the *odium theologicum* but *politicum* also, far more pestilential at present, which has marked you out as an infecting person." Lindsey assures him, "I am truly mortified to be able to be of so little use to one of such superior talents and abilities and . . . with dispositions to serve both God and Man with them." Continued effort and the aid of friends, he hopes, will provide "a means of emerging."

In another letter Lindsey rejoices to hear of Frend "being so happy and chearful; which must be wherever you are, for I know none who has so little gloom and a more constant fund for variety and entertainment."

This is consoling for his biographer, for it might be expected that anyone in Frend's position—with no fixed work, spied on and suspected, debarred from academic positions for which he was so well qualified—might have been depressed. But he seems always to have been able to occupy himself, and in the last months of the century he was busy re-editing his Algebra, writing "Animadversions", a treatise in answer to Bishop Pretyman's *Elements of Christian Theology*; preparing a pamphlet on Paper Money and its effects on the price of provisions; and pursuing the study of astronomy and of economics with unflagging zeal.

A letter from Mrs Reynolds of Paxton on 9 January 1798 shows indirectly that Frend was also engaged in more frivolous occupations and that he had friends in high places: "Your mechanical experiments must have been very amusing, and it is well when anything occurs to take the attention from the present melancholy state of public affairs, the assessed taxes make me sick whenever I think of them & I think Lord Oxford's Organ could put them out of my Head."[1]

* * *

If at any time Frend did feel down-hearted he was always sure of comfort and cheer from the good Mr and Mrs Reynolds, who constantly wrote him chatty letters telling him the local news and pressing him to stay with them, "when your numerous engagements will permit you to traverse little Paxton Hills."

The Reynolds would come with their "whisky" and fetch him from Huntingdon coach stage, Mrs R. talking incessantly as they drove, if one may so presume from the poem she addressed to Frend on one of his visits (presented with a bouquet of flowers from her garden):

Leave then the Town, its Smoke and Noise
And seek the humbler village joys,
    Leave Politics awhile alone
    Let Algebra be scarcely known;
With Mirth and Freedom let us talk
Nor yet forget the Morning Walk

The pony is lame, Mrs Reynolds says,

But in the Whisky you may ride,
And talk while driving by my side.
Talk, did I say? With shame, I fear,
You scarce can talk when I am near . . .

On another occasion, "I have a thousand things to tell you and am too much inclined to talk, but a little hint will

[1] Reynolds to W.F., 9.1.1798.

silence me"; and again, "Mr Pearce talked more than I did, so I could not sleep!"

Whether Frend found her conversation enjoyable or tiresome, he was very fond of the Reynolds' and returned to Paxton and its garden again and again. Between visits his hosts kept him informed of all their doings, which were those of country gentry living through difficult times but making the most of their rural pleasures.

"Flowers have been in high perfection this summer and the Garden still looks in some Beauty";—"We have hitherto had a most delightful harvest and at Little Paxton the Wheat is already in. Harvest Cakes come to us in plenty, I have wished you here to eat them & have always thought of you whenever we have had an Apricot Pye . . . "—"Our Hay is likely to be good . . . I never remember so early or so fine a Summer . . ."[1]

They entertain or are entertained: one evening they "drink tea and play at Whist with the great Dr Parr." "I never saw such a man as the Doctor," says Mrs Reynolds: "He is fierce to a degree on the subject of Politicks & I think it will be lucky if he does not get shut up in Prison, unless indeed he should play his cards in a Gaol as well as Wakefield and Flower." Dr Parr "is a most curious figure, in a curious Wig, and much inclined to talk nonsense to Ladies."[2]

Country gentlemen had their troubles, and these are recounted at length, from "Rheumatick Pains and the Cramp" brought on by hunting, to legal proceedings over enclosures of land. Frend is asked in one letter (12 July 1799) to call on Reynolds' solicitors in Southampton Buildings—"Pray pop in and ask them . . . when I may expect that Mr H. will take my Estate, or refuse it . . . "

Besides the expressions of affection and admiration in these letters, a very solid token of Paxton's esteem for Frend has survived in the form of a mahogany cabinet, made by the local carpenter at the instructions of Mrs Reynolds' cabinet-maker,

[1] Reynolds to W.F., 9.8.1798.

[2] Reynolds to W.F., 5.12.1799.

which has descended to Frend's great-granddaughter, complete with its twelve drawers and the poems by Mrs Reynolds which accompanied it. One of these has a charm and directness which entitle it to be quoted, apart from the useful advice it imparts:

> Accept this plain cabinet, honest Will Frend,
> Twill teach thee I hope in exactness to mend.
> Tye up with red tape all the Bills you have paid,
> The undischarg'd few may here also be laid.
> On Letters receiv'd put the date & the name,
> The useless destroy or your head I shall blame . . .

Besides the many letters from Paxton Hall are those from Stanton written by John Hammond, who also had his troubles, domestic, financial and political. At the end of the century what mainly worried small farmers was the question of enclosure—would they get a good piece of land, would the cost of fencing, draining, tilling, eventually be repaid, what would happen to the poor village folk who were already suffering from shortages and the high cost of living? Two years later Hammond wrote to Frend: "Nothing is to be talked or thought of but the inclosure . . . I feel myself as much adverse to it as ever."[1]

We shall return to Hammond's laments later—for in the decade that followed the turn of the century, small farmers, squires and labourers alike found their worries increasing; the early years of the nineteenth century were perhaps the most troubled in the history of agricultural England, and Huntingdon's rural population suffered like the rest. Very many letters from Stanton and Paxton to Frend reflect the anxiety, and Frend's own writings show that he—like William Cobbett, if less dramatically—was very much concerned with the radical change in social conditions caused by the alteration in the countryside as well as in industry, now assuming a new significance for him.

[1] Hammond to W.F., 1801.

But before we leave the eighteenth century and follow Frend into middle age, we should perhaps look back at one aspect of his life in London in the 1790's—the friendships he made and enjoyed when he was a bachelor, an unattached intellectual, moving among some of the most interesting figures of his time.

14

LITERARY FRIENDSHIPS

I William Godwin, Mary Hays

IT WOULD BE pleasant to think that Frend had time for gaiety and feminine society as well as for his very serious occupations; he was after all only thirty-seven when he left Cambridge in 1793, and was still disposed to enjoy himself. But his Unitarian acquaintances were not greatly given to merriment, and his literary cronies—Lamb, Dyer, Rutt—each had personal troubles at this time, even had they been the kind to introduce him to young ladies.

The only member of the opposite sex, apart from his own family, whom Frend knew at all well during the years following his "banishment" was the highly strung London lady, Mary Hays, who was more remarkable for her brains than for her beauty (if we are to accept Coleridge's judgement) and was not likely to offer him cheerful companionship. Miss Hays, daughter of Nonconformist middle-class parents, was something of a theologian as well as a novelist and historian. She had suffered greatly when her lover, a gentleman of Tunbridge Wells, had been killed in a post-chaise accident in 1780; she had been infatuated with poor John Eccles, had corresponded with him for over ten years, exchanging over 130 letters, and in 1792 she still believed she would never love any man again.

After the tragedy of his death, she threw herself into the writing of magazine articles and historical biographies instead of love letters. She had also become "through Robert Robinson a Unitarian and a very zealous political and moral reformer",[1] and in 1792 embarked, under the name of "Eusebia", on a pamphlet on the question of social worship in the Unitarian church, partly in answer to a recent

[1] H. Crabb Robinson: *On Books and their Writers*, p. 5.

publication of Gilbert Wakefield's condemning popular forms of public worship. Her pamphlet circulated and met with approval among the fellowship of Essex Street chapel, and a copy found its way into the hands of William Frend.

Frend was impressed by it and rashly wrote to congratulate the author, thereby stirring up much trouble for himself—and for her too, poor lady, for she was incurably romantic, and at the same time exceedingly lonely.

Although Frend could not have known this, or suspected it from her discussion of theological questions, his letter to her (dated 18 April 1792) from Jesus College, was rather injudicious. He spoke of his "agreeable hopes of being introduced on my next journey to London to the acquaintance of a Lady who entertains the highest esteem for the writings of revelation," and examines them with "freedom of candor" in her "elegant pamphlet".

Referring to his recent ordeal, he says that "to one who has been . . . listening to the wranglings of contending parties . . . wearied with ineffectual struggles against the power of interest and prejudice" there is "no higher gratification . . . than that of hearing sentiments unsophisticated by scholastick learning and drawn . . . from the source of truth." He becomes more and more complimentary: "Eusebia has given the world a proof that she has dedicated her time and talents to the best employment." He hopes "she will permit him to number himself among her friends, and thanks her for the pleasure he received in reading the pamphlet." He rambles on, and after discussing the Unitarian creed, and describing his visit to the mountains of Savoy where "one Sunday I stepped into a church crowded with healthful and happy peasants", comments on the methods of the pastor, and suggests that "the plain tale of such a pastor would be lost among the refinements of a London audience . . ." He signs himself Eusebia's "unknown though sincere well-wisher".[1]

Whether he intended it or not, this letter was taken as an

[1] Wedd: *Love Letters of Mary Hays*, pp. 220–222.

invitation to develop the acquaintance. It was some time before Mary found a way of meeting him. They had several mutual friends who could have introduced them in 1792, but Cambridge was a long way from London where Mary was living, and it was not until Frend came to live in town that they became more than pen-friends.

A letter to Mary from George Dyer, on a visit to the Hammonds near Cambridge, shows that she was trying hard to get in touch with Frend even during the very busy late summer of 1793: "Mr Frend you must forgive. His hands are full, and he will do himself the pleasure of writing you an epistle soon, which I shall bring with me to town."

It is to be feared that the rest of the letter, though it gave a nice picture of Dyer on holiday ("I am now at Stanton in Huntingdonshire, quite retired, and leading just such a life as is agreeable to me among books and trees and one or two friends . . . ") was not of such interest to Mary, but she must have felt gratified, if not satisfied, by his "Farewell—with my best compliments, in which Mr Frend unites, I remain, dear Madam . . . " The postscript tells her that Frend's account of the trial "will be out in about three weeks", and so will Dyer's own latest book, *The Complaints of the Poor People of England* (a moving account of social evils of the day, which somehow had escaped the Treasury Solicitor's eye): "I wish to make up a little sum for one or two cases of distress that have fallen in my way," writes the kind George: "if therefore you know any persons . . . who are likely to want any of my books, you'll oblige me by letting me know."[1]

On 28 February, Dyer wrote to Mary again, this time from 45 Carey Street, to tell her that Dr Joseph Priestley was in town, before emigrating to America. "The doctor leaves London in a few weeks' time, for ought Dyer knows in a few days. The doctor invites Mary and Elizabeth Hays to give him the favour of their company the first day of next

[1] George Dyer to Mary Hays, *Correspondence* (Mss. Dr Williams' Library), July 1793; and Wedd: *op. cit.*, p. 226.

week to tea . . . the doctor is very busy packing up, and will probably be engaged after the 3rd . . . Dyer therefore should be happy if they can make it agreeable, he will do himself the pleasure of attending them, and will also mention it to William Frend whom he shall see today."[1]

Frend was on cordial terms with Mary during 1794, and we find him writing to her about philosophy and art. In the late summer of that year he tells her, "I am at present in the Chambers of a friend, I have again a decent show of books around me. My attention has however been chiefly arrested by Godwin on Political Justice. The first hundred pages please me exceedingly and, if he continues in the same manner, I might venture to presage that his book will in a few years operate as great a change in the political sentiments of our nation as Locke's famous treatise on government."[2]

These comments aroused Mary's interest in Godwin, and led to her writing to him on 14 October, quoting Frend, and telling Godwin of her "ardor for the perusal of this book" and of the difficulty she has had in obtaining it. "I had recourse, but in vain, to various circulating libraries, being informed that the work was too expensive for their purposes." She frankly confesses "that the same cause renders it inconvenient for me to purchase it . . ." and, proclaiming herself "a disciple of the truth", she asks the author to lend her a copy of his book. Her letter might serve as a model for any prospective borrower approaching a writer, in its blending of flattery and self advancement:

"I must not say that I will *promise* to preserve the books and return them with punctuality—but I will assure Mr G that from the first dawnings of reason, amid all the disadvantages of worse than neglected, perverted, female education, the governing principles of my mind have been an ardent love of literature and an unbounded reverence for truth and genius . . ." and "these associations have mechanic-

[1] Dyer to Mary Hays.
[2] Wedd: *Love letters of Mary Hays*, p. 228.

ally produced in my mind a thirst after books and a sense of their value."[1]

This was the beginning of a correspondence and close friendship based on mutual interests and convictions, and made closer by Mary's introducing Godwin to Mary Wollstonecraft whom she had got to know at the house of Johnson the publisher.

"I will do myself the pleasure of waiting on you on Friday", he writes, "and shall be happy to meet Mrs Wollstonecraft, of whom I know not that I ever said a word of harm, and who has frequently amused herself with depreciating me."[2]

Mary Hays had known Mrs Wollstonecraft for several years, and had often consulted her on literary problems. The authoress of *The Rights of Women* had always answered her in a forthright manner: "I have just cast my eye over your sensible little pamphlet and found fewer of the superlatives, exquisite, fascinating, etc. all of the feminine gender, than I expected . . . "

She was strongly feminist in her advice: "Your male friends will still treat you like a woman, and many a man . . . even Dr Priestley, have insensibly been led to utter warm eulogiums in private that they would be sorry openly to avow without some explanatory ifs. An author, especially if a woman, should be cautious lest she hastily swallows the crude praises," of her male friends.[3]

Not long after Mary Hays had introduced Godwin to Mrs Wollstonecraft the two set up house together; and in April 1797 Godwin wrote to Mary that they had got married:[4] "My fair neighbour desires me to announce to you a piece of news which . . . consonant to the regard that both she and I entertain for you, you should rather learn from us than from any other quarter." He reminds her of how she

[1] Wedd: *op. cit.*, p. 229.
[2] *Ibid.*, p. 232.
[3] *Ibid.*, p. 225.
[4] *Ibid.*, p. 241.

"pressed him to prevail upon her [Mary] to change her name". "We found there was no way so obvious for her to drop the name of Imlay, as to assume the name of Godwin. Mrs Godwin (who the devil is that?) will be glad to see you at No. 29, Polygon, Somers Town, whenever you are inclined to favour her with a call."[1]

From then on Mary Hays was a constant visitor at Godwin's house, finding a double fascination in the philosopher's conversation and his wife's company. She described him, under the name of Francis, in her novel *Emma Courtney*: "Mr Francis was in his fortieth year, his figure slender and delicate, his eye piercing and his manner impressive." He seemed "the antagonist of the man of fashion".

Emma's conversations, first with the conventional young ladies, then with "Francis", are probably pretty true to life:

The Misses Morton "rallied me on being found tete a tete with the Philosopher", and she retorted that Mr Francis appeared to her "a rational man". Godwin (alias Francis) later in the chapter gave her a lecture which seems to echo the letters he really wrote her: "You have talents—cultivate them and learn to rest on your own powers."

Godwin and Mary Hays had a "contract" by which, as Godwin said on 7 September 1795, "you (Mary) shall communicate your sentiments by letter, and I will answer you in person." The result was that Mary poured out her troubles and hopes and ideas to Godwin, in embarrassingly detailed letters of great length.

* * *

London literary society was enough of a closed circle at this time for writers and philosophers to be constantly meeting at each other's houses. Mary Hays must have met Frend in many different settings: at Lindsey's, at Godwin's and at the Disneys'. One of their mutual acquaintances was Thomas Holcroft, and Mary may have occasionally met Frend at one

[1] Wedd: *op. cit.*, p. 241.

of "Holcroft's evenings", (though not at a dinner—usually all-male—such as is described in Holcroft's diary for 9 July 1798, at which Frend was present and mathematical puzzles were discussed).[1] As Holcroft was a specialist in music and both Mary Hays and Frend enjoyed it in an amateurish way, it is not unlikely that they were invited; "I should like to meet you," Mary wrote to Godwin on 8 March 1796, "one day at Mr Holcroft's when there is not too much company. Mr H. need not trouble himself to procure ladies to meet me, his daughter is sufficient. I am more used to, and therefore more at ease in the company of men—I wish to hear Miss H. on the harpsichord . . ."[2] Godwin of course was a frequent visitor at the Holcrofts', Thomas being one of his best friends, and the first reviewer of *Political Justice* in the *Monthly Review.*

Another frequenter of literary evenings, whom Mary might have met at Dyer's or at a Unitarian home, was Henry Crabb Robinson, and it is to his diary that we owe the revelation that Mary Hays was in love with Frend, had been for many months, and was desperately unhappy because he did not and could not return her feeling.

"She confided to me on our first acquaintance that she was wretched, the consequence of an attachment where union was impossible . . ." The man whom she accused of deserting her was William Frend. "It was of course quite untrue that she was deserted", says Robinson: "the love-making was all on the lady's side", and it seems she was as impressionable, romantic, and lacking in self-control at thirty-five as she had been in 1787.

Mary obviously suffered very deeply from her unrequited passion; she found some comfort in telling Godwin about it, but her only real relief was, it seems, to pour her soul out in her novel, *Emma Courtney*. She did this all through 1795, risking her good name by writing what, according to Crabb Robinson, "had some reputation as a novel of passion but was

[1] Hazlitt: *Life of Holcroft*, Vol. iii, p. 177.
[2] Wedd: *op. cit.*, p. 233.

thought to be heretical on the great question of marriage, and which brought her into disrepute among the rigid", though quite undeservedly.

So self-lacerating and revealing a book can seldom have been written by a woman well known in the literary circles of her time. It is really a case history, and may justifiably be examined here for the light it throws on Mary herself and on Frend, who is portrayed surprisingly clearly and fairly; apart from the fiction of his marriage to another woman, Augustus Harley is a life-like picture of Frend, as seen of course through Mary Hays' eyes, in the unlikely situations which the author devises for him.

Emma, the heroine, is a friend of Augustus' mother; she knows the young lawyer from descriptions and a portrait of him, but does not meet him till, travelling in a coach one evening, there is an accident; a passenger, Mary's admirer, John Montagu, is badly hurt; and Augustus Harley, passing by, gives help, conveys Montagu to safety, but is himself overcome by exhaustion. Emma nurses him, and falls passionately in love in the process.

They spend a few weeks as neighbours and she becomes more and more infatuated. They talk philosophy and science and literature, and Harley appears kind and affectionate, but in no way enamoured. When he announces his departure for London she is dreadfully upset, and describes her feelings at length; the worst is the uncertainty of not knowing his sentiments towards her:

"Augustus was silent, but fixed his penetrating eyes on my face with an expression that covered me with confusion." She suffered "the most cruel inquietude", knowing that "he was about to mix in the gay world—to lose in the hurry of business or of pleasure, the remembrance of those tender rational tranquil moments together. Would the idea of timid affectionate Emma ever recur to his mind in the tumultuous scenes of the crouded metropolis?" Unable to bear his absence, Emma decided to go to London too, and stayed with relatives; she determined to confess her love, and when he visited the house one day she "awaited him in the library with a beating heart" and thrust into his hands an eight-page letter, quoting poetry, and passages from Holcroft's latest play *Anna St Ives*, and telling him she loved him—not for "personal graces" but for "the virtues and talents of the individual—for without intellect, virtue is an empty name."

"From this period he continued to visit me (I confess, at my solicitude) more frequently." They resumed scientific pursuits, read together, or discussed various topics. "At length he grew captious, disputatious, gloomy and imperious. He disapproved my conduct, my sentiments; my frankness offended him. In company his manners were studiously cold and distant, in private capricious, yet reserved and guarded." Poor Emma blamed herself for "the painful and delicate situation in which I had placed myself" and was quite honest in admitting that the gentleman had given her no cause for hope.

In the midst of all the pathos and sentiment there is a vivid and amusing description of a dinner party at the house of a rich planter, recently returned to England from the West Indies, almost certainly drawn from the life. Emma and Harley were both present. The conversation turned on the army. The hostess, a very shallow woman, asked, "Do you not think, Miss Courtney . . . that soldiers are the most agreeable and charming men in the world?"

To which Emma retorted, "Indeed I do not, Madam; their trade is *murder* and their trappings, in my eyes, appear but the gaudy pomp of sacrifice." The hostess insisted that "there have always been wars in the world . . . there always must be . . . " and the discussion (like countless similar ones even today) fizzled out in an agreement to differ. But the next subject that arose was equally controversial: the hostess, fresh from the West Indies, complained of the slaves and "wished there were more of these *murderers* [soldiers] to keep the slaves in subordination; who since absurd notions of liberty had been put into their heads were grown very troublesome and refractory and in a short time would become as insolent as the English servants."

"This is a land of freedom, my dear," the planter reminded her. "Servants here will not submit to be treated like the slaves in Jamaica"; and Emma suggested that the servants might "happen to think their superiors unreasonable," which brought the quick answer, "What have servants or women to do with thinking!"

We are told that Mr Harley then "pleaded the cause of freedom and humanity with a bold and manly eloquence", and we can imagine William Frend in his element, while Mary Hays hung on his words: "I listened with delight as Augustus exposed and confuted the specious reasoning . . . of his antagonists. Exulting in the triumph of truth and justice, I secretly gloried . . . in the virtue and abilities of my friend."

Still he gave her no encouragement, and still she went on hoping: "My heart obstinately refuses to renounce the man to whose mind my own seems akin." Next day she sent him a 15-page letter, asking him to tell her plainly whether "the obstacles which oppose my affection are absolutely and altogether insuperable"; she warned him: "early tomorrow morning a messenger shall call for the paper which is to decide the colour of my future destiny." She spent a sleepless night, tormented by her emotions, and next morning she waited for the return of the messenger "in a state of mind difficult to be conceived."

Poor Emma: the answer was that "Mr Harley desired me to tell you 'he had not had time to write'."—"Gracious God!" she wailed, "I shudder even now to recall the convulsive sensation."

She wrote "a short incoherent note" entreating "to be spared another day, another night like the preceding. I asked only *one single line*."

The messenger went and came back, with the laconic message that Mr Harley "would write tomorrow". Emma exploded: "Barbarous, unfeeling, unpitying man!"

The next day a letter arrived, "coldly confusedly written" and with no comfort for Emma. "To write had always afforded a temporary relief to my spirits—the next day I resumed my pen," she says. The result was ten pages of highly emotional outpourings.

For two weeks she had no answer. She wrote again (four pages) quoting *Anna St Ives*, but this was equally fruitless. Then she suddenly received a call to visit Mrs Harley (Augustus' mother) and found the good lady in a state of great agitation: she had just had a lawyer's letter saying that her son must give up a hoped-for legacy, because "he had contracted a marriage three years before, with a foreigner with whom he had become acquainted during his travels."

In this, the worst of the many crises in the book, Emma nearly collapses, but is comforted by Mr Francis (as she imagines Godwin might have comforted her) on one of his rare appearances; in return for his kindness she almost immediately afterwards writes him a fourteen-page letter. The shock of the lawyer's communication is altogether too much for Mrs Harley who succumbs and dies. There is an awkward moment at the deathbed, when Augustus arrives. "He behaved toward me with distant cold respect", Emma says, recording their final parting after the funeral.

The story hastens to its close; Montagu turns up again, and persuades Emma to marry him; but realizing that her heart will always belong to Harley he contrives to kill his rival, making it appear an accident. Augustus commits his infant son to Emma's care and he dies. Montagu shortly afterwards throws himself under a postchaise. And that is the end of the sad tale, which however melodramatic and long-drawn-out has moments of truth and certainly paints an extremely realistic picture of Emma's overwrought state.

Mary Hays' preface tells us that she set out "to delineate the consequences of our strong indulged passion or prejudice . . . " and wished to represent Emma Courtney as a human being "loving virtue while enslaved by passion."

"Whether the incidents of the character are copied from life is of little importance," says the author. Perhaps not for her—but for us, the fact that they are so evidently copied is today their main and not inconsiderable interest.[1]

The novel was reasonably successful. Crabb Robinson's comments on it are probably typical of the average intelligent reader:

"I have recently read some interesting works. Emma Courtney does not stand high in my estimation, it promises more than it executes. We do not sympathize with Emma's love for Harley for we see no cause for such extreme attraction ... and we are dissatisfied with the explication of the riddle of his Conduct." However, Anthony Robinson, Crabb's brother, "thinks it superior to Anna St Ives, he esteems it much."

During the spring of 1796 Mary Hays was gradually recovering from her infatuation, writing to Godwin on 8 March that "though very far from happy, I am better than I have been", thanks largely to Godwin, who seems to have been very good to her: "Your friendship is one of my greatest, and most unmixed consolations", she tells him, and "from you I have received nothing but acts of kindness." She describes a visit made to "the man who had been the subject of my confessions"—presumably Frend—in order to show she had renounced any claim on his heart.

This must have been a great relief to the beloved; and when Mary invited him, with two other friends, to tea, "he assented without hesitation." The tea-party went off well and helped to restore Mary's calm. She explained her motives for it at length to Godwin: " ... as I conceived I had not been faultless, and as it is particularly painful to me to cherish severe feelings, where I have before felt affection, I do not repent of what I have done, but feel myself relieved by it ... My hopes have now, *entirely ceased*, and with them, some illusions appear to be losing their force—my mind

[1] M. Hays: *Emma Courtney*, Preface.

seems regaining a firmer tone—it is no longer *convulsed with uncertainty.*"[1]

The theme of a letter two days later is Frend's unkindness, and Godwin's sympathy: "I do wish you had been in love (but not as I have tasted only its bitterness) and then you wou'd always understand me, which you are yet, I doubt, notwithstanding your delicacy and sensibility, too wise and too reasonable to do."

She clearly is recovering, for she finishes this letter anticipating "some hours of calm repose", counting her blessings: "I have moral and intellectual powers, I am free from the sting of remorse . . . and there are still some who look with an eye of tenderness on my faults and who love my virtues—a gentle and kindly emotion swells my bosom—*I am not miserable this evening!*"[2]

Unfortunately for Mary Hays, she seems to have been unable to enjoy her peace of mind for long; having recovered from her passion for Frend, she became equally infatuated a few months later with Charles Lloyd, the poet, a far from estimable character.

Coleridge said of him, "he is unfit to be any Man's Friend and to all but a very guarded Man he is a perilous acquaintance." He might have added, "and especially perilous to an unguarded woman"—for Mary Hays had by her behaviour aroused his ridicule, and he had openly made game of her, something which could never have happened with the kind and considerate Frend, however much she tormented him.

At the end of 1797 Godwin tried to check the affair, by voicing his disapproval of Lloyd in no uncertain terms: "I am much obliged to you for what you add respecting the person whose confidence you at present enjoy. I believe such confessions are fairly due, and wish I had known it sooner. That man has something in him that instinctively repels me, and I should despair of being upon terms of unbounded

[1] Wedd: *op. cit.*, p. 234.
[2] *Ibid.*, p. 237.

cordiality with any one of whom he was the chosen companion. Do not construe me in this to mean more than I do. I have a great regard for some persons that cultivate his society, and for you I entertain a real esteem."

Lloyd's behaviour was censured even by more tolerant acquaintances than Godwin. Coleridge wrote to Southey, on 25 January 1800, that he had seen Miss Hays; "Charles Lloyd's conduct has been atrocious beyond what you stated —Lamb himself confessed to me, that during the time in which he kept up his ranting sentimental Correspondence with Miss Hays, he frequently read her Letters in company, as a subject for *Laughter*—and then sate down and answered them quite à la Rousseau!"

Both Southey and Coleridge were doubtless shocked at this treatment of poor Mary, Southey because he greatly respected her, and Coleridge in spite of his reservations as to her literary gifts. He told Southey that "of Miss Hays' intellect I do not think as highly as you—or rather to speak sincerely, I think not contemptuously, but certainly very despectively thereof. Yet I think you likely in this case to have judged better than I—for to hear a Thing, ugly and petticoated, exsyllogize a God with cold-blooded precision, and attempt to run Religion thro' the body with an Icicle—an Icicle from a Scotch Hog-trough! *I* do not endure it!—my Eye beholds phantoms—and nothing is but what is not."[1]

Southey, in spite of Coleridge's deprecating remarks about Mary Hays, seems to have retained his respect for her; he wrote two kind answers to her request for advice and a recommendation to the booksellers, saying his recommendation "might be of some avail if they referred a manuscript to me, but it is of none in introducing a book to them, for this reason—that they regard *subject* as the main thing, and consider themselves the best judges of that, which probably they are. If the subject be likely to succeed among other winter fashions, then they think about the execution, and

[1] Wedd: *op. cit.*, p. 11.

refer it to some professor of criticism which, in contradiction to cobbling, may be called the ungentle craft."[1]

He gave her some advice on translating, but attempted to dissuade her from such work: "I should be sorry to see you employed in translation nor is it easy to point out any work of merit which has not already been made English." However he draws her attention to "a wild Ariosto-like romance by Cazotto called Olivier". ("Perhaps the author's name might give it a salable notoriety . . . ") and offers to lend her the book.

However a second letter says "I am sorry you should have laboured at Olivier in vain. With the name of Cazotto and the praise of Gibbon? I should have thought any bookseller would have willingly purchased the translation." Southey repeats, "your powers of language ought not to be wasted on translation," and he closes extremely cordially: "Mention if you can make me in any way useful, and command me freely—the points on which we differ are fewer than those on which we agree, and our hopes of mankind are the same."[2] (If this was so, Miss Hays' radicalism must have faded considerably since the vigorous defence by Eusebia of liberty of conscience, for by 1803 Southey was a respectable Establishment man. Yet the above lines show him to have been a kind and helpful one, and must have meant a lot to the troubled authoress.)

It was Mary Hays' misfortune to be born so far ahead of her time in ideas, and without Mary Wollstonecraft's personality and charm. She might well have felt frustrated, but we know from Crabb Robinson that "she is content to be a useful writer and does not lose feminine excellence and virtues while she seeks literary fame."[3] In 1813 he wrote of her, "I wish her happiness wherever she goes; but I fear an over-strained sensibility joined to precise manners . . .

[1] Wedd: *op. cit.*, p. 244.
[2] *Ibid.*, p. 246.
[3] H. Crabb Robinson: *op. cit.*, p. 843.

make her offensive and ridiculous to the many, infinitely below herself in all essential qualities."[1]

An intellectual woman could too easily be a laughing stock or a target for abuse if she had not feminine charm or a husband, and Mary has been mainly and unfairly remembered through a few caustic lines in Coleridge's letters.

By giving her an honourable place in the company of the Godwins, Lindsey, Dyer and of course William Frend, dare we hope we may redress the balance, putting her back where she would most like to be found?

[1] *Ibid.*, p. 131.

15

LITERARY FRIENDSHIPS
II Lamb, Dyer, Coleridge

Friend of the friendless, friend of all mankind,
To thy wide friendships I have not been blind;
But looking at them nearly, in the end
I love thee most that thou art Dyer's Frend.[1]

So wrote Charles Lamb, and not just for the pleasure of punning. Frend had indeed an unusually wide circle of people attached to him through common interests and convictions, or through services which he had rendered—this is shown by surviving letters of thanks to him, and the frequent mention of his helpfulness to men and women of all kinds.

George Dyer was at the very centre of his affection, and Dyer himself had a great number of acquaintances, which extended Frend's circle further. Through the scholar-poet, Frend met Miss Hays, he came to know Lamb, and he kept in touch with Coleridge, to whom Dyer was greatly attached. In February 1795 Coleridge concluded a letter to Dyer with the words "to Mr Frend present my most grateful respect—God Almighty bless him"; in March, he asked "Is Mr Frend in Town?", and on 30 December 1796 sent "affectionate Regards to Mr Frend if you see him."

Up to that time, Coleridge still shared Frend's ideas; he was even in 1796 producing passionate verse against tyrants, for freedom and justice, and pressing the republican Flower to publish it in the *Cambridge Intelligencer*, while Dyer hawked copies round London booksellers; but as the magic and idealism of 1789 faded he withdrew farther and farther from the hard facts of political struggle, the rationalist thinking that was the basis of the French Revolution, and from the

[1] S. De Morgan: *op. cit.*, p. 80.

day-to-day activity of the English Radicals, prosaically pushing pamphlets and collecting funds for Pitt's victims.

Frend did not feel at ease with people who did not share his convictions, particularly if they had formerly proclaimed themselves on his side, and he saw little of Coleridge during those difficult years; but it seems that after two decades had passed, and political passions had somewhat abated, the two men met and conversed amiably enough; Sophia, Frend's daughter, wrote many years later, "My remembrance of Coleridge is vague and shadowy, but I have heard him talking *to* not *with* my father for many hours when I, being a child only, wished he would stop . . . as much as when, years after, I went with my father to call on him at Highgate, I wished he had been well enough to let us hear him talk."[1]

Frend, being a practical person and no mystic, felt more at home in the company of Charles Lamb than in that of the *literati* of the Lakes, whom he must have considered to have abjured their former ideals. Coleridge, who had become a Trinitarian; Wordsworth, author of a most moving poem greeting the French Revolution and now a confirmed anti-Jacobin; Southey, now poet-laureate to an arch-reactionary régime—what had he in common with these erstwhile enthusiasts for reform? Lamb on the other hand had never professed political zeal, but his heart, as far as Frend was concerned, was firmly lodged in the right place; he was good through and through, kind, humorous, a Unitarian, and when Frend's children began to grow up he was like an affectionate uncle to them.

Recalling her early family life, Sophia Frend wrote that "Charles Lamb felt much esteem for my father" and occasionally visited the house. Sophia had the impression that Lamb did not care to have guests at his own house, where poor Mary Lamb was suffering, on and off, from mental troubles. He wrote several charming verses in Sophia's album "in his firm neat writing". One was an intro-

[1] S. De Morgan: *op. cit.*, p. 68.

duction to the whole collection, and is so neatly turned that it might well serve as a model to anyone faced with the task:

Little Casket! Storehouse rare
of rich conceits to please the Fair
Happiest he of mortal men
—I crown him monarch of the pen—
To whom Sophia deigns to give
the flattering prerogative
To inscribe his name in chief
on the first and maiden Leaf.[1]

Another contribution to the album is a skilful and truly poetical acrostic on the name Sophia, which shows that Lamb really put his mind to pleasing the young Frends.[2]

Frend and Lamb met frequently at the rather dingy rooms inhabited by George Dyer, to whom they were both greatly attached—Lamb having known him as a small boy at Christ's Hospital, Frend as a struggling scholar and teacher at Cambridge. As common friends of the Lindseys, and worshippers at Essex Street chapel, they constantly met in London during Frend's first year's "banishment", and later became close friends. During the first decade of the nineteenth century, Sophia Frend tells us, George Dyer "lived in the ground-floor chambers of an old dirt begrimed house in Clifford's Inn, near the old gateway . . . He was supposed to be cared for by relations, who received money for taking no care of him. Several friends, among them Joseph Jekyll, Charles Lamb, John Rickman . . . and my father, some of whom had helped Dyer in his college days, saw and lamented the neglected state of the poor scholar, and my father made many efforts to procure comfort and cleanliness in his daily life."

He was generally loved, with a love blended with pity for his poverty, respect for his devotion to scholarship and his

[1] S. De Morgan: *op. cit.*, p. 80.
[2] *Ibid.*, p. 81.

fearless radical convictions, and amusement for his almost unbelievable absent-mindedness.

Countless stories circulated about Dyer's adventures and misadventures, chiefly retailed by Lamb, Frend, Crabb Robinson and Bowring, as a result of which he became almost a legend. Unfortunately for him there was usually a solid basis for fact in the stories: his mind, being constantly on higher things—composing a poem, thinking up a polemic, solving a knotty historical or theological problem—he did not notice what he was wearing or eating, or even where he was or had lately been. Once, he had spent an evening at Leigh Hunt's house, and after going half-way home turned back and roused his host who had retired for the night, in order to find one of his shoes, which he had shuffled off under the table, and had only just noticed was missing. Another time, when visiting friends, he took up the coal-scuttle in mistake for his hat, and coals fell out in all directions.[1]

His short-sightedness was partly to blame; it led him into worse trouble than these little incidents and practical jokes by friends.

One day, on his way to visit Charles Lamb, he nearly drowned himself by walking into the New River at Islington. Lamb described the adventure in *Amicus Redivivus*, claiming that he himself plunged in to pull Dyer out, portraying the scared and dripping poet as he emerged, and delivering a short, sharp little sermon on the dangers of myopia.

"I protest, George, you shall not venture out again—no, not by daylight—without a sufficient pair of spectacles—in your musing moods especially. Your absence of mind we have borne, till your presence of body came to be called in question by it. You shall not go wandering into Euripus with Aristotle, if we can help it. Fie, man, to turn dipper at your years, after your many tracts in favour of sprinkling only"—an allusion to Dyer's strong Unitarian and non-Baptist opinions.[2]

[1] Rodgers: *Georgian Chronicle*, p. 186.
[2] Lamb: *Essays of Elia. Amicus Redivivus.*

There is an amusing glimpse of Dyer on one of his forays after knowledge, in a letter from Lamb to Thomas Manning, mutual friend of theirs and of Coleridge and Frend, then teaching mathematics in Cambridge: "That worthy man and excellent Poet, George Dyer, made me a visit yesternight, on purpose to borrow (a copy of your Algebra) . . . He is just now diverted from the pursuit of Bell Letters by a paradox, which he has heard his friend Frend (that learned mathematician) maintain, that the negative quantities were *merae nugae*, things scarcely in *rerum naturae* and smacking too much of mystery for gentlemen of Mr Frend's clear Unitarian capacity." Lamb implores Manning to send Dyer a copy of Manning's Algebra "with a neat manuscriptum on the blank leaf, running thus FROM THE AUTHOR! It would save his wits and restore the unhappy author to those studies of poetry and criticism which are at present suspended, to the infinite regret of the whole literary world. N. B. Dirty books, smeared leaves, and dogs' ears, will be rather a recommendation than otherwise."[1]

Dyer's literary activities were almost as much of a byword as his day-to-day misfortunes. Not that any of them were anything but admirable—his verse was sincere and often sensitive, his biography of Robert Robinson was a model of its kind; nobody would laugh at his painstaking research into academic archives for the History he planned to write of Cambridge, even though Lamb could describe it very amusingly; many people could praise his pamphlets on religion, and everyone with any heart could applaud his *Complaints of the Poor People of England*. But when it came to literary criticism, even his best friends could not take seriously the flood of comments and ideas which he poured out and which he tried so strenuously to get published, writing and calling on everyone he knew to raise subscriptions for this purpose.

There must have been very mixed feelings among the faithful few who agreed to be drawn in to help him. Letters

[1] Lamb: *Letters*, 21.8.1800 (Everyman edition, 1945), p. 152.

from Lindsey, and Disney to Frend, and vice versa, show the constant preoccupation with the question of Dyer's works and of their distribution.

Frend appears to have been a middleman between Essex Street and Dyer, besides raising money from all sympathetic Unitarians he felt he could touch for help. Lamb helped him by passing the word on to his literary friends when any new works of Dyer's were about to appear. He wrote to Coleridge, on 14 August 1800, announcing "that George Dyer hath prepared two ponderous volumes full of poetry and criticism. They impend over the town and are threatened to fall in the winter . . . O George, George! With a head uniformly wrong and a heart uniformly right, that I had the power and might equal to my wishes: then would I call the gentry of thy native island and they should come in troops, flocking at the sound of thy prospectus trumpet, and crowding who shall be the first to stand in the list of subscribers! I can only put twelve shillings into thy pocket (which I will answer for them will not stick there long) out of a pocket almost as bare as thine . . . "[1]

As a poet, in the estimation of his obituarist in *The Gentleman's Magazine*, forty years later, "Dyer evinces much spirit and genuine feeling, and adorns his verse with graceful and judicious imagery."

To modern readers the poems seem at their worst stilted and artificial, at their best distinguished by a pleasant observation and a genuine love of nature. His trouble was, as Lamb points out, that "the gods by denying him the very faculty of discrimination have effectually cut off every seed of envy in his bosom. To G.D., a poem is a poem. His own as good as anybody's, and (God bless him) anybody's as good as his own: for I do not think he has the most distant guess of the possibility of one poem being better than another."

But he could on occasion be self-critical to the highest degree; for instance, in 1800, when a volume of poems with a preface of some seventy pages had gone to the printer, he

[1] Lamb: *Letters*, 14.8.1800, p. 151.

discovered, according to Lamb, "that he had set out with a principle of criticism fundamentally wrong, which vitiated all his following reasoning. The Preface must be expunged, although it cost him £30 . . . In vain his real friends remonstrated against this Midsummer madness. George is as obstinate as a Primitive Christian—and wards and parries off all our thrusts with one unanswerable fence: 'Sir, it's of consequence that the *world* is not *misled*'."[1]

However, it seems that he could not find the thirty pounds, because in the end the poems went to the printer without any preface: Lamb tells the story of what happened to the original offending one in a letter (1801) to John Rickman:[2]

"Twas on Tuesday week the poor heathen [Dyer] scrambled up to my door about breakfast time. He came through a violent rain with his neck cloth on, and a beard that made him a spectacle to men and angels, and tap'd at the door, Mary open'd it and he stood stark still and held a paper in his hand importing that he had been ill with a fever.

"He either would not or could not speak except by signs. When we went to comfort him he put his hand upon his heart and shook his head and told us his complaint lay where no medicine could reach it. I was dispatched for Dr Dale, Mr Phillips of St Paul's Churchyard, and Mr Frend, who is to be his executor. George solemnly delivered into Mr Frend's hands and mine an old burnt preface that had been in the fire, with injunctions which we solemnly vowed to obey that it should be printed after his death with his last corrections, and that some account should be given to the world why he had not fulfill'd his engagment with subscribers . . ."

It turned out that Dyer was really ill, chiefly owing to malnutrition; Dr Dale gave him some white powders, and the Lambs put him to bed and nursed him for several days;

[1] Lamb: *Letters*, 27.12.1800, p. 176.
[2] *Ibid*., Nov. 1801, p. 200.

after which Charles made him promise to eat with them regularly, saw to it that the £20 voted to Dyer by the Literary Fund was spent "on his own carcase", "assisted him in arranging the remainder of what he calls Poems"—we know that Lamb was the most kind-hearted of men, but his goodness to Dyer was exceptional by any standards; and unlike some loftier intellectuals he stuck to his old friend until his own death. The story of the slight difference over remarks in a literary journal belongs to a later chapter, in which we shall meet Dyer and Lamb again, still liberals and "one-God men" and attached to Frend despite the passing of time.

* * *

The course of true love between Dyer and Coleridge on the other hand ran less smooth. While Coleridge was an enthusiastic undergraduate applauding Frend, preaching Unitarianism, writing pro-Revolutionary verse and trying to get it published and sold, Dyer was a great friend and a useful one. In September 1794 Coleridge wrote to Southey describing their first meeting: "Dyer showed me some poetry and I showed him part of the first Act (of *Robespierre*) which I happened to have about me—He liked it hugely . . . offered to speak to Robinson his bookseller—he went to Johnson's & to Kearsley's—the former objected, because Dyer (who is a Reviewer) had confessedly only read the first act. So on Saturday he called on me, and I gave him the whole to look over . . . and tomorrow morning I breakfast with him."[1] (The drama was eventually published by Benjamin Flower.)

A few days later, Coleridge told Southey that he was ill and his finances exhausted—"Ill as I was I sat down and scrawled two guineas' worth of Nonsense for the Booksellers—which Dyer disposed of for me . . . "[2]

[1] Coleridge: *Letters*, p. 97. O.U.P., (ed. E. L. Griggs 1956.)

[2] *Ibid.*, p. 105.

In February 1795 Coleridge wrote Dyer a long letter "pouring my heart out before you as water", telling him about his Pantisocratic Plan and asking Dyer's advice as to taking a tutoring post: "What am I to do with regard to the Earl of Buchan? Am I to live in the house with the Erskines? Is this a necessary accompaniment of Tutorage?" and closing the letter with "My dear Sir! Believe me, my heart beats high with gratitude to you—I know you will write to me as to a Brother."

At the same time Coleridge shows that he is still a "Jacobin". "Since I have been in Bristol I have endeavoured to disseminate the Truth by three political Lectures—I believe I shall give a fourth, but the opposition of the Aristocrats is so furious and determined that I begin to fear that the Good I do is not proportionate to the Evil I occasion—Mobs and Mayors, Blockheads and Brickbats, Placards and Press Gangs have leagued in horrible Conspiracy against me—the Democrats are as sturdy in the support of me—but their number is comparatively small—two or three uncouth and unbrained Automata have threatened my Life—and in the Last Lecture the Genus infimum were scarcely restrained from attacking the house in which the 'damn'd Jacobin' was jawing away . . . "

There is a p.s.: "I am glad to see your Book advertised—I have placed orders for ten—Cottle the Bookseller here has sent for them . . . Southey speaks of you . . . "

In March (1795) Coleridge quotes "a sentence in your last letter which affected me greatly—'I feel a degree of languor . . . and by seeing and frequently feeling much illiberality acquire something of misanthropy.' It is melancholy." Coleridge condoles with him "to think that the best of us are liable to be shaped and coloured by surrounding Objects—and a demonstrative proof that Man was not made to live in great Cities!"[1] He goes on to say "God love you, my very dear Sir! I would that we could form a Pantisocracy in England, and that you could be one of us. The

[1] Coleridge: *Letters*, p. 154 seq.

fine-fibred Heart, that like the statue of Memnon, trembles into melody at the sunbeam touch of Benevolence, is most easily jarred into the dissonance of Misanthropy. But you will never suffer your feelings to be bent by the Torpedo Touch of that Fiend—I know you—and know that you will drink of every Mourner's sorrows, even while your own Cup is trembling over its Brink!—"

Again, in March, he wrote, "Southey desires his remembrances to you in warmth of esteem . . . I receive great pleasure from your Letters—write soon."

But two years later he had cooled off considerably: on 9 March 1798 mentioning that "George Dyer is going into Scotland with that booby Arthur Aikin", and when talking about his proposed "little colony", he does not suggest that Dyer should join Tobin, Wordsworth, Davy and the other elect. By then, Coleridge's ideas had begun to take a very different direction from Dyer's, and Coleridge found the characteristics which were previously endearing now rather irritating. He wrote to Southey, on 19 December 1799, on an exasperated note: "Why did not George Dyer (who bye the bye has written a silly milk-and-water Life of you, in which your Talents for *pastoral and rural* life are extolled, in which you are asserted to be a Republican) why has not George Dyer sent to the anthology that Poem in the last monthly magazine—it is so very far superior to any thing I have ever seen of his and might have made some atonement for his former transgressions. Bless him—he is a very good man: but he ought not to degrade himself writing lives of Living Characters for Phillips; & all his Friends make wry faces, peeping out of the Pillory of his advertisements."[1]

As Coleridge grew older and more and more critical, so Dyer's lack of discrimination became more distasteful to him. He thought his poetry poor, and was frankly scathing about his literary criticism.

Coleridge's copy of Dyer's *Poems* is liberally scattered

[1] Coleridge: *Letters*, p. 392.

with marginalia proclaiming his devastating opinions, particularly of Dyer's excursions into criticism: for instance, on p. 325, the author remarks "that the principal and immediate aim of poetry is to please, has been opposed by Julius Scaliger and some other critics"; and Dyer seems inclined to agree with Scaliger: Coleridge scribbles all round the page "Damned Nonsense—But why does it please? Because it pleases! O Mystery!—If not some cause out of itself must be found. Mere utility it certainly is not, nor mere goodness. Wherefore there must be some third power and that is Beauty, i.e. that which ought to please. My benevolent friend seems not to have made an obvious distinction between end and means. The Poet *must* always aim at Pleasure as his specific means but surely Milton did right to aim at something nobler as the end, viz to cultivate and predispose the heart of the Readers."[1]

Again, when Dyer states that "Sappho's ode . . . is produced by Longinus as one of the noblest and completest examples of the sublime", Coleridge notes in the margin, "No such thing. L. was no very proper critic—but he was no blunderer.—Of the energetic, of the language of high excitement, elevated from paper, in short of the [excellent?] it was, is & probably ever will be the most perfect specimen. But as to sublime, you might as well call it Blue or Snub nosed. STC."[2]

Further on he scribbles "Pindar—and who? Horace!!! and pray good George Dyer in what ode in Horace does . . ." —the sentence ends illegibly, as though S.T.C.'s exasperation had got the better of his pen.[3]

In 1804 Dyer committed an indiscretion which infuriated Coleridge and seems to have dealt a mortal blow to their friendship. He wrote an article, one of a series in the Monthly Magazine, called *Cantabrigiana*, in which the following passage occurred:

[1] Dyer: *Poems*, B.M., C. 45, f. 18(2), p. 325.
[2] *Ibid.*, p. xxvi.
[3] Dyer: *Poems*, B.M. copy, p. 214.

"The poetical abilities of Mr Coleridge, formerly of Jesus College, are well known. He obtained one of the prizes at Cambridge, and but one for the Greek ode. Being once in company with a person who had gained two prizes, the latter carried himself with an air of superiority and triumph and seemed to estimate his own abilities above Coleridge's in the ratio of at least two to one. A person in the company growing at length indignant at the vaunting airs of the conceited young fellow, exclaimed, "why, zounds, Sir, a man's leg may as easily be too big for the boot as yours just fitted it."

Coleridge wrote off to Dyer obviously in a state of acute annoyance: "Dear Sir, if you *knew* me you would know that I am not of the genus irritabile: and must resign all claim to the poetic inspiration, if irritability be an essential character of it"—"I felt no resentment or offence on my own account", he says, denies the truth of the anecdote, and repeats that "my concern was for *you* not for *myself*—on general principles, not the consequence of a particular Feeling. Good Heavens, my dear Sir! who would dare open their mouths in your presence, if it were generally known that you would without their knowledge or consent publish any anecdote of them and with their names— . . . besides the reluctance to be named in a public journal is a valuable characteristic of an Englishman, and should neither be invaded nor on light grounds given up."

Coleridge says he never felt and therefore does not retain the least offence—though the tone of the letter belies this—"but one *demand I must make* . . . that you do not correct the account *at all nor in any way* repeat my name, nor in any way attempt to draw back the attention and recollection of the Readers of the Dyerhoea Cantabrigiensis to that anecdote . . . "[1]

Three days later he repeats his pun on Dyer's name in a letter to John Rickman: "I will forgive you tho' you should suspect me of having caught the Dyerhoea explanatoria,

[1] Coleridge: *Letters*, 15.3.1804.

sive morbus hyperbotheratorium symptomaticus ... a disease not quite so bad to the Patient as Water on the Brain, but more troublesome to his Friends ... "

Why, one may ask, did Coleridge turn so fiercely against Dyer, when he had previously been so fond of him? He had called him "My elder brother under many titles, Brother Blue, Brother Grecian, Brother Poet, ... a man who has never in his long life, by tongue or pen, uttered what he did not believe to be the truth from any motive, or concealed what he did conceive to be such from other motives than those of tenderness for the feelings of others." [1]

Was it that Dyer's disorderliness, vagueness, other-worldliness, exasperated Coleridge? Was it that he was too sick, too preoccupied, too important, now, to have time for someone of humble standing? In his youth he had taken full advantage of Dyer's help and even when he was really ill had written him letters of a friendly tone.

One has the impression that Coleridge, flushed with the excitement and enthusiasm of the years immediately following the French Revolution, took to his heart all those who felt the same, without regard for their literary ability or overall efficiency. While the poet shared Dyer's idea of social justice and reform, and was like him a practising Unitarian, he took Dyer's work and literary efforts seriously; but when he dropped out of the active political movement, he withdrew at the same time from those who were still "committed". One suspects that a slight but persistent feeling of guilt, of having in a sense deserted or being thought to have deserted, took the form of abusing those former friends, and of putting himself in the right. Wordsworth had also rejoiced in the new Dawn, but had been less involved, and had fewer radical friends—disappointed in the turn of events in France, and depressed by the outbreak and continuance of war, he took up an a-political attitude, but never felt responsibility (and hence recrimination) vis-à-vis former "brothers". Southey, from being an active and zealous

[1] Coleridge: *Letters*, 18.3.1804.

"Jacobin", veered to the opposite extreme; his changes of opinion did not weigh on his conscience which was far less tender than Coleridge's, he felt no sense of guilt, for to win success for Southey was his main object in life—and this, with the Laureate's crown he may be said to have achieved.[1]

Coleridge, having turned his back on politics, consorted mainly with purely literary people and artists. He kept in touch with Benjamin Flower, the publisher, for a while; and he corresponded for many years with John Thelwall, whom he really esteemed as a poet and a man—but few of the letters touch on politics; they are much more concerned with personal, religious and philosophical questions, and very exhilarating they are to read— but they do show how completely Coleridge had cut himself off from the social and economic questions which had, when he was a student, under Frend's influence, so absorbed him, and partly explain his attitude to his former friends.

Dyer, incapable as he was of resentment, probably did not even realize how he was being snubbed by Coleridge, and would have been the first to defend him from a charge of disloyalty. His amiability was proverbial and extended to exonerating even a notorious murderer with the words "He must have been rather an eccentric man".[2]

Whatever Coleridge felt, Dyer retained the warm friendship of many distinguished people; Crabb Robinson frequently mentions him as being present at parties in London; Holcroft met him at dinner; and it is known that he was a co-founder and longstanding member, with William Frend, of a Club for literary and scientific discussion which met at the Chapter Coffee-house in Paternoster Row. Among the members were Samuel Rogers, the poet; Maltby, the Librarian of the British Museum; "Conversation" Sharpe; Hoppner, Henry Tresham, Shee, of the Royal Academy, causing Lamb to write to Dyer "How these painters encroach on our province!" He did not think the arts ought to be

[1] cf. Cestre: *Les poètes anglais et la revolution française.*

[2] Rodgers: *op. cit.* p. 184.

mixed: "No large tea-dealer sells cheeses, no great silversmith deals in razor strops: it is only your petty dealers who mix commodities. If Nero had been a great emperor he would never have played the violoncello. Who ever caught you, Dyer, designing a landscape or taking a likeness?"[1]

One can be sure that this remark delighted Dyer, as Lamb's quips usually did, while he was vaguely aware that his leg was being pulled.

Many years later he was really hurt by one of Lamb's whimsical articles, though even that was made up between the two good friends, but that is a story of the 1820's for which we must wait. We will leave Dyer in the Chapter Coffee-house, and return to William Frend about to enter a new and important period of his life.

[1] Lamb: *Letters*, ?15.7.1808, p. 307.

PART III

CHANGING EPOCH

16

PROSPECTS FOR THE NEW CENTURY

1800 DAWNED ON an England suffering from troubles worse than at any time in the previous century, even in its last grim years. Half a decade of war had brought hardships and shortages unfamiliar in rural England where previously the country folk, though poor, at least had enough to eat. Now, owing to the enclosure of more and more common land, the old yeomanry were hard hit, and cottagers forced off their smallholdings to become hired labourers, or to seek employment in the towns on a starvation wage.

In 1800 the exorbitant rises in the price of corn caused riots in the cities, while in the villages the Speenhamland measures created paupers. Many solutions were advanced: while the Reverend Thomas Malthus advocated letting the children of the poor die off, the newspapers abounded with recipes for saving malt in brewing beer, or for adulterating wheat in making bread. The Government exhorted the better off to be frugal. This was very distasteful to the rebellious old radical Richard Reynolds, who wrote to William Frend from Little Paxton on 10 December 1800, that "we have not yet begun to stint and diet our family as all our neighbours do, not that we are not willing to try to alleviate and take a share of distress with the needy; but I feel a repugnance to comply with all commands from a certain quarter." Yet Reynolds took the lead in relieving local distress, and reports a vestry meeting at St Neots where it was "agreed to purchase a good Stock of Wheat & Barley to grind it & sell it out to the Labouring Poor; besides Allowances in Money weekly".[1]

Frend took a keen interest in these problems and in 1801 wrote an article enquiring into "The Causes and

[1] Reynolds to W.F., 10.12.1800.

Remedies of the late and present Scarcity and the High Price of Provisions." Among other factors he blamed "the uncommonly cold and rainy summer and autumn of 1799 . . . the misdeeds of middlemen, the depreciation of money, and increased consumption in consequence of the war—330,000 soldiers, sailors and prisoners of war consume double the quantity they otherwise would do . . . Expensive loans and increased taxes . . . unsettle for a time the due ration between wages and the price of provisions . . . Agriculture was not keeping pace with manufactures."

Richard Reynolds provided him with facts about local conditions: "The Bench at Huntingdon agreed that 2/3 per head in a family of Labourers is a requisite sum for their maintenance. If a Labourer has a Wife & 4 Children he earns 9s pr Week, Wife & Children earn 1/6—total 10/6—then the Overseer must add 3s. Tithe Wheat sold last Thursday at the enormous price of £3.9.0 pr Load—The Maltsters . . . will get a fortune by selling their Malt above the price which they bought at last year & they are said to be discontented with this, but they mix new Barley with old",[1] making even bigger profits.

Owing to all these manoeuvres, to the enclosure acts and the demand for home-grown corn, the big farmers prospered. Their interests were protected by the Board of Agriculture (set up at the start of the war) and now more scientific farming ensured better crops and good prices. The new industrialists were doing well, too, with cheap labour flooding in from the countryside, modern machinery increasing production, and contracts to supply the army with everything from guns to uniforms, bullets to buttons.

Some of their workers, ground down by long hours and low wages, banded together in primitive trade unions which were soon smashed by Pitt's Combination Laws. Radicals still languished in jail—Gilbert Wakefield was held from 1798 till 1801 in Dorchester prison, and released only to die. Political action was difficult if not impossible, and during the

[1] Reynolds to W.F., 29.12.1801.

first years of the century even the indefatigable Frend seems to have given up campaigning for reform or for peace.

A gleam of hope brightened the year 1802, when the Treaty of Amiens was signed on 25 March and resulted in a truce between Britain, France, Spain and Holland. It was agreed that Britain should restore Egypt to Turkey, while keeping Trinidad and Ceylon. The French undertook to leave Naples, and Portugal's independence was guaranteed.

However, a few months later, Napoleon's intervention in the German States and his election as President of the new Italian Republic caused the Allies some alarm. Britain announced that she would now hold on to Malta for ten years, and demanded French evacuation of Holland and Switzerland. Napoleon refused this, and war broke out again on 16 May 1803.

This time it must have seemed even to pro-Republicans in Britain a national duty actively to oppose Napoleon, who no longer appeared to represent the fine aspirations of 1789, but to be intent on the conquest of Europe and the invasion of England. William Frend temporarily abandoned his anti-war position and, as his contribution to the recruiting campaign, wrote a 36-page essay on the history of patriotism from Alexander the Great onwards; he concluded this with a poem appealing for volunteers to the militia. Poetry, he explained in his preface, "is designed to inspire the mind with lofty and noble sentiments and by the melody of numbers to fix them more deeply on the soul."

He ended his twenty pages of verse with the following stirring lines:

Awake: attend! be indolent no more—
For friendship, social peace, domestic love,
Arise! your country's living safety prove
And train her valiant youth to watch around her shore.

At one point in his pamphlet Frend remarks: "In Kent it is a very pleasant sight to see a game of cricket which lasts the whole day, and the spectators are much interested in the scene before them . . . How much greater would that be supposing twenty thousand volunteers to be drawn up in Hyde Park!"

The fear of invasion must have been strong and prevalent for the normally calm Frend to catch the contagion. He certainly did not welcome or support the resumption of the war, nor did he have any faith in the British government which was directing it. He shared the general feelings of Reformers, reflected in a letter from his friend Hammond, asking what Frend thought "of the present politics" and giving the writer's own views: "If we may judge from its opening we never had a more insipid Parliament . . . The present ministry is too insipid and insignificant to stand, but all parties seem as a rope of sand." Hammond hoped that their mutual friend Mr Raine, recently elected to the new House, would "give a helping hand to cleanse the augean stable." [1]

Richard Reynolds wrote that "if I am not mistaken you have the military ardour, I feel no spark of it. The violation of the Treaty and the infinite absurdity of rushing into the war are uppermost in my thoughts." [2] The old gentleman got into trouble for refusing to pay £100 towards the cost of cavalry horses, and his letters to Frend are peppered with angry digs at the militia and reserves invading Huntingdon. John Coke, M.P., the well known Norfolk landowner and agriculturist, was also censured for not believing in the danger of invasion and for withholding his support for local volunteers. But these independent-minded men were few and far between.

Presumably Frend saw that France was entering an expansionist phase, and he thought the measures for national defence necessary, but from whatever motives he supported the raising of the militia for once he was on the fashionable side. Everywhere the top people were backing the recruiting campaign. Miss Raine, sister of the M.P., confirms this

[1] Hammond to W.F., 18.12.1802.
[2] Reynolds to W.F., 16.11.1803.

wittily in a description of a visit to Alnwick Castle: "Lord Percy is an amiable young man and much beloved by all who know him. His military talents may perhaps be tried in due time, for his father has placed him at the head of a thousand of his tenantry who are . . . to be maintained at his expense during the present war. My eyes & ears are tired of red coats & drums, but I am told I am blamably insensible to the dangers with which we are threatened."[1]

Mrs Theophilus Lindsey for her part wrote: "It is very happy that the country is so generally roused to a sense of danger from without & getting ready to meet it which probably may discourage the attempt. Francis [her brother] is quite right in joining the volunteers. His example is an encouragement to the lower orders."[2] And an amusing undated letter from the learned Godfrey Higgins shows that even antiquarians turned soldier in their country's hour of need:

"You talk of Volunteers: damn it Sir I have been encamped upon Elmstead Heath all Summer and am now in Winter Quarters in Colchester Barracks . . . would any man ever believe it but it is true. I took arms the moment the Consul overran Switzerland . . . I have some fears in my mind that you are (when you tell me of your leg) a malingerer. I should laugh to see you shoulder a Musket . . .

"I have no doubt the Volunteers will show themselves the support of their Country's Cause whenever the time shall arrive for calling on them. We had an alarm about a fortnight before we came into Quarters, nothing could exceed the alacrity of our men, they would not wait for the delivery of the ball cartridges but they broke the Barrels to pieces and helped themselves; after the alarm the whole Regiment was ready to march away in twenty minutes in every respect ready for action about midnight."[3]

One is reminded of Thomas Hardy's Granfer Cantle who

[1] Miss Raine to W.F., 29.9.1804.
[2] Mrs Lindsey to W.F., 13.8.1803.
[3] G. Higgins to W.F., 1804.

in *The Return of the Native* expressed the feelings of the average volunteer: "Why, afore I went a soldier in the Bang-up Locals (as we was called) in the year four . . . I didn't know no more what the world was like than the commonest man among ye—and now, jown it all, won't say what I baint fit for, hey? . . . Nothing came a miss to me after I joined the Locals in '04".[1]

* * *

Besides helping in the national effort Frend was busily, though not very successfully, writing and publishing economic and theological pamphlets. His *Present State of National Banking* was criticized in a *Refutation* by Mr T. S. Surr, a fellow economist ("This, I confess, is not the logic expected from a Mathematician of Mr Frend's celebrity")[2] and Robert Tyrwhitt wrote cantankerously about various tracts which Frend had sent him. It was all rather discouraging, but Frend refused to be down-hearted. He considered starting a journal and wrote round to get support, from Hammond, for instance, who replied:

"I like the plan of your periodical publication very much and should be happy to be an occasional contributor to it."

This venture, "The Gentleman's Monthly Miscellany" was launched in 1803, but only lived for a few months. After this Frend devoted his energies to producing a monthly series of articles entitled *Evening Amusements* which described the changing night sky throughout the year, and appears to have been highly successful. It ran from 1805 to 1824 and was praised by astronomers and amateurs alike. There is an unsolicited testimonial to the series in the *Monthly Repository* of May 1808:

"I cannot refrain from thanking Mr Frend for the instruction I have received . . . It was he who first taught me to discern order amidst the apparent confusion which the heavens

[1] Hardy: *The Return of the Native*, Bk. i, chap. 3, iv. 7.
[2] T. S. Surr: *Refutation*. British Museum.

nightly present to the eye, and who pointed out the most magnificent display of the wisdom and omnipotence of the Creator."

Evening Amusements was widely read, and it has been suggested that a passage in one of the issues of 1814 may have inspired lines in Blake's *Milton*:

The Sky is an immortal Tent built by the Sons of Los
And every Space that a Man views around his dwelling-place
Standing on his own roof or in his garden on a mount
Of twenty-five cubits in height, such space is his Universe . . .

Frend knew Blake in the early days of the century, and it is quite possible that they met and talked about the marvels of the universe—and that out of such discussion came the seed of the poem, to flower a decade later.

Freelance writing and teaching did not satisfy Frend, although he enjoyed them. He applied for the post of Lucasian Professor of Mathematics at Cambridge, competing, ironically, with Isaac Milner who, personally supported by Sir William Scott and other influential figures, was bound to succeed.[1]

Notwithstanding his disappointment, Frend continued to hanker after a post in Cambridge; this is apparent in a letter from Tyrwhitt in 1805 which begins: "You ask me to give ocular demonstration of your position in the list of Theological Respondents." Brusque as ever, Tyrwhitt dashed Frend's hopes: "You desire me to do what is impossible, for, as I prepared you to expect, you have no place in it . . . If you ask me why you have no place among them, perhaps the reason may be that they are all senior to you and therefore your turn is to come . . . If you should at least be called into the schools, you will have the pleasure of seeing one of

[1] Mary Milner: *Life of Isaac Milner*, pp. 169–170.

your Cubicks in the Chair, Dr Ramsden who strange as it may appear now sits as Deputy Professor."

Another letter from Tyrwhitt (1 February 1806) reflects Frend's continuing but frustrated interest in Cambridge affairs—this time the election of an M.P.: "I was disappointed in not seeing you here at the usual time last year, and should be glad to see you at our Election. But as your attendance may be in some respect or other rendered disagreeable to you & cannot be of any real importance, I do not envisage it . . . I shall probably take no part in it, as I always have thought with you that such Elections are very ill suited to the character of the Electors and therefore should be discouraged."

* * *

Frend's main source of income at this time was coaching the children of several well-to-do families in mathematics, and we catch a glimpse of him at Lord Oxford's and the Duke of Cumberland's homes. But his favourite pupil was Annabella, Byron's "princess of parallelograms", daughter of Sir Ralph and Lady Milbanke, a clever little girl to whom he taught algebra and Latin. The Milbankes had a London house though their seat was at Seaham; they were progressive land-owners and staunch Unitarians. Frend's correspondent Miss Raine stayed with them in 1804 and it is probable that she provided the introduction that resulted in Frend's teaching Annabella and in the long friendship which followed.

The precocious only child was nine years later to marry Lord Byron and be a tragic centre of interest for her time and for posterity; but at this period she was an earnest adolescent with a surprising love of lessons. She devoured Cicero, solved Euclid and asked for more—in short, the perfect pupil. Added to this she idolized her tutor, who had so dramatically defied authority during the witch-hunt of the 1790's and was still something of a hero to young radicals.

The pupil-teacher relationship developed into a friendship which lasted through the stormy days of Annabella's marriage till Frend's death, as a file of some seventy letters proves. Two of these from this early period show Frend's attitude towards his pupil. Clearly amused by the precocious letters which she had sent him, he wrote in mock deference on 25 November 1806: "Mr Frend is very much concerned that a variety of occupations has prevented him from noticing the receipt of Miss Milbanke's communication." She had evidently missed some lessons, for Frend presumed "that the business of elections might engage some of her attention." He congratulated Sir Ralph on his success "though the next parliament may present to the world very extraordinary scenes & will require the exertions of every honest man." Hoping that "from this time Miss M.'s exercises may be resumed & will in future suffer no interruptions" Frend pats her on the back for completing the fourth book of Euclid, and discusses her further studies: Astronomy, algebra, Latin, and geometry.[1]

The following autumn he writes from Ramsgate telling her that "your translation of Cicero is good but it wants the english polish. Perhaps you meant that it should be rather literal than elegant . . ."

He had evidently set her a composition on Current Affairs, for he asks, "How came you to hesitate so much on the action off Copenhagen?" and delivers a little lecture on international law.

Annabella's literary gifts were less developed than her mathematical ability which was remarkable; she was making strides in astronomy and had plotted the passage of Halley's Comet so accurately that, though Frend was unable to see it—"the evenings having been remarkably hazy"—"through her observations he can make out its progress tolerably well."[2]

In 1806 Frend was offered a regular post as Actuary to the

[1] M. Elwin: *Lord Byron's Wife*, pp. 81–82.

[2] W.F. to A.B., 8. 10. 1807.

newly formed Rock Life Assurance Company. This office job, less amusing perhaps than his freelance writing and teaching, offered good prospects and was in fact more exciting and challenging than it might appear.

Life insurance was a comparatively new business, and an important step forward in social security. There were only four companies in existence in 1806 and they had all been founded by public-spirited men who saw the need for this kind of insurance where none had previously existed, as a remedy for much insecurity and misery.

One of the main protagonists of life insurance was the celebrated Dissenter Dr Richard Price, who took a keen interest in social questions; besides his many philosophical and political tracts he wrote pamphlets on "Reversionary Payments" and "Equitable Assurances" as early as 1769, and with Baron Maseres worked out a scheme for personal insurance which was passed by the House of Commons but rejected by the Lords, in 1772.[1] Three years later, however, it had passed both Houses; as a result, the first insurance company, the Equitable Society, was set up under Dr Price's guidance, by his nephew William Morgan (also a Unitarian). This proved extremely successful, and in the formation of the Rock Company Morgan was consulted, and was instrumental in Frend's appointment as its first actuary. The two men knew each other well and had previously worked together in advising friendly societies (which were among Frend's many good causes). It is clear that Frend respected Morgan, for he later adopted many of his ideas in modelling the Rock Company.[2]

The first meeting of the Rock (today amalgamated into the Law Union and Rock Insurance Company) was held at the London Tavern on 11 March 1806, and a subscription opened for forming a Proprietary Life Assurance Company. Twenty-one directors were chosen, with Sir Charles Price, son of Richard, as Chairman. Frend was appointed Actuary,

[1] *D.N.B.* Dr Richard Price.

[2] M. E. Ogborn: *Equitable Assurances*, pp. 197–198.

and a residence provided for him in the Company's house, in New Bridge Street, near Bridewell, from where, in these days "open ground could be reached in a moderate walk." From the windows of the office, the Rock Centenary Year Book tells us, "there was in clear weather an uninterrupted view of the Surrey Hills. Unfortunately, it was the centre of London smoke, at that time heavier and thicker in proportion to the size of the City."[1] One of Frend's many pamphlets deals with the problem of "How to allay the smoke in the City of London", a subject obviously very near his heart; he suggested that the height of chimneys and the power of furnaces should be controlled, but in the *laissez-faire* of the time nothing came of it.

* * *

One reason for Frend's taking the regular employment at the Rock was that he was thinking of getting married, and could hardly hope to support a wife and family on freelance work. His intended was Sara Blackburne, grand-daughter of the eminent Archdeacon who although a loyal Churchman had made a courageous stand in 1785 for the rights of Dissenters. One of his daughters was the wife of Dr Disney and his step-daughter Hannah had married Theophilus Lindsey; it was no doubt through this connection that Frend met Sara.

The future Mrs Frend was good-looking, intelligent, a gifted painter, shared William's ideas, and proved to be an excellent wife and mother.

Some letters of congratulation on their marriage early in 1808 survive. John Hammond wrote on 25 January that he had seen the news in the Cambridge paper—and expressed his great pleasure. He says, "It was a matter of regret to me whenever I reflected on the subject, that one endued with so many social qualities, should continue in a life of celibacy. I remember Dr Priestley . . . recommends matrimony as

[1] *Rock Centenary Year Book*, 1906.

productive of benevolent affections by the natural tendency it has to divert attention from self... I rejoice to see the hope which I have long cherished of seeing you married and comfortably settled, now realized. From the revered name of Blackburne, I augur everything great and good ...

"I think from what I have seen in both your Characters that I should not be much out of the Way in pronouncing that you will meet with comfortable days."[1]

Godfrey Higgins, his old Cambridge friend, told him: "By this day's paper I learn that you are married, indeed with great surprize I learnt it, I thought you a confirmed old batchelor ..." He wishes the Frends "every happiness which it is possible to enjoy in this nether sphere" and "three as cherry cheeked noisy brats as I have now at my elbow, as healthy, as lively and as handsome." He goes on to reminisce about "Poor old Kipling" and to comment on the "ruin of our cursed foreign commerce", on Napoleon and—surely with tongue in cheek—on "the heresy of Cobbettism and Burdettism with which many people in this country are tainted."[2]

Such letters show that Frend's new domestic happiness was not likely to prevent him from keeping up with current affairs. Though Hammond wrote in 1808, "When a man is settled his family becomes as it were a little world to him, where his principal cares and tenderness are centered", he does not dwell on Frend's domestic affairs, but goes on to discuss the French Revolution—"a perfect phenomenon in the history of the world; I cannot account for the turn it has taken, from the principles of philosophy or the nature of the human mind" ... "that so much blood should have been shed and such misery occasioned for such an end ... is truly mysterious and utterly inexplicable."[3]

[1] One former friend who did not rejoice was Mary Hays. Crabb Robinson's diary (30.8.1819) contains the entry: "Frend's sudden marriage with Miss Blackburne was a severe blow to her." *op. cit.*, p. 235.

[2] Higgins to Frend, 26.1.1808.

[3] Hammond to W.F., 5.4.1808.

Frend in fact was following current affairs more closely than ever before, chiefly for the purpose of writing a regular feature article for the Unitarian *Monthly Repository*. From 1808 on, his life was divided between his work and three ruling interests: politics, the Unitarian church, and his family and friends. On 10 November 1808, the first of his seven children was born—Sophia, the apple of his eye, who, as soon as she could walk and talk, was taken everywhere with him, and taught, first, reading and writing, later Hebrew and philosophy, and introduced to all his famous friends.

Sophia in her memoirs recalls some of them—scholars and politicians and poets who came to the hospitable Frend house and endlessly discussed current events and literature and philosophy: Lamb, Coleridge and Dyer; Baron Maseres, who had known Dr Johnson and Dr Parr, and told stories about them; Mr Robert Hibbert, the founder of the Hibbert Trust, who gave Sophia sticks of barley sugar from his plantation in Jamaica; John Landseer (the painter's father), Thomas Taylor the Platonist, Henry Crabb Robinson, and many more.

Sophia's most interesting recollection is of meeting, while on a walk with her father in the Strand, "a man who had on a brown coat and whose eyes I thought were uncommonly bright.

"He shook hands with my father and said: 'Why don't you come and see me? I live down here'; and he raised his hand and pointed to a street which led to the river.

"Each said something about visiting the other, and they parted." Sophia asked "who that gentleman was", and was told "He is a strange man; he thinks he sees spirits."

"Tell me his name", Sophia said—and was told "William Blake."[1]

[1] S. De Morgan: *op. cit.*, pp. 67–68.

17

THE NEW REFORM MOVEMENT

ONE OF THE closest friends of the family was Sir Francis Burdett, the debonair, aristocratic politician who had been an ardent supporter of the radical Horne Tooke, and at this period was still considered something of a "Jacobin". In spite of this he was described by Byron as "sweet and silvery as Belial himself and I think the greatest favourite in Pandemonium [the House of Commons]."

Perhaps Burdett liked the intellectual but homely Frends as a change from politicians or from the gay and brilliant society in which he normally moved with his wealthy wife Sophia, daughter of the banker Coutts.

Whatever the reason, Frend was very closely involved in the dramatic events between 1807 and 1811 in which Burdett played a leading part and which made him the focus of political activity at that time.

It was when Frend was collecting for prisoners' families in 1798 that he first met Burdett, then a young M.P. who took a keen interest in prison conditions and exposed the appalling state of things at Cold Bath Fields gaol (thus discrediting Wilberforce who claimed that all was perfectly well there). After amassing 210 affidavits and letters from prisoners Burdett forced an enquiry into the management of the gaol, and a commission was appointed, which won some concessions to justice and humanity—the first of many of Burdett's victories in this field.[1]

Though a Whig, Burdett did not consider himself tied to the party and pursued an independent line, which endeared him to Frend, who helped him in his campaigns, in the capacity of adviser, press agent and public relations officer. In his monthly feature article in the *Repository* Frend gave

[1] Patterson: *Sir Francis Burdett and his Times*, p. 428.

full coverage to Sir Francis's battles for Parliamentary Reform and against corruption. Their friendship kept him in close touch with day-to-day political life and actively involved him in the revival of the Reform movement. This had been in the doldrums for over ten years but was now stirring into life partly owing to popular revulsion against the weak and inefficient government, and largely thanks to Burdett's energy and dynamic personal leadership.

The election of 1807, following the fall of the Grenville Ministry, brought Burdett to the fore when he stood for Westminster and topped the poll with 5,134 votes, on a programme of free and honest elections.

This is not the place to tell the complicated story of the campaign, in which Francis Place played an important part and which was noted for its rows, skirmishes and duels. Burdett's victory was the important thing, and the populace turned out in force to acclaim it. "London had never seen such a triumphal progress as that given him", wrote William Frend, describing how half a million people joined in the demonstrations and 2,000 attended the celebration dinner.

In the *Political Register* of 14 February, Cobbett demanded: "Name any other man in this kingdom . . . who could find 1500 people volunteer to give 10/6 each for the sake of a dinner with him." Toasts included "that honest and incorruptible representative of the people"; "Purity of Election"; "The People". Replying to the last, Burdett remarked that "both parties laugh at the people. They despise the people. And those who have robbed us most have the most contempt." But, he claimed, "the People" had given their answer that day to both the parties and to the government. It was the first time for years that anybody had used such language and it was greeted with delirious enthusiasm. From then up to 1815 Burdett was the embodiment of the new spirit of Reform; his stand, backed by a radical group in Parliament and by progressive writers (Cobbett in particular) was largely responsible for the ensuing battle against the prevalent corruption, war profiteering and incompetence.

Letters to Frend from Major Cartwright and Christopher Wyvill show that he was working with these old stalwarts to promote the cause.[1] We find him in 1808 writing long articles on everything from home affairs, trade, industry, to the course of the war in Europe, events in America, Asia and the Middle East, showing how all these things were interrelated. He had an extraordinary grasp of the situation both at home and abroad and revealed tellingly how commerce in the East was affected by "jobbing" in London, our Peninsular policy by religion in Spain, military and naval disasters abroad by scandals at home—of which in 1808 and 1809 there were plenty.

Frend had inside information, gleaned from Burdett's circle, and his articles were often highly defamatory, particularly so in relating the most spectacular of the current scandals: that involving the Duke of York (Commander-in-Chief of the Army) and his mistress Mrs Clarke. This lady was discovered to be obtaining preferential posts for her friends through her royal paramour. The revelations of immorality and graft in high places shook the government and the establishment itself. The Radicals trumpeted the sensations in and outside Parliament. The Tories foamed at the mouth: "A conspiracy exists to ruin the royal family in the public estimation and by running them down to destroy the constitution . . . It is carried on by Jacobins who abuse the liberty of the press."[2]

The accusers stuck to their guns. Frend wrote in his article of December 1809 that "a footboy who used to wait on (Mrs Clarke) and the Duke of York was rewarded by a command in the army"; someone else "had a son who was made Lieutenant Colonel by the time he was of age . . . It is evident that corruption has prevailed to a very great extent."

Reform was vital: " . . . Jobbing for seats in Parliament, trafficking for places, unlimited confidence in ministers,

[1] cf. *Letters*, Montagu Papers, Bodleian Library.
[2] Patterson: *op. cit.*, Vol. i, p. 223.

wasteful expenditure, are the natural fruits of the violation of the constitution."

On top of the Duke of York scandal came the disaster of the July expedition to Walcheren (decided on by Castlereagh as a diversion to aid Austria by capturing Antwerp where France was building ships). It was an ill-fated decision, dividing England's military strength which was already over-extended by the Peninsular campaign; for in Spain and Portugal a large force of men under Wellesley (the future Lord Wellington) were, for the time being, unproductively pinned down. In the circumstances, and thanks to delay, bungling and misunderstanding between the commanders of the operation, the Walcheren expedition ended in complete catastrophe and the loss of many men in the swamps of the Scheldt.

Public feeling was deeply stirred. Frend quotes the words of a backbencher, Mr Ward, which expressed the general anger and anxiety: "All the calamities and disasters ... were the consequences of measures of men ... that would fill up the peerage in reward of useless victories and send out forces to treacherous and unwilling Allies, whilst they exhausted the means of their own defence at home." Samuel Whitbread, a staunch radical, denounced "the ignorance, imbecility, bigotry" of these men "for the fate with which providence visits their measures."

Our enemy, said Whitbread, "could not select men more suitable to his ends, or more pernicious to our interests."

Numerous meetings and petitions showed the popular support for this position. Following heated debates there were proposals, early in 1810, for enquiries into the conduct of the war, and into the necessity for Reform. The announcement of these was the prelude to the Burdett affair, which was to rock the country throughout that spring and summer.

Frend wrote: "When these enquiries were due to take place the public were naturally anxious to hear them. But Mr Yorke, member for Cambridgeshire, succeeded in having all strangers excluded from the Gallery." This led "a local disputing society" to protest, and to abuse Mr Yorke by means of placards affixed to Westminster's walls.

The Hon. Member complained that this was a breach of privilege and, says Frend, "on his motion the House decreed the placard to be a libel and committed its author Mr Gale Jones to Newgate, thus acting as prosecutor, judge and executioner in its own cause."[1] This happened on 21 February. Burdett was absent, suffering from gout, but, highly indignant about the whole business, he rose from his bed of sickness, hurried to the House and moved a motion against these undemocratic proceedings.

The motion was lost, so Burdett wrote a strong letter to his constituents "making certain expressions . . . offensive to those persons who came into their seats by means at present needless to describe," as Frend says, referring to the buying and selling of parliamentary places.[2]

Burdett's letter was published by Cobbett in the *Political Register* of Saturday 24 March and at once (on Monday 26 March) stigmatized as a libel by Mr Yorke and his friends. This produced a Commons debate on Thursday 5 April which lasted from 5 p.m. till 7 the next morning. In spite of "a severe struggle" the motion "that Burdett's letter was scandalous and libellous and violated parliamentary privileges" was carried without a division. Sir Robert Salusbury then moved that Burdett should be committed to the Tower, and obtained 189 votes for, 152 against.

In Frend's words, "the Speaker signed the warrant (for Burdett's arrest) and the news was quickly spread through the Metropolis, exciting no small degree of alarm and curiosity to see in what manner so extraordinary a proceeding would terminate."

The story of the Baronet's resistance to arrest is a fascinating one but it can only be told here in bare outline. He barricaded himself into his Piccadilly house, while the people of London crowded to his support, blocking the streets all

[1] *Monthly Repository* (*M.R.*), March 1810.

[2] *M.R.*, April 1810.

around, and 50,000 troops, with artillery, took up positions in Green Park. Eventually, after three days, soldiers broke into his house. He was conveyed, "an immense body of troops going before and following after", to the Tower where he was delivered to the custody of the constable, Earl Moira, "who received him with great politeness" and ushered him into a private suite (such as prisoners of the government could enjoy if they had the private means).

Outside, "the soldiers were irritated at the hootings of the populacc, occasionally accompanied with the throwing of whatever came to hand, and used their swords and pistols very freely." Many people were injured, and at least two died.

All this "immediately excited a considerable ferment in the city of Westminster", Frend tells us. A meeting of over twenty thousand assembled in the Palace Yard, resolutions were passed, and petitions sent to the House of Commons urging Burdett's release. This however was too much to expect. From the government's point of view "the great object was secured. The army . . . gradually separated and returned to their former positions. Everything was quiet in the metropolis, and at a large meeting in the city . . . the health of Sir Francis Burdett was drunk with the greatest enthusiasm."[1]

The Baronet was held in the Tower for three months, and during that period the government were provided with striking proof of the prisoner's popularity, both as a person and as a symbol of Reform. One of John Hammond's long chatty letters to Frend, dated 24 April, testifies that lively public interest in the affair was evinced even in the out-of-the-way fenland village of Stanton:

"There is nothing now talked of in the country but the imprisonment of our great and beloved patriot Sir Francis Burdett. I hear my labourers discussing the subject every day; and what surprizes me is, that they all seem perfectly to understand it, and regard the cause in which he is engaged as

[1] *M.R.*, April 1810.

their own. The imprisonment of Sir Francis will, by the blessing of God, be the means of renovating the Constitution and re-establishing our liberties. The prayers and blessing of every honest man in the kingdom attend him & his righteous cause. It is owing to such men that we sit under our vine and figtree in the enjoyment of liberty and peace."

Hammond, a man not merely of words, adds a P.S.: "I see by the newspapers that a Subscription has been opened for the benefit of Mr Gale Jones, and I have herewith sent you . . . my mite of a Guinea for his use."

The country, from Cambridgeshire to Newcastle, from Liverpool to Canterbury was seething with pro-Burdett demonstrations and meetings; petitions for his release poured in to the House of Commons. Frend commented of his home town that "it is singular that at Canterbury, a place abounding with clergymen, not one signed the petition, though it contains a thousand and sixty four signatures, among them the most respectable inhabitants of the city."[1]

Meanwhile, Sir Francis was not doing too badly. Being affluent, he occupied comfortable apartments in the Tower, was allowed to wander about the premises and to receive visitors. His agent, Richard Crabtree, kept him informed on estate matters;[2] Lady Burdett came and brought him clean linen; William Frend came and discussed politics; even children—his own and others—were permitted. Little Sophia Frend was carried to visit him by her nurse who taught her to answer the question "Who put Burdett in the Tower?" with an emphatic "Naughty men-folk!"

One day William Frend received an urgent note asking him to visit Burdett at once, and hurried to the Tower, leaving the insurance business to look after itself. He found Sir Francis in a state of great agitation. Taking his daily exercise he had seen a prisoner being flogged—a terrible and shocking sight. In Sophia's words, recalling her father's account, "the man more dead than alive was at length

[1] *M.R.*, April 1810.

[2] Berkshire County Records.

taken away to the hospital and the prisoner determined that no effort of his should be untried which might prevent a repetition of such horrors."[1]

Burdett wrote to Frend the same evening, " . . . There is no end to the meanness and cruelty of this atrocious system. The scenes of this morning have filled my mind with sensations difficult to describe & will make the remainder of my residence here much more painful than before."[2] Expressing horror to his wife in another note Burdett mentions that the authorities were "not a little embarrassed by my presence, & a young man who has a place here in the Ordnance Office, a nephew of Mr Frend, who happened to call upon me with Mr Frend, and who walked out with me when these executions were going on, got thereby into a scrape . . . "[3]

Sophia Frend wrote later that "Sir Francis begged my father again to go to him to consult with other friends upon the best means of getting the practice of flogging in the army abolished or made less terrible . . . To his earnest efforts in the House of Commons, was due a searching inquiry . . . with the result of getting flogging much reduced."[4] Shortly after this, in July 1810, William Cobbett was imprisoned in Newgate for protesting in the *Political Register* against the flogging by German militia of mutineers at Ely.

Nonetheless, thanks to these efforts, two years later circulars against the use of flogging were issued by the Duke of York to commanding officers. And the final prohibition of this barbarous practice can be attributed largely to the protests of 1810.

At last Burdett's imprisonment ended, owing to the prorogation of Parliament in June. Frend wrote in his Survey that "the inhabitants of the metropolis were eager upon this occasion to pay the desired tribute to the champion

[1] S. De Morgan: *op. cit.*, p. 2.
[2] *Ibid.*, p. 5.
[3] Patterson: *op. cit.*, p. 285.
[4] S. De Morgan: *op. cit.*, pp. 4–5.

of Magna Carta. For this purpose a grand procession was prepared to accompany Sir Francis on his liberation from the Tower. Great preparations were also made by the administration. The veterans in the Tower were changed for Scotch regiments and forces were collected from all quarters to preserve the peace of the metropolis." [1]

At 3.30 on 21 June Earl Moira "communicated to Burdett the intelligence that he was at liberty to quit the Tower. This permission was immediately accepted, and Sir Francis took a boat at the Tower Stairs, went a little way down the river, and then mounted his horse to take the way to his country-house." Frend in this article does not mention that he and another friend of Burdett's were with him in the boat. Nor that an enormous crowd of supporters were extremely annoyed that their hero had not appeared to lead a triumphal procession through the streets of London. Frend says, "the procession moved forward, not without some disappointment on the part of those who formed it." This understatement is complemented by a letter addressed to Burdett later by an anonymous participant: "I looked forward to a glorious day . . . I filled my pockets with stones for the evenings business and went to my club at 9 a.m. We found a large basket of blue ribbands sent us annonymously. We drank confusion to the ministers and sallied forth. I waited patiently till I had nearly dropped with fatigue having been appointed standard-bearer to the party, and after having lugged about a large blue flag upon a pole until my arms ached I heard that you were gone by water. I confess I was angry, I swore a little, and might have said it was a shabby trick." [2]

The press pounced on Burdett's conduct and did its best to portray the day's events as more absurd than they were; Gillray drew a scurrilous cartoon captioned "The Burdettites Hoax'd or One Fool makes Many", in which Sir Francis's disgusted supporters have balloons coming out of

[1] *M.R.*, June 1810.
[2] Patterson: *op. cit.*, p. 289.

their mouths commenting "A pretty take in, to be sure!" and "Poh! d—m, that's all gammon. No gentleman would go to serve gentlemen so ungenteel!"

Sophia's account, as given her by her father, explains Burdett's action for which William Frend was largely responsible. Frend "had gone direct to the Tower, where according to agreement he had met Sir Francis's brother. They had been very apprehensive of the consequences of the immense gathering of people, for outbreaks and riots were of every day occurrence, and the conspicuous place designed for the hero of the day would expose him to the danger of well-aimed shots from adverse hands, and would be likely thus to endanger peace; and under such circumstances, an excited street mob, partly composed of helpless women and children was a matter to be contemplated with terror . . . As soon as Sir Francis had his discharge the three walked down to the Tower stairs, where they found a wherry engaged by them, waiting for the released prisoner . . . They had to go through a rather crowded part of the river, and it was five miles to Putney. They all sat quiet until they had cleared the craft and shipping, then my father, who enjoyed the situation, began addressing the boatman: 'Well, I think you must wish to see the show today in the streets?'

" 'No, Sir, I don't.'—'How's that?'—'Well, I'm not so sure Burdett would get through all right. I'd rather we had him here.'—'What would you do if you had him here?'—'I'd pull a strong oar as I'm doing now.' "[1]

In the July number of the *Repository*, Frend justified Burdett's behaviour: "His friends were eager to show their hero triumph, and mortified at not being indulged in this assuredly very justifiable wish; but they did not sufficiently reflect in what a particular situation he stood, and how much it became him to prevent his enemies from the triumph they would have enjoyed if the military had been called in and scattered woe and dismay upon innumerable families . . .

[1] S. De Morgan: *op. cit.*, pp. 7–8.

He was to be commended for preferring the public good to any private enjoyment."

Sir Francis's own explanation to thirty-two members of the Westminster Committee was that "his enemies had been base enough to charge him with the bloodshed when he was taken to the Tower", and that he did not want to risk any more bloodshed.

Sir Samuel Romilly's comment, in his journal for 22 June 1810, was that Burdett "did well not to appear in the triumphal cavalcade that was prepared for him; but he would have done much better if he had declared his intention beforehand; and if he had not suffered it to be imagined, as he did . . . that it was with his privity and approbation that the procession had been publicly announced." [1]

Cautious man that he was, Romilly declined an invitation to the celebration dinner. "I cannot think that the circumstance of Sir Francis Burdett being discharged from the Tower because the House of Commons which placed him there is no longer sitting, is an event which can with any propriety be celebrated as a matter of public triumph." [2]

Perhaps Burdett's bitterest critic was Francis Place, who had played a major part in organizing the abortive demonstration, and had been made to look ridiculous. He accused Burdett of being "a damned coward and poltroon",[3] which seems a little unfair in view of Burdett's usual intrepid courage.

Up to the time of the baronet's arrest, he and Place had been reasonably friendly, or at least had respected one another; but Burdett now believed that Place had betrayed him by delaying the arrival of the civil power on the morning of his arrest, and even thought Place might be a government spy, and could have arranged with the Government to have him shot as he rode in the triumphal car.

This may seem far-fetched, but Place, it appears, was not

[1] Sir S. Romilly, *Memoirs . . .*, p. 340.
[2] *Ibid.*, p. 341.
[3] Henry Hunt, *Memoirs*, ii, p. 423.

above suspicion. There had been a scandal in May 1810 involving the Duke of Cumberland. William Frend, one-time tutor to the Duke's children, suspected the Duke, as many people did, of murdering an Italian valet who, jealous of the ducal advances to his wife, had attacked and wounded him. Writing to Rev. John Tate, Frend commented that "English husbands would not have been so terribly violent. It is remarkable that the regrets excited by the catastrophe were not so strongly expressed as might have been expected."[1] At the inquest on the valet's death Francis Place was the foreman of the jury that returned a verdict of suicide, and cleared the Duke of Cumberland. It was generally believed by the Radicals that Place had been bribed by the Court to screen the Duke. Henry Hunt in his *Memoirs* mentions that "since that period Place has been a *very rich* man, but before it he was a *poor*, *very poor* democrat."[2]

As for Burdett, he was full of suspicions and for nine years did not speak to Place; he even wrote, in 1814, to the Committee of the West London Lancastrian Association demanding Place's expulsion from the committee as a Government spy.

But to return to 1810: the "Burdett affair" came to a spectacular end with a great public dinner at the Crown and Anchor at which his constituents demonstrated their loyal support. Sir Francis made a fighting speech urging Reform and criticizing Lord Grey (who had been an ardent Reformer in 1793–94) for his present caution. His Lordship had said that experience had made him wiser; Burdett declared that men whose principles can change as they advance in years "cut up and destroy all confidence."

"A principle once formed remains for ever the same: it does not alter by time . . . When a man once pledges himself to certain principles he has stamped on himself the character which he intends shall belong to him; and if he departs from those principles it is impossible for any reasonable man ever

[1] W.F. to Tate, 10 June; quoted by Patterson: *op. cit.*, p. 291.
[2] Hunt, *Memoirs*; quoted by Patterson: *op. cit.*, p. 291.

after to put trust in him." Lord Grey had protested "against men, who under pretence to Reform would drive us into extravagant theories, but I have always been a friend to moderate Reform." Grey had described Burdett as "a misguided man lending himself to doctrines to the tendency of which he was blind"—Sir Francis replied that "practice without vision" would lead to disaster.[1]

Frend must have joined in the enthusiastic applause for this speech; himself a man of unwavering loyalty to his cause, he was deeply to regret Burdett's later change of heart and of principle—for as the baronet grew older he apparently forgot his stirring words, and eventually became a true blue tory and pillar of the Establishment.

One of Frend's biographers wrote in 1841 that "Mr Frend used to defend Sir Francis's conduct in slinking away from the Tower of London, but had he lived to see the reverse in the Banner Baronet, once 'Westminster's pride and England's Glory', he would have resigned his defence into other hands".[2] However Henry Frend contradicted this: "Even if my father could have been so unreasonable as to have disapproved of a step previously taken by his advice, he had no occasion to have resigned his defence of it to other hands: for he was living and in full possession of his faculties for many months after Sir Francis had publicly avowed the change in his political sentiments. And although he deeply regretted that change, yet his personal regard for the Baronet was so great, that he was never known to utter any expression from which it could be inferred that he considered Sir Francis to have been actuated by any other motives than a sincere adoption of Conservative principles."[3]

Sophia Frend says that "during the last years of his life Burdett and my father did not meet. The views of the politician had changed and he was no more 'the man of the people' held up by them as 'England's pride and West-

[1] Patterson: *op. cit.*, pp. 292–293.
[2] *Christian Reformer*, 1841, ii, p. 607.
[3] *Ibid.*, ii, p. 769.

minster's glory.' But his exceeding kindness of heart never altered and he was always ready to give to the needy and deserving." In 1835 he gave Sophia £20 for one of her good causes—vagrant children's homes; "and" says she, "I could tell of cases in which his purse was ready for the assistance, to a large amount, of friendless young men to whom an education would be provision for life."[1]

Burdett, for all his kindness, was clearly a politician first, and a radical second; he trimmed his sails to the political wind. Frend never trimmed his sails but till the end of his life forged ahead as his Unitarian conscience bade. He was, of course, a radical first, and a politician second, unwillingly, knowing politics to be the only available means to the longed-for end, Reform.

[1] S. De Morgan: *op. cit.*, pp. 17–18.

18

REPORTING WAR AND PEACE

NOTWITHSTANDING ALL THE excitements at home, Frend managed to keep up with international events, and his *Monthly Repository* reports on the course of the Napoleonic Wars show an astonishing grasp of world affairs; they are also very readable, vivid and liberally spiced with his tangy personal comments.

For a picture of the man, and his view of the stormy outside world of his day, one could hardly do better than quote some extracts from the series showing his political perception, his moral fervour and his imaginative ability as a reporter; he gives the impression of actually living through the events he describes.

Take for instance the bombardment of Flushing in the summer of 1809: "The fire was occasioned by the most tremendous cannonading, and showers of rockets from several posts at a small distance from the town. The distress of the inhabitants cannot be conceived but by those who were eye-witnesses of it . . . Driven from their houses by the falling of the roofs and walls, death seized them in every direction. The noise of the cannon, the crash of houses, the bursting of bombs, the screams of the women and children, struck horror in every breast for two nights and a day . . . "

After further details of "the scenes produced by war", Frend exclaims: "Lamentable state of the human race! Yet it cannot always remain so, and in spite of the infidelity of the present day, we look forward to the time when reason shall have its due influence with mankind . . .

"The instruments of destruction will be converted to their proper purpose, the subduing of the earth to the benefit of mankind . . . Who that looks upon the destruction of Flushing and the noble road cut through the Alps by the

Duke of Savoy would not wish that the money and labour employed to overthrow the works of human industry were expended in giving facility to the nobler exertions of peace?"[1]

The Peninsular War caused Frend much heartbreak. Though a British patriot he was strongly anti-Roman Catholic, and sincerely believed that our support of the Bourbon régime was to be condemned, and that the Spanish people would eventually accept the more enlightened régime with which Napoleon proposed to supplant Inquisition and Junta. "The Spanish people", he wrote in February 1810, "have redeemed their character by burning down the Inquisition at Valladolid . . . the inhabitants rejoiced at the destruction of the abominable building and its horrible engines of torture . . . The Spaniard will be little likely to sigh for the return of a Bourbon, to carry him back to his former bigotry and slavery . . . "[2]

Yet the Spaniards continued to resist Napoleon—nationalism being stronger than the desire for religious freedom, or perhaps the catholicism of Spain more deeply rooted than Frend knew.

In the December *Survey* he writes that "Spain and Portugal still present a scene of horror to every civilised mind. Destruction follows the steps of the great armies and innumerable guerillas."

And at a time of widespread tragedy he found the news from Spain particularly harrowing: "Nothing can be more afflicting to a well-bred mind", he wrote at the beginning of 1811. "Spain and Portugal continue to present such horrors as could not exist in a christianised world. Vast districts have been laid waste, and fire and the sword have destroyed populous cities and villages with their inhabitants. Such is the fate of war, that is, of the folly and wickedness of man . . ."

Although deriving some small comfort from the fact that "the Peninsula is in such a state that a new system must take

[1] *M.R.*, July 1810.

[2] *Ibid.*, February 1810.

place, the old system cannot be restored". Frend describes Massena's defeat and retreat in almost biblical terms: "He carried with him havock and desolation; and the land through which he passed must long mourn his progress."[1]

During the years 1811 and 1812 Russia and Turkey were at each other's throats. Frend wrote in November 1811, "The Turkish provinces of Europe continue to feel all the horrors of war. Immense armies are ravaging them . . . It is doubtful from whom they receive the greatest injuries, their friends or their enemies . . . Turkish armies are said to amount to 400,000 men and Russians to about half that number, but the numbers are little better than an armed rabble . . . It is rumoured that peace is likely to be obtained on the Turks ceding Wallachia and Bulgaria to their enemy."

A month later, the sack of Constantinople "presented a scene of most dreadful disorder. Insurrection among the Janissaries was quelled by an immense slaughter; ten thousand fallen in battle only in the streets, and three thousand by the hand of the executioner; the Grand Seignior compelled to quit his seraglio. But a victorious (Turkish) army has marched from Damascus to enter in triumph into Grand Cairo."[2]

At long range Frend surveyed the New World, linking events in Europe with developments in the Americas, north and south.

"One result of the Spanish troubles", he wrote prophetically in August 1810, "will be the independence of the Spanish colonies. The South Americas will begin to make a figure upon the globe. They will carry on an extensive commerce . . . introduce new ideas, new competitions. Happy will it be for them if they establish the liberty of the press, emancipate themselves from priestcraft, and make themselves a proper use of the rich and fertile country. The benefits to Europe are incalculable, if we leave them to themselves and are contented with the advantages of trade."

[1] *M.R.*, January 1811.
[2] *Ibid.*, December 1811.

Again: "The various interests of the old inhabitants, the descendants of the Spanish settlers and the native Spaniards, will give rise to various competitions and combinations . . . With prudence on the part of Great Britain a very extensive field is open for its commerce." (July 1810). And six months later: "An enlarged policy is requisite in the rising countries of America, which when liberty and civilisation have quitted Europe, will hold out very different views of government and religion . . . to our dark ages." [1]

Frend was bitterly disappointed by developments in the United States from which he and other British Radicals had hoped so much.

The Americans, it appeared, were just as foolish and greedy as other men. An incident between British and American ships in June 1810 produced the comment, "War desolates the finest regions in Europe. The passion of man may extend the evil, and we look with fear and trembling on a transaction in the Atlantic."

Peace hung in the balance for over a year, and in August 1811 Frend wrote happily, "No war yet with America! Every month of peace is a joyful acquisition . . . We cannot see any good reason for the two nations fighting, though plausible pretences in abundance will be found on either side, whenever they choose to unsheath the sword." Cautiously he added, "In America, as well as in England, there are a sufficient number of malignant spirits to stir up contention, who care not for the life of man or the ruin they cause to the peaceful manufacturer, agriculturist and the merchant."

The "malignant spirits" won the day, and in August 1812 America declared war, which lasted for two years. Frend lamented, "We will allow them causes of complaint, but what do they all amount to, compared with the mischiefs of a single campaign?" and he foretold the invasion of Canada, with "the usual devastation and distress."

At the same time he was watching Napoleon's ominous

[1] *M.R.*, January 1811.

moves eastwards in Europe: "Buonaparte has placed himself advantageously on the frontiers of Russia. He has seized that part of Poland which Russia in so barbarous a manner tore away from its ancient rulers. Buonaparte's army is posted along the Dwina and the country between it and the Beristhena . . . There is reason to believe that the resistance of the Russians is greater than he expected and may prevent his progress to any great distance into the interior of the country."

Frend, in his dislike of religious superstition, clearly hoped that French enlightenment might eventually replace "the debasement in religious matters" imposed by the Tsar and Church on the Russian people. "However much this country may deplore the success of Napoleon", he opines that "no one can hesitate in rejoicing that the chains of so disgraceful and base a superstition should be broken."[1]

He conveys in his monthly features of September, October and November something of the fascinated horror with which observers watched Napoleon's advance into Russia:

"The great conqueror is advancing with rapidity towards Moscow. The last bulletin states that his army has reached Wiasma . . . In the way, the town of Smolensko has been laid in ashes in the sight of the two armies, between which there was a very sharp conflict and the Russians were defeated . . . The guns of the French were playing upon the town, spreading fire and desolation in every quarter, and the ravages of the flames were increased by the Russians themselves when they found they were obliged to quit the place.

"Ye who have husbands, wives, parents, children . . . conceive to yourselves a moment a city in flames and a shower of balls falling in every direction upon the devoted inhabitants . . . Little do the men of this world accustom themselves to contemplate war in its true aspect. The proud trappings of an army dazzle the sight, but we do not think of the shrieks of the dying virgin, the wailings of the orphan, the groans of the wounded . . . A fine town is erased from the

[1] *M.R.*, August 1812.

catalogue of cities. It is no longer of use but in a military point of view . . . It serves as a depot for ammunition and its palaces are converted into hospitals. How many towns and villages must share the same fate before the ambition of the conqueror is gratified?"[1]

Frend opens his account of the burning of Moscow with a heartfelt cry: "Horror upon horrors! Battles, murders, conflagrations call for the deepest feelings of sorrow on the one hand, whilst painted dolls and infatuated superstitions and blasphemous inventions excite on the other contempt and indignation.

"Smolensk had exhibited a scene which harrowed up the soul. From this place the conqueror marched in the utmost confidence of victory to the entrenched camp of the Russians at Moskwa, about 70 miles from Moscow. A battle of two days [Borodino] decided the contest, a murderous battle, which, dreadful as have been those which this age has witnessed, exceeds them all in the horrid work of war, in carnage and destruction. The Russians fled in every direction and left the road open to Moscow. The conqueror lost no time, and a few days after was seated in the Kremlin, the interior of the city, a fortress like the seraglio, that was the ancient seat of empire.

"The erections of Moscow are chiefly of wood . . . Many of their streets have also wood instead of stone for their pavement. Scarcely was the conqueror lodged in the Kremlin when the town around him was fired in every direction by [Russians] appointed for this purpose. All the engines had previously been removed, and the destructive element had unlimited sway for several days . . . The greater part of this unhappy city thus was reduced to ashes" and those "who had devised the plan had the pitiful satisfaction of knowing that they had produced infinitely more misery than the conqueror ever intended."[2]

In the following months' *Surveys* Frend vividly describes

[1] *M.R.*, September 1812.

[2] *Ibid.*, October 1812.

Napoleon's retreat westward, "pursued by numerous hordes of Russians and Cossacks", his arrival at and departure from Dresden, and his battle against the Confederates at Leipzig, with "the loss of an immense number of men, nearly all his ammunition, guns and baggage".

"With the wreck of his army, between 70 and 80,000 men (having lost 60,000) he made the best of his way back towards France."

But the war was by no means over—the Allies had also suffered severe losses, and Napoleon's introduction of conscription raised 300,000 French soldiers, "apparently willing to continue the fight." [1]

Throughout 1813 there was a strong movement in Britain in favour of peace, which it was felt could now be obtained by agreement.

Meetings were held and petitions presented imploring the House of Commons "to reflect on the miseries which this continued and widespread war has inflicted on mankind", stressing "the alarming and unprecedented decay of trade" in various towns, declaring that the people "will be unable to bear the excessive weight of public and parochial taxes, much less sustain these additions . . . if war is persisted in." Frend observed that "the pressure of the rates, while insufficient to help the poor, constantly reduces others to similar distress . . . Peace alone can alleviate the industrious poor, wholly or partially deprived of that employment by which they were accustomed to support their families."

In November Frend declared that the British were sick of war, and suggested that this was a moment when the French might come to some agreement. But the Prince Regent pronounced that peace could not be attained "without further exertions and great pecuniary supplies for the subsidies to the allies." And so the war with its bloodletting and its taxes and levies went on for another five months.

But at last Napoleon's position became apparently hopeless. Wellington arrived at Bordeaux from Spain, and the

[1] *M.R.*, November 1813.

Confederates' armies entered Paris. The Treaty of Paris was signed, and Napoleon packed off to Elba. In March's *Survey* Frend wrote exuberantly, "The sound of peace has been heard. Delightful sound! May it be restored to distracted Europe and may the events of the last twenty years teach men to be more careful how they interfere in the government of other states, and to value the gains of peace and industry above all the plunder to be obtained by war and slaughter." But he was disturbed by many of the treaty's provisions: "France should not be allowed to exercise the slave trade", he protested—it was a means of re-introducing "this monstrous species of commerce" here by a back door. With the restoration of the Bourbons he feared that Popery would return. "In Spain it erects its head with boldness", and "processions are to take place in France" he writes, in June, adding mournfully: "When we contemplate the Inquisition in Spain, the restoration of superstition in France, the invasion of Norway, the prison ships of the slave trade and the wars excited in Africa, Europe seems to be unworthy of its blessings, and we fear that that cannot be lasting which is contaminated by so many horrors."

The Congress of Vienna met in the autumn of 1814 and continued its deliberations well into 1815. Frend followed the proceedings so closely that one is tempted to imagine he was present; but it is unlikely that the *Monthly Repository* sent a roving reporter to Austria, and it was simply his knack of presenting events in his articles that made them appear like first-hand accounts.

Frend scoffed at the elaborate religious ceremonies that dignified the proceedings: "The adoration of the wafer-god was performed with great pomp and solemn devotion"—but otherwise he took the Congress very seriously. He had a low opinion of the journalists covering it, "men with maps before them and scissors to cut out portions as it suits their fancy."—"One principle alone seems to guide the political writers, namely that mankind was made for sovereigns, not sovereigns for mankind . . . The good of the people is the last thing that enters the minds of these sagacious politicians."

The most important proposal that emerged was, he felt, that of the Emperor of Russia "that the number of the military in every country should be diminished." And he commented, "doubtless such a diminution would be of great benefit to every country . . . Europe has presented the most odious and despicable picture that can be contemplated by a reasonable being. The work of blood has been holden in the highest honour, and kings in friendly visits to each other have been entertained with military arrays, each vying with the other in showing the state of preparation he is in for hostile aggression or self-defence. In such a state of mankind it is ridiculous to talk about the blessings of peace . . . When such numbers of men are living by the sword it cannot be long unsheathed . . . "

Frend puts in a plea for general disarmament: "If man is so degraded that each kingdom feels . . . the necessity of being ever prepared for war, then the nations, whatever names they may give to their treaties . . . are living in fact in the state only of armed truce. This is a state contrary to the real end of man on this earth, and it must be corrected by a further advance in civilisation; he is only a half-tamed savage if he is kept within bounds by the fear of the bayonet."[1]

The following month Napoleon escaped from Elba, and Frend rather melodramatically commented, "The name of one man, aided by only a thousand troops, struck a terror in every court in Europe."

Frend believed that the French people supported Napoleon. "Are we," he asked, "to maintain perpetual war to seat a family on the throne of France, contrary to the wishes of the people? . . . If we refuse to make peace with Buonaparte, Europe is doomed to another war." He forecast gloomily "the hordes of Cossacks, the disciplined legions of Prussia, English troops, being reassembled; and the addition of a thousand

[1] *M.R.*, February 1815.

million to the national debt could not be viewed without considerable agitation."[1]

With characteristic courage Frend stuck to the view that Napoleon would be a better, more progressive ruler than the Bourbons:

"Buonaparte has decreed that the slave trade shall no longer be carried on by Frenchmen; he has openly declared for the freedom of the press; . . . declared freedom of religion to be irrevocable. Why are the French not to be allowed the right of settling their internal government as they please? and why are they to be dictated to in this respect by foreign nations?"

After Waterloo, however, Frend admitted that the battle was "most decisive". "The ruin of the [French army] was complete, and the conquerors followed up their victory with such rapidity that Paris fell into their hands without a blow . . . The Emperor of Russia arrived in time to save the bridge of Jena, which Blucher had made plans to destroy (because it recalled a French victory over Prussia). Paris had many similar monuments to the heroism of its great military chief, but their names have been changed, and thus the fury of the conqueror has been averted."

"The thrones of the Bourbons are re-established", the *Survey* admits sorrowfully in July 1815. "They are now sovereigns at Paris, Naples and Madrid, and their conduct in their different seats of government will form very curious pages of future history."

In August Frend again shakes his head over the position in France: "The Bourbons were brought back by the bayonets of an enemy and it is problematical whether this stay would be secure if these bayonets were withdrawn."

* * *

So the long era of European war ended, with things no better for the majority of the populations, and in some

[1] *M.R.*, February 1815.

countries far worse. For England, peace meant a state of crisis and poverty except for the *nouveaux riches* and war profiteers who could live off their recent pickings. Europe, our market for munitions and war supplies, now took no more of these or of many other goods.

The Continent established itself again and in Britain, as exports fell off, unemployment spread like a blight. Manufacturers attempted to solve their problems of high costs and dwindling profits by cutting wages, lengthening the working day, intensifying labour—but even these harsh measures failed to bring in orders. In fact they increased distress by reducing purchasing power at home.

Following good harvests in 1814, corn prices had fallen, and farmers were now demanding new laws to insure their profits. When the Corn Laws were passed, popular agitation became uncontrollable; misery and starvation drove labourers and countryfolk to far more widespread and violent rioting than in 1811 and 1812, when there had been alarming "risings". The panic-stricken government rushed troops and yeomanry to the disturbed areas, where labourers accused of rioting or of burning property were arrested, and tried on the evidence of spies and informers. The magistrates conducting the trials were pro-Government clergy, who had little sympathy for the accused and meted out sentences of hanging to many of the ringleaders as an example to the disaffected.

There were of course manifold proposals and much activity to alleviate conditions, ranging from the establishment-sponsored "National Society for the Relief of Distress" (which Reformers mocked for its inadequacy, and to which Cobbett pointed out that "what the labourers wanted was not charity but higher wages") to the radical Spencean group which called for direct action.

The latter organized a mass meeting on 15 November 1818 in Spa Fields, where Henry Hunt spoke in fiery terms. In spite of his tirade the crowd was orderly and the resolution and address to the Prince Regent mild. This sedate behaviour failed to produce anything but an expression of regret from the Home Secretary, and a donation towards the Spitalfields Soup Committee.

Undeterred, the same group called another meeting, on 2 December, and this time there were 100,000 people present in Spa Fields, determined to obtain some result. Hunt urged that there should be no violence and that another petition for Reform be sent to Parliament. But he was forestalled by a group of Spencean revolutionaries who held a meeting of their own in a corner of the field, and made off towards the City in a riotous crowd. (It seems probable that the disturbances were engineered by provocateurs to bring disrepute on the radical Reformers.)

William Frend, living in the heart of the City, wrote to Annabella Milbanke—now Lady Byron: "I fear the papers tomorrow will give an account of riot, confusion and bloodshed."—"A meeting had been advertised in Spa Fields, but the notoriety of it seem'd to me to dissipate any cause of alarm & the march of troops last night by my house convinc'd me that government was fully aware of the danger & prepared to suppress it.

"I was surprised however on stepping out to find most of the shops in Fleet Street, Ludgate Hill & Cheapside shut up . . . in consequence of a party of rioters appearing at the top of Fleet Market who broke into a gun shop in Skinner Street, wounded the Shopman & seized a quantity of arms; thence they went down to the Tower & a gentleman come from that quarter told me that he heard the reports of guns, but whether they had encountered the Military or not is not known. A party is also said to be in Moorfields where the military are said to have fired upon them.

"Another party is reported to have gone to the Kings Bench prison to release Lord Cochrane but the great body is in Spa Fields & of its proceedings I have not had any accounts.

"I pass'd a party of light dragoons five & twenty in number stationd at the top of Cheapside, which will be sufficient guard to the avenue from Newgate Street. The night will scarcely pass over without some temporary tumult at some part of the town but the vigilance of the Lord Mayor will I think preserve the city quiet & the military will soon dissipate the rioters in other quarters."[1]

Frend was not in favour of revolutionary violence, and he remarked on this occasion, "It is melancholy to think that there is such a spirit in the lower orders." But he was still in heart a radical, understood the reasons for this "spirit" and laid blame where it belonged—particularly on the new Corn Laws.

"The passing of the Corn Bill has been in my opinion the occasion of a great injury to the country", he wrote early in December. "The land owners in pursuing their private interests were not sufficiently attentive to the general welfare of the kingdom . . . "

On 13 December he told Lady Byron, "We are all perfectly quiet in London thanks to our Lord Mayor who is beyond all praise. The parliament may however produce confusion. It has an awful task to perform. May God grant our Senators wisdom!"[2]

Frend's prayer was not heard; the Senators showed extreme folly in tackling their "awful task". They appointed Committees to examine evidence of conspiracy against the government, despite Lord Cochrane's amendment denying that the Reform meetings were disturbing the peace.

On 4 March 1817, panicky at the unrest and growing clamour for Reform, the government passed four laws, suspending Habeas Corpus, restricting freedom of assembly and suppressing radical societies. William Cobbett sailed away to America just in time to avoid the wave of arrests of "subversive" editors and writers. Although William Hone, the satirist, and Thomas Wooler, editor of the *Black Dwarf*, were acquitted by special juries in 1817, many were less lucky, when the "gagging acts" (as Place called them) began to take effect.

[1] W.F. to A.B., 2.12.1816.
[2] *Ibid.*, 13.12.1816.

The Radical leaders who might have headed a movement to restore some sanity, Hunt, Place and Burdett, had quarrelled and were hardly on speaking terms; it was not till after two years of repression when brutality culminated in the Peterloo massacre of August 1819 that they closed their ranks, and then they were not free to organize effective opposition.

Hunt, who had addressed the Manchester meeting, was imprisoned and later sentenced for conspiracy, and Sir Francis Burdett, who protested vigorously against the massacre, was arrested and arraigned at Leicester in March 1820. After several more months' litigation, the letter Burdett had addressed to his constituents urging "the gentlemen of England to head Public Meetings . . . to put a stop in its commencement to a reign of terror and blood", was pronounced a libel. The baronet was fined £2,000 and gaoled for three months—this time in King's Bench prison, where as before he was allowed books and visitors (though the less affluent Hunt suffered third degree treatment in Bristol gaol).

The faithful Frend visited Burdett regularly, taking on one occasion nine-year-old Sophia and a Bible—in which, the little girl noticed "he did not show any interest."[1] But it would have taken more than a lack of interest to discourage Frend from what he considered right.

* * *

Throughout the troubled decade 1809 to 1819 Frend was consistently loyal both to causes and to people: there are letters to him from Cambridge contemporaries with whom he kept up: cheerful letters describing leisure occupations in rural retreats, mournful communications telling of illness and death (Theophilus Lindsey had died in 1808, Matthew Robinson in 1810, the Duke of Grafton in 1811), and neat reports (which sometimes accompanied a turkey or farm

[1] S. De Morgan: *op. cit.*, pp. 10–12.

produce) from John Hammond, on the progress of his children at school, or his efforts to politicize Fenland.

One letter is written on the blank side of a printed form petitioning Parliament on Dissenters' rights, sent to Hammond "by Dr Disney in order to procure signatures in his neighbourhood." This was brought to Frend by George Dyer, who often acted as postman for the Fen Stanton and Paxton households; "Mr Dyer", Hammond wrote, "will explain to you in what state he left good Mr Reynolds. It appears from a letter . . . written by his Hairdresser but dictated by Mr Reynolds himself that he still continues confined to his bed and in great pain."[1]

Richard Reynolds, the champion of the poor of Huntingdonshire, died soon after, to Frend's great sorrow.

Another kind of sorrow is reflected in Frend's correspondence of 1815 and 1816—that between him and Annabella Milbanke, newly married to Lord Byron. The notes wishing her future happiness in her marriage, with tributes to Byron's genius, have a sad retrospective irony. Frend had had high hopes and had predicted, according to Augusta Leigh that "you [Annabella] and B will not be a vulgar fashionable pair". (Augusta had added that "the idea that you found it more *comfortable* to return home after the Play instead of going to a Party and Ball is *very unfashionable*.")[2]

A few days after the wedding Frend sent "heart-felt congratulations on the change in your situation . . . To this event I have been looking forward with that anxiety which I feel for your welfare."

He added "I perceive by the papers of today that Lord B.'s name is put in connection with some Hebrew melodies. Nothing could afford me greater pleasure than to see the Lyre of David & Esaiah [*sic*] resting in his hands, for who so able to do justice to the sublimest poetry?" He asked to be remembered to his Lordship "as one whose prayers to heaven will be for your mutual happiness . . ." Lord B.'s *Childe*

[1] Hammond to W.F., 28.1.1811.

[2] M. Elwin: *Lord Byron's Wife*, p. 308.

Harold was not particularly to Frend's taste, but he tried hard to give the poet the benefit of the doubt: "I have no doubt of his surpassing himself when he contemplates man in the more dignified point of view . . . & in his lays commemorates those who have been the ornaments of our species."[1]

"I look forward with pleasing anxiety to the day when I may salute you a mother", he wrote on hearing that Annabella was expecting a baby. Ada Byron was born on 10 December 1815, and in January 1816, after just a year of unhappy marriage, Annabella left Byron and went home with the baby to Seaham. Sir Ralph Milbanke wrote to tell Byron that she would not return. Whoever was responsible for the break up, Frend's sympathy lay entirely with Annabella, and he wrote offering "all the support of friendship in my power—no instance of your confidence will be abused."

On 11 April 1816, he "rejoices to hear that you are so near the termination of the business", and hopes "that past events will not prey too much on your mind." In May, he "hoped that you begin to feel yourself relieved from the fatigue and anxiety which were the results of late occurrences. Such a trial as you have undergone could not but produce some temporary effects both on the frame of your body and your mind . . . As for your mind I am convinced that this rough encounter will tend only to fix more deeply in it the good principles with which it is embued."

Frend had on a previous occasion given Annabella advice on managing her income—"Little did we think then that a reverse of circumstances might seem to render it superfluous", he sighed.[2]

Thereafter he was always ready to help her in her financial affairs as well as in matters concerned with her (to his mind) erring husband who was trying to contact her. Frend expressed anxiety on 4 May, "that you had received a letter from a certain quarter with intimations also from other

[1] W.F. to A.B., 17.8.1815.

[2] *Ibid.*, 4.5.1816.

persons . . . I am fully convinced that they are designed to ensnare you & thus prepared you will be upon your guard . . . I should be extremely cautious how I committed myself upon paper & in fact I scarcely see how any correspondence can be kept up without danger to yourself. There have been instances when parties separated have communicated with each other their feelings respecting those objects which are interesting to both, but yours is a very particular case & requires much more circumspection."

Annabella received many letters from Frend that summer, advising her to travel, recommending Barmouth for a holiday, telling her not to give up mathematics, urging her to learn Hebrew, or if she preferred "a living language, Welsh", to take her mind off her troubles. His disapproval of Byron was restrained but evident: "I have not seen the farewell to England & do not feel my curiosity excited", he wrote on 21 June 1816. "It will probably fall in my way next week, when I shall give it a perusal."

He had however read two volumes of the *roman à clef* by Caroline Lamb, *Glenarvon* (but "not the third volume in which your ladyship is said to make her appearance".) "Since my return to town a key has been given to me of the characters in this horrid tale which is read I find according to the vulgar expression by everybody."

On 16 December he wrote that "I dined in company the other day with a gentleman who was on the lake with Lord B. in one of those gales in which it seems he takes delight but I should have been better pleased with my old friend if he had been less attach'd to talent & more to moral character."

To Annabella's letter expressing anxiety lest Ada should inherit her father's nature, Frend answered, "it is evident that children do not always inherit the disposition of the parents, for very virtuous characters have been unfortunate, if I may use that term, in their parents. But whether there is any of the sort of influence you allude to I am sure that providence has left us the means of counteracting it." [1]

[1] W.F. to A.B., 21.6.1816.

In spite of his rather priggish and preaching attitude, Frend must have been a source of comfort and strength to poor Annabella; one hopes that she was able to follow his advice on her troubles, particularly that of 21 August 1816: "There is only one way of seeing these things. Place yourself in the Sun & all the irregularities which we think we observe in the planetary motions disappear."

* * *

Apart from these, Frend wrote few letters at this period except for those connected with the Rock or Unitarian business. There are pages and pages covered with mathematical formulae and problems of premiums and life-probability, but not the long discursive screeds of earlier—and subsequent—times.

When not working out calculations he was fully absorbed in his other work—his articles for the *Monthly Repository*. And one has the impression, as one turns over the material accumulated during the terrible years of the Napoleonic wars and the anxious peace, that Frend's life in Blackfriars was that of a working journalist—the family and social background nebulous, the real setting the stormy scene of war and political upheaval: Frend himself, as it were, very much alone with his thoughts and his conscience on a bark riding the roaring waves.

From 1820 on, the letters, journals, reminiscences, take us into an utterly different world, which we enter with a certain feeling of relief.

19
COUNTRY LIFE

IN 1820 IT seemed as though Sidmouth's strong-arm tactics had worked and that the government was in control of the situation. In fact, the people were no more amenable, but the economic state of the country was healthier, life slightly more tolerable.

Popular discontent still found expression in the irrepressible *Black Dwarf* and other pamphlets, but riots had ceased and though many "agitators" were in gaol there were no major political trials after that of Henry Hunt in March. Cobbett who had sailed away to America in 1817 thought it safe to return to England in late 1819, and write the *Political Register* though in a less fiery vein than formerly. A comparatively peaceful decade lay ahead.

William Frend, though as keen as ever on Parliamentary Reform, was now in his sixties, very busy in the Rock Office, and less active in politics, more concerned with his home life and in bringing up his seven young children than in journalism.

That year the family moved from Blackfriars to the small country town of Stoke Newington, some seven miles from the city centre.

For William it had the advantage of being within reach of his office and of his many London friends; and for the children it was a much healthier environment than the gloomy insalubrious district of Blackfriars.

Their new home was a fine old house adjacent to fields which extended beyond King's Cross. It had at one time been the home of Dr Isaac Watts and also of Daniel Defoe and boasted a secret door in oak panelling through which Defoe used to escape from his political persecutors. It had beautiful wooded grounds, a garden which provided flowers and vegetables and a field big enough to keep not only chickens but two cows.

Sophia Frend "greatly delighted in its clean, white, wainscoted rooms with clusters of roses peeping in at the window, its spacious recesses and unsuspected nooks and cupboards, and above all its large beautiful garden full of trees such as we seldom see near London."[1]

Family letters from Stoke express delight with everything. Mrs Frend wrote to Sophia in May 1824, that "we are all much interested with our garden and have procured some new plants", while her husband boasted of his flowering shrubs: "Last Saturday we made an excursion to Kew Gardens & notwithstanding the fine show we saw, my own Rhododendrons & Azalias did not lose their attraction and I can enjoy the caradrons & other Mays now in all their glory."[2]

There were fauna as well as flora for their delectation: "Frances (the second daughter) has two broods of chickens to take care of, one of six, the other of five." On 2 June "Frances is completely occupied with her chickens", though "she is rather unfortunate, having lost some little ones. Henry's little black bantam hen too died with the heavy cold rains . . . " Mrs Frend had bought "a very pretty little cow . . . as good a milker as the finest cow we have had & quite a beauty in the field."

The children were blissful: "Harriet & Alicia are very happy at school & Frances seems more satisfied now that Mrs Lewis comes to her." Richard, the delicate boy, was becoming stronger; Henry, happy as a sandboy, apart from the loss of his bantam; and the baby in fine form: "Dear little Alf has been running about with us all breakfast time, he is very well and looks quite rosy", according to his proud mother. "He is becoming a perfect parrot: upon his Papa's and Uncle's coming in from town together, he looked from one to the other and pointed at his Papa and said 'Papa',

[1] S. De Morgan, *op. cit.*, p. 86.

[2] W.F. to Sophia Frend, 2.6.1824.

and then at his Uncle—'More Papa'. And has called him 'More Papa' ever since."[1]

Sophia was now seventeen, old enough to go visiting on her own; her father wrote her long gossipy letters about domestic happenings.

"We had a famous thunderstorm the night before last. Great anxiety for Frances and Mother who had walked to Clapton & returned just as we were sending emissaries in quest of them. The grass plot was a perfect lake." He tells her that "we cut our first melon yesterday at dinner & the Misses Hart came in the evening to finish it."

Melon, he regrets, does not agree with him but "they say it was excellent." He mentions that "I dined in company with Sir Francis Burdett the other day, who pressed me much to come to him in Wiltshire."

On the eve of Sophia's first ball, at her uncle's house in Somerset, her parents were almost as nervous as their daughter: Mrs Frend wrote that she had not the least objection to this Ball "which cannot be considered as a *coming out* but as an accidental thing," and trusts her aunt to assist her in choice of dress.

William did not presume to advise Sophia on what to wear but he offered a few tips on correct deportment: "Young as you are, yet I can trust you in a ball-room without any fear of your being guilty of impropriety: yet there are a few things worth your knowing . . . The main point is to avoid affectation of every kind, whether in walk, gesture or talk . . . In the common modes of dancing you have had instruction enough, and of them I say nothing. Anything like romping in dancing is to be carefully avoided. There is a certain distance to be moved over in a given time. I have seen girls hurrying through twice that distance and thinking they had done a great feat; but in fact they only made themselves ridiculous, and looked like hoydens. Mind your time and the figure of the dance . . . Few are there that can make either a good bow or a good curtsey. I care not whether it is a low

[1] Mrs Frend to Sophia Frend, 2.6.1824.

one, as in my time, or a nod, or a clip, as is now the fashion ... The great secret is to carry with you a cheerful and innocent heart, desirous of giving and receiving all the satisfaction which the amusement is capable of affording ..."

Life in Stoke Newington seems to have flowed along smoothly and pleasantly for the young Frends. They were healthy happy children, apart from Richard, the second boy who, though exceptionally intelligent, was a cripple and always delicate. The rest led a carefree normal life, attending the Stoke dame school, or having tuition from visiting teachers, with special lessons from their father in his favourite subjects. There were frequently family outings, to London museums, to Kew, to exhibitions. They went for long walks or for picnics in the fields "under a hedge in the favourite spot, Prospect Hill."[1]

It may have been on one such outing that Frend saw the birdcatcher snaring goldfinches by a cruel operation which moved him to write his *Memoirs of a Goldfinch*—a rather touching little poem, much superior to the *Appeal to the Volunteers*. Frend was no poet, but he evidently felt deeply what he saw and compared the sufferings of the birds aptly enough with those of the human prisoners he had so often championed.

The poem is preceded by an attractive "Note" showing Frend's power of observation and his love of nature:

"The bird is an eager devourer of the winged seed of the thistle, from which it takes one of its names—the thistle-finch. A flock of goldfinches is frequently seen in the bright weather of early autumn, detected, perhaps, first by the trembling of the rigid stalks of the crop of dry thistles; when, as the observer approaches the spot, numbers of little golden wings glitter in the sun, and, after a short flutter, are hidden again at a little distance by the downy tops of an adjacent cluster of the weeds, the chearful call being repeated, as the birds hang on the quivering branch.

[1] W.F. to Sophia Frend, 18.6.1824.

"The bird-catcher finds dry seedy thistles an excellent lime for the goldfinch and accordingly sticks them about the nets. The 'net' is 'tight-strained' on two separate rectangular frames . . . with a space between them which they are capable of folding over . . . A smart jerk given by a long cord held by the birdman at a distance causes them to rise quickly and fold over the space between them."

The thistle plants bedeck'd the ground,
The tight strain'd net in ambush lay;
The well trained brace-bird peck'd around;
The call-birds summons issued gay.

Down merrily the youngsters flew—
The dext'rous fowler jerk'd the strings.
In vain th'astonish'd captive crew
Batter'd the twine with crumpled wings.

In grated prison foul'd and dreary
Where motley crowded captives lay,
The stronger trampling on the weary
In wild confusion and dismay
And why or how to us unknown,
In darkness closed, our mournful throng
With frequent justling shocks o'erthrown,
Heated and faint was borne along.

On the occasion of one country walk Frend demonstrated his sense of justice and his physical strength when nearing the age of seventy: his grand-daughter recalls how "coming home across a lonely path in company with a scientific friend" Frend met a young girl who was being molested by a man and who appealed to him for help.

"Bidding his companion take the offender by the feet, himself took him by the shoulders and carried him to an adjacent pond to be chastized . . . My grandfather chose a green corner of the pond, covered with weed, and at his instigation the unhappy man was ducked therein."[1]

* * *

One of the main attractions of Stoke Newington was its cultural and social life. Since Mrs Letitia Barbauld the poet and some of her close friends had settled there, it was the gathering ground for many intellectuals who came out to visit and were entertained by the local people. Frend had many guests, and himself went calling, taking a selection of children with him.

Mrs Barbauld was a broad-minded woman, very welcoming and kind, and she put Sophia and Frances up at her home, down the road from their own, while Defoe's old house was being re-decorated. Sophia remembered her as "a very thin old lady, small and delicate-looking with a kind and pleasant face, wearing a 'front' of flaxen curls, a white cap, and dress of slate-coloured silk with a short train . . . "[2]

The poetess had a passion for highbrow parlour games, which the young Frends found "too intellectual and too little fun" and made Sophia "feel a dunce and a failure." But there was the consolation of meeting all kinds of interesting people, some of them strangers but others who were old friends. Charles Lamb came (a "small man quaint and old-fashioned-looking") and Crabb Robinson, and of course George Dyer, eccentric as ever, who would arrive "sadly uncouth and slovenly in appearance." Mrs Barbauld's niece, Anna, once saw him picking up a coal-scuttle in mistake for his hat, and on another occasion, when alone in the parlour, entering into a conversation with a marble bust of Diana in mistake for his hostess.

Anna said "he always had a fatal habit of kissing us on his arrival which we always tried to avoid."[3]

[1] S. De Morgan: *op. cit.*, p. xxxii.

[2] *Ibid.*, p. 87.

[3] Rodgers: *Georgian Chronicle*, p. 186.

But everyone loved Dyer, and there was much rejoicing among his friends when it was said that he had been left a legacy by Lord Stanhope, whose children he had once tutored. Dyer refused the legacy, to everybody's regret, but he was persuaded to accept a small annuity instead. This led Lamb, in one of his teasing moods, to ask Dyer "if the common report was true that he was to be made a Lord?" Dyer was terribly upset: "Oh dear no, Mr Lamb, I couldn't think of such a thing!"—"I thought not", said Lamb, "and I contradict it wherever I go." But he scared Dyer by declaring that the Government "would not ask a person's consent, but would raise one to the peerage without any warning."

Frend teased him too, but was devoted to him. The incident described by Lamb of Dyer falling into the river is well known but it may not be remembered that it was William Frend who was called by Lamb to Dyer's bedside when he seemed in danger of succumbing to his ducking; for Frend was his executor, and for fifty years his adviser and close confidant.

It was to Frend that Dyer came for advice about a proposal of marriage which was made to him, late in life, by a worthy widow, Mrs Mather. The lady had been married three times before, and, according to Sophia Frend, her father went in some alarm to the chambers of the designing widow who had already buried three husbands. "But she was so simple, so open, and so evidently kind-hearted that, after examining and comparing all the circumstances he [Frend] thought that his old friend's happiness would be secured by the marriage. It took place shortly after, in St Dunstan's Church in Fleet Street." Sophia goes on to say that "when the newly-married pair came to visit us at Stoke Newington we were pleased to find her a sensible kind-hearted woman who had made of our neglected old friend a fine-looking well-dressed elderly man, beaming with kindness and happiness."[1]

This is confirmed by Cowden Clarke, who voiced "the

[1] S. De Morgan: *op. cit.*, pp. 75–76.

great general gratification of Dyer's friends to see how the old student's rusty suit of black, threadbare and shining with the shabbiness of neglect, the limp wisp of jaconet muslin, yellow with age, round his throat, the dusty shoes and stubbly beard, had become exchanged for a coat that shone only with the lustre of regular brushing, a snow-white cravat neatly tied on, brightly blacked shoes and a close-shaven chin, the whole man presenting a cosy and burnished appearance like one carefully and affectionately tended."[1]

Besides Dyer and Lamb, many literary people and philosophers of various nationalities visited Stoke Newington between 1819 and 1826. Sophia mentions an eminent Indian religious reformer, Rammohun Roy; she was impressed by his "dark sparkling eyes" and his flowing oriental robes, and "rejoiced in the beautiful bit of colour on our green lawn and still more when I listened to his conversation." One of the local Dissenters, of a poetic turn of mind, observed that "the star of the East shone over our humble Suburb"; but the chief Unitarian minister was very suspicious of all the foreign visitors and disapproved of Frend. At a tea-drinking party of the ladies of his congregation, this reverend gentleman pronounced that "if there is a queer fish in the world he will find his way to Frend's house." To which, Sophia with great presence of mind demurely replied, "Pardon me, sir, I do not remember our having had the pleasure of seeing you there."[2]

* * *

During the years he lived at Stoke Newington Frend devoted much of his leisure to one of the subjects nearest his heart—the advancement of education. He was interested in all its aspects, from the upbringing of his own children to the experiment of Joseph Lancaster, from the reform of the Public

[1] Cowden Clarke, quoted in Emmanuel College Magazine, 1905, p. 213.

[2] S. De Morgan: *op. cit.*, p. 96.

Schools and universities to the forming of Mechanics' Institutes. His letters to Lady Byron are packed with reflections and maxims on the subject: "There is nothing like experiment . . . "—"If we were better taken care of in our early years, the effects would be seen in each generation"—"Education is not to be confined to the early period of life; we are throughout in a state of education, always finding something to learn"—"If in our progress we never think of the most important subject but take upon trust what has been poured into us in youth, we remain children through life." [1]

He put his theories into practice with his own girls and boys and reported progress to Lady Byron, who in her turn frequently asked his advice on her own little daughter, Ada's, education. Frend's opinions on particular forms of schooling were just as decided as on general education. He strongly disliked the emphasis on classics in British schools. "The faults of our publick schools are notorious", he told Lady Byron, in February 1829: "At Eton, Winchester & Westminster the whole of their attention is paid to what is called classical literature & the instructors are in general tolerably proficient in that branch of knowledge, but I very much doubt that there is one of them if addressed by a person in Latin could keep up a conversation with him & as to Greek, to think of asking him to write a letter off hand in that language would argue a perfect ignorance of the system in those schools. As to the boys themselves, not one in ten acquires anything like a tolerable proficiency in what they are supposed to be learning, and as to morals and manners they are still more deficient."

He praised the method of Joseph Lancaster's schools for poor children. "If a scale were laid down to be given to each boy for his attainments in classics, mathematics and Natural Philosophy", Frend said, "I would pit 100 of the best boys in this school against 100 selected from any of the public schools of equal ages."

[1] W.F. to A.B., 27.2.1829.

To prove his point, he added that "I heard of an instance of the publick school teaching the other day in a young lad just come from one of them who felt sensibly the waste of his time, & feeling it, had the courage to begin . . . his education anew."

One thing Frend was quite sure about: "The first thing to be done . . . is to get education out of the hands of the Clergy; and in this opinion I was glad to find one of the best Tutors in one of our Universities coinciding with me, & he desired no other reform in them than that the restraint on fellows of Colleges with respect to [holy] orders should be taken off." Soon, he thought, "you would have instructors unembarrassed by the garb & habits of a fictitious character. Their minds would be improved by literature & knowledge of the world; & if at a later period of life they went into the Church they would not make the worse clergymen."[1]

As to higher education, his Cambridge experiences had made him into a crusader for religious freedom and toleration, and, as Sophia says, "he was well qualified to estimate the value of university training and the great loss and deprivation sustained by young men . . . who were unable from religious belief to receive it." Frend looked forward to the day "when good conduct and compliance with rules should be the only conditions of admission."

He had aired his conception of a University "in which the highest academical teaching should be given without reference to religious differences" in some letters signed "Civis", published in a monthly periodical edited by John Thelwall in 1819. Sophia firmly believed that these letters led to the founding of London University.[2]

"A short time after the publication of the letters, Mr Thomas Campbell the poet first visited Frend, and informed him that Mr Brougham and Dr Birkbeck with himself and one or two others believed that the time was come to make the attempt. I was about twelve years old when Mr

[1] W.F. to A.B., 27.2.1829.

[2] S. De Morgan, *op. cit.*, pp. 102 207.

Brougham dined with my father to consult upon it. Some meetings took place, other liberal men joined them and after some delay the first active committee was formed."

Frend was prevented by a severe illness from taking an active part in the first meetings—he fell sick in 1826, and had to retire from the Rock Co. and all other work for two years. But on his recovery he joined the general committee, became a shareholder, and on the election of a council and officers he was appointed one of four auditors. Sophia wrote that "the establishment of University College, called at first the London University, promised to fulfil the hopes of all friends of education and was hailed as a forerunner of religious freedom. My father took the liveliest interest in its progress."[1]

This interest is expressed in two letters which survive, from Frend to Mr Thomas Coates, the Registrar: "I am very sorry" he says "that a particular engagement prevents me from attending the session of the Council today. I should be very happy in forwarding to the utmost of my power the object in view . . . " But he foresees trouble: "I am fearful that the design of the building sent round to the Proprietors will have a bad effect as the inevitable expence of it may discourage many & the length of time before it can be completed is a still further objection."[2]

This and a later note reflect some of the difficulties, economic and otherwise, besetting those responsible for constructing and administering new universities, in the nineteenth as well as in our own century. "The University begins well, but it requires time and much exertion before it can vie with the older institutions", says Frend, and makes various suggestions for the Council's consideration. Certain inefficiencies in the clerical department might be avoided: he had been requested for a contribution which he had already given and had had receipted. They had not acknowledged a gift of books: "I gave directions to my bookseller three months ago to send some Mathematical and Philo-

[1] S. De Morgan: *Memoir of Augustus De Morgan*, pp. 22, 23, 24.

[2] W.F. Letter, University College Library, 3.6.1826.

sophical works that came into my possession to different persons and institutions and among them intended the University of London. Have you received them? The astronomical society acknowledged the receipt by a printed letter & if you have not such a plan I beg leave to recommend to you the adoption of the same plan."

Frend goes on to mention that he had, as executor for Robert Tyrwhitt, transferred £4,000 to Cambridge University which was used to found three scholarships of Hebrew literature, in the name of the giver. He suggests that "a few scholarships of this kind would be very beneficial to the new institution & a Rothschild's foundation for the Hebrew would be a trifle to him & creditable to his name. But if we cannot expect these gifts & bequests immediately, a beginning might be made in another way & some prizes form'd to be given away immediately after the summer vacation." Ways and means had been worked out with Frend's usual mathematical accuracy, to be put before the Council for consideration. Frend assures the Registrar that he "has the prosperity of the University much at heart and the greatest confidence in its ultimate success."[1]

The story of the University's not untroubled early years has been told elsewhere, but perhaps a passage from Sophia's memoirs may throw a little extra light on the reason for its difficulties.

"A few of the most liberal thinkers of the time gave their best help to the completion of the design, but the large body of men who had been trained under University discipline held aloof from an institution from which religious tests were excluded and which might at some time compete with the two Universities (Oxford and Cambridge) bound up as they were by old usage with the interests of the Established Church . . . Thus, with the exception of the few enlightened scholars who generally held out a hand to their less fortunate brethren, the founders of the London University were either liberal politicians, not always familiar with the details of

[1] W.F. Letter, University College Library.

academic discipline, or mercantile men . . . with little experience of securing concord and due balance in the relations of governing body, teacher and pupil."[1]

However the teething troubles eventually came to an end, and Frend's confidence was amply justified.

* * *

Over the years Frend had assembled his ideas on education and written them up in the form of "Letters to an hitherto undescribed Country", which he "intended to be left to the discretion of executors to throw into the fire or to publish." The original manuscript has disappeared but extracts from it were published in a little book called *A Plan of Universal Education*, in 1832.

Here Frend's ideal school is presented through the eyes of a visitor, who describes every day in the academic week: Monday, for instance, "Slate, writing and repetition schools & a holiday"; Tuesday, "Viva voce and minor schools"; Wednesday, "Boys' lecture, riding school—land surveying," and so on. The audience at the "boys' lecture" consisted of "about fifteen hundred" assembled in the school theatre to hear several boys discourse on topography, overshot mills worked by forcing pump, "the application of water to machinery of various kinds", illustrated by models, including a small artificial lake. Scientific equipment for demonstrating applied science was a most important part of education—and expense, in Frend's ideal community, no object whatsoever.

The one absolutely essential factor in education, he considered, was the combination of theory and practice; he insists on the pupils attending the "experimental school" where all sorts of scientific experiments were carried out, showing for instance "the effects of various modes of loading waggons and carts as they were to move on plane ground or up and down hills." The visitor is made to remark, "I could

[1] S. De Morgan: *Memoir of Augustus De Morgan*, p. 24.

not but observe among the spectators several who appeared to be farmers' servants or draymen: and . . . it is a common practice for farmers to give their men an opportunity of being at this school & thus overcoming the prejudices which are prevalent in that class in many countries."

It is not quite clear whether the farmers or the servants were prejudiced, but Frend, anti-bigot as always, was determined that his system should break down barriers and be thoroughly democratic.

He considered (as he writes in this booklet) that "Man has been degraded . . . from the sordid selfishness of the few and the brutal ignorance of the many" and this state of things must be replaced by universal and equal education if the world is to become a happier place.[1]

With characteristic precision Frend had worked out the means by which his scheme could be implemented; first of all by appropriating the revenues of the cathedral and collegiate churches of the realm. (Was he, one wonders, subconsciously taking revenge on the race of prelates, some of whom—Ely, Carlisle, Llandaff—had bitterly opposed him in the past?) He suggested trying out his plan at his home town of Canterbury, using his own old school: "The present school, the chapter-house and another building . . . will give accomodation for more than five hundred boys. The professors and teachers must at first submit to temporary inconvenience and be lodged in the town." But they would later take over the houses of the canons and prebendaries; "the deanery would of course be preserved when vacant, for saloons", while "the open spaces about the cathedral would be easily converted into excellent play-grounds; and it need not be here repeated that play-grounds are, in the education of youth, of as much importance as schools." [2]

He defended his plan for expropriating the surplus income of the Church by inviting anyone interested to "Visit a cathedral on a week-day and see how few persons are present,

[1] Frend: *Universal Education*, p. 119.
[2] *Ibid.*, pp. 114, 115.

and then determine which is the best mode of employing an income: that for singing and praying . . . or for instilling into youth the information necessary for good conduct in future life. The successors of the deans and prebendaries will not be inferior to them in moral, religious and literary attainments."[1]

One cannot help feeling that Frend was out to shock—and he probably succeeded; he was as much an *enfant terrible* in his seventies as in his twenties when he was rebelling against authority in Cambridge. And if Isaac Milner happened to read his booklet, so much the better! But behind his apparently unrealistic and outrageous proposals there was much good educational sense and some principles which could well be applied in the world today. As for instance, "Opinions here (in the ideal school) are free as air, and man is judged only by his actions"; and "The education of the females was as much attended to as that of the men, however it might be directed also to objects more peculiar to them."[2]

* * *

The Frends decided in 1830 to go back to live in London. There were good reasons for this, but it was a wrench to leave Stoke Newington. Sophia doubtless spoke for her father as well as herself when she wrote in her *Memories*, "It was a sorrow to me in many ways when we left our old house . . . Every blossoming tree—and there were many of rare beauty —had been a friend and companion."

For Sophia "the greatest grief of all was to bid farewell to the large spreading oak in the field", which had a seat among the branches, up to which she used to climb on fine mornings and read voraciously: Spenser's *Faerie Queene*, books on natural philosophy and chemistry, and "better than all, metaphysical works such as Thomas Browne's Essays and Cousin's Histoire de la Philosophie."

It was "far from being a systematic course of intellectual

[1] Frend: *Universal Education*, p. 117.
[2] *Ibid.*, p. 50.

training", Sophia admits[1]—but one of which her father (if he knew of it) must surely have approved.

The family spent a winter at Hastings, where William worked on a system of decimal coinage, helped in the organization of a co-operative store, and talked Reform to the fishermen, while Sophia studied and went for long walks on the hills with the poet Thomas Campbell. They settled in Tavistock Square in London towards the end of 1831—a time of hectic political activity and countless meetings and debates preceding the First Reform Bill.

Frend's interest in politics had revived, and he emerged again, at the age of seventy-four as an enthusiastic crusader for Reform.

[1] S. De Morgan: *Three Score Years and Ten*, p. 108.

20

LIVELY OLD AGE

AFTER MANY YEARS of active service and two serious illnesses, William Frend might now have been expected to opt out of public life. He had had to retire from the Rock Co. through sickness in 1826, and had a relapse in 1829 which he told his friends would probably be fatal. He feared he would not live to read his antiquarian friend Godfrey Higgins' new book, he said. Higgins wrote a reassuring letter: "I see no reason why you should not live as long as old Maseres and be to the last as healthy. If I had you to manage and *could* manage you I would make you live as long."

He offered good advice about posture: "You should have a chair exactly like mine" and "a table with a drawer in it to rise and fall, so that when you write you would have your paper almost up to your chin . . . When I write over a common table I soon have a severe difficulty of breathing from bending down but I know how to prevent it."

Another friend wrote some weeks later that "the account you give of yourself towards the latter part of your letter made up for the fright the first four pages kept me in & I hope you will now enjoy the otium dig for many many years to come."[1]

Otium cum dignitate is defined by Brewer as "Retirement after a person has given up business and has saved enough to live upon in comfort."

This was to be Frend's happy lot, if indeed the whirl of activity into which he threw himself on recovery can be described as retirement.

Between his return to health at the end of 1829 and 1840 Frend seems never to have relaxed or put his feet up. He travelled a good deal (there are letters from Brighton,

[1] Miss Cooper to W.F., 29.7.1829.

Exmouth, Ramsgate, Hastings, Bristol) which in pre-railway days itself demanded no small physical exertion. His epistolary output was astonishing. His letters—mainly to Lady Byron—describe innumerable meetings of all kinds of societies: the Statistical, the Astronomical, the Literary, the British Association, Unitarian groups for good works, committees of London University. And, as already mentioned, his interest in politics revived and he plunged into what he considered progressive campaigns with the same fervour and devotion as of old.

The pressure for Parliamentary Reform was at this time becoming so strong that Frend felt certain his long-deferred hopes were soon to be realized: he was glad to see the people at last demonstrating their wish for proper representation in such a way that this could not long be withheld.

Up and down the country industrial workers and country labourers were becoming impatient and there were outbreaks of rioting, machine breaking and rick-burning throughout 1830, culminating in the Bristol riots of October. Although Frend could hardly be called a revolutionary he would not condemn the direct action to which people were resorting. Much as he deplored violence, he saw the reason for it and strongly denounced the government's refusal to concede the necessary reforms, and its methods of brutal suppression.

Following the rioting in Kent during November 1830, he wrote to Lady Byron that he had been staying in the county and "was a witness to the stupor of its inhabitants on the breaking out of the trouble such as no one can have any conception of" who had not seen it. "Sir E. Knatchbull and his brother magistrates have much to answer for on this occasion. The evil has long been ripening. The payment of the labourers out of the poor rates was a very ill-advised measure but it naturally followed from the system of depriving the poor man of every comfort belonging to a cottage. The poor laws, game laws, corn laws must undergo a thorough examination. All of them have tended to bring us into the present state. The land holders intent only on their own peculiar interests have forgotten that they & all of us derive our comforts from labour & the labourer is worthy of his hire."

Frend rejoiced that the cause of reform was now "in the hands of government where I always wish'd it to be, having been firmly convinc'd that if it was not taken up in that quarter the task would be performed by those more likely to break the machine in pieces than to render it suitable to beneficial purposes." He saw that rioting had achieved a useful purpose: "... Out of the present tumults may arise some good, that other people may have their fears & that oligarchy which has resisted all reform may now consent to give up a part lest they should lose the whole."[1]

A month later, on Christmas Day, he returned to the subject: "I perceive that Kent which labours under some disgrace from the troubles having first burst out in that county, is setting an example to other counties by the formation of a yeomanry corps. The list of officers appointed is published. I do not augur any good either from the nature of the corps or the individuals that compose it. Instead it appears to me that if the plan is generally adopted there will be a civil war in the country." He added, in a minor key unusual for him, "my mind is a good deal oppressed & praying for better times."[2]

Frend had abandoned none of his strong views on the unsatisfactory state of the House of Commons, which still only represented a small minority of the population, and he still held to what he wrote in 1817: "The landed interest is the great supporter of the usurping oligarchy that rules the house of Commons & in this it manifests its ignorance of its true dignity ... To the present system, moreover, we are indebted for ten million a year of unnecessary taxes, i.e. we are now paying these millions a year in consequence of the present constitution of the House." Frend thought, in 1817,

[1] W.F. to A.B., 29.11.1830.

[2] *Ibid.*, 25.12.1830.

that "this wretched system would be continued because it is the interest of a few great landed proprietors who have contrived to cheat the great bulk of the middling class & to raise an outcry of mad dog against all those who see the true cause of the evil & endeavour to remove it . . ."

He had foretold what seemed to be happening in 1830: The usurpers would in their own defence "keep up such restraining laws on the liberty of the subject as are entirely alien to the spirit and feelings of this country." No wonder that watching the Kent Yeomanry in formation he felt his worst forebodings were being realized. To restrain the liberty of the subject (he had prophesied) "a strong military force will be necessary. We shall sink into a military government & then Commerce & Manufactures will flee away & the landholder may enjoy his depreciated lands in sullen tranquillity. I am not however convinced that the Usurpers will get the better in the present struggle." He remembered the troops and the gibbets he had seen in Belgium in 1789, and was more than ever convinced that repressive measures are "far from being a solid bulwark to any administration."[1]

Frend's interest was not academic; he closely followed the debates on Reform inside and outside Parliament, and took an active part in the campaign which was gathering momentum to force the Reform Bill through the House. In April 1831, although seventy-four years of age, he was prepared to travel from London to Cambridge to register his university vote for Cavendish and Palmerston: "In these spirit-stirring times neutrality would be a crime", he tells Lady Byron on 29 April, explaining that "as I apprehend there must be much uncertainty from the voters being engaged in their respective cities & counties, who can come & who cannot, it is most probable that I shall go down. The crisis is not without its alarms & if the King & people should be beat I tremble for the consequences."

Even when on holiday in Hastings, Frend attended "a general meeting to petition the house of Lords in favour of

[1] W.F. to A.B., 13.3.1817.

the Bill, which was very respectably attended & conducted, the Mayor being in the Chair." He tells Lady Byron that "the petition was carried unanimously & the meeting broke up after thanks to the Mayor & four hearty cheers for the king."[1]

The petition, like other petitions of that time and this, failed to have any immediate effect (though who can say that it was useless?) The House rejected the Reform Bill and the campaign forged ahead again.

In May 1832 Frend was in the thick of it, this time in London. "I am paying the penalty for my patriotism", he wrote. "Last Thursday about 12 o'clock a neighbour informed me that at one was to be a meeting of the middle districts of reform & invited me to go with him. We had a coach immediately & the Committee requested me to take part in the proceedings & gave me the choice of the resolutions, the first having been dispos'd of. I like a simpleton took a late one & in consequence sat in a very cramped situation in a crowded booth for about three hours before my turn came to address the audience. I could scarcely get to the front of the booth & the pain curtailed my oration. The resolution however was well seconded & passed as did all the rest unanimously & it was a very gratifying sight to see upwards of twelve thousand hands held up in support of them." No mean feat for a man of over seventy-five.[2]

On 4 June 1832, the First Reform Bill was at last passed by both Houses. Radicals all over England rejoiced, and in London Reform was toasted at the Annual Westminster Dinner on 27 June, and at a great Reform Festival in the Guildhall which we may guess Frend attended with his old fellow-fighter Hobhouse. Burdett, who of all "reformers" should have been there, was conspicuous by his absence.

The unreformed Parliament came to an end with its dissolution in December 1832. The elections to the new House passed quietly, though it was evident that some candidates did

[1] W.F. to A.B., 26.9.1831.

[2] *Ibid.*, 20.5.1832.

not see eye to eye with the populace, by their refusals to give pledges to repeal taxes.

Frend for his part expressed his delight and hopes in a letter to Lady Byron. He wrote, sitting by his fireside after an attack of gout "enthroned in all the dignity of flannels" to wish her a happy New Year "whatever may happen on the great theatre of the world."—"This is the first day of the New Year. It begins with better auspices than any that I ever remembered. We have got a Cobbett in the new parliament and got rid of a Hunt . . . In gentility and in intelligence the new parliament will not be inferior to any that has preceded it."[1]

During the months following the passing of the Reform Bill Frend hoped for great changes, and was disappointed that the rate of progress was not faster. He was ready to give the government the benefit of the doubt. He supported Peel's policy on the Malt Tax, and was hopeful about other aspects of conservative policy, particularly church affairs: "If he succeeds on the Church question he will immortalise himself", he wrote, adding "Sophia says I am ratting, but if Peel does what the Whigs either could not or would not do it seems to me to be folly to reject the boon. I have nothing to expect from either party & in wishing for the good of the whole you will I am sure concur . . ."[2] Inter-Church relations did indeed improve during the next few years. Whatever contributed to burying the hatchet was welcome to Frend and in October 1835 he declared "I am lost in astonishment at the changes I have witnessed. This year is truly annus mirabilis! A catholick sheriff of London succeeded in his office by a Jew—a catholick proclaiming liberty of conscience in a presbyterian kirk of Scotland—an advertisement in a town signed by two clergymen and seven dissenting ministers uniting to exhort their flocks to celebrate the translation of the Bible—a toast given to the dissenting ministers of the county—the tercentenary celebration

[1] W.F. to A.B., 1.1.1833.
[2] *Ibid.*, 6.10.1835.

disfigured indeed by the abuse of the papists but presenting the extraordinary union of churchmen & dissenters. The wolf is assuredly lying down with the lamb. If I had foretold this fifty years ago I should have been looked upon as a madman."

It may be remembered that just under half a century before, in 1787, Frend, as a young Cambridge don, had tried to persuade the University to grant equal rights to dissenters, and been called a "heretick" for his pains.

Referring to the city elections in which councillors of many denominations were returned he writes, in February 1836, that "I am rejoiced in much I have witnessed & trust that the coming generation will be far better than that to which I belonged . . . I exult in the great change of our municipal government not on account of the victory over the Tories, preservatives, or by whatever name they are to be called, but on the manifest change of publick opinion on the great right of private judgment. I see in the list of councillors Catholick, Lowchurchmen, Presbyterian . . . Quaker, Methodist, Unitarian." He reflects that "this is as it should be. By mixing with each other they will learn that a man may be a good subject & a good citizen though one goes to a place of worship with, & another to one without, a steeple & some go to no place of worship at all."[1]

He indulges in a dig at the Tories who try to slow down the progress of Church unity: "Bumpers are filled & glasses are rattled to the toast of Church & King, which means nothing more nor less than May our Party be dominant. They have no idea what the word Church means, much less are they interested in the spread of truth, but in vain do they cherish their prejudices . . . The word of God runs securely along & brings to pass in its proper time the destined effects."

Notwithstanding his firm belief in future progress through the word of God and the Reform Bill, and despite a sceptical attitude towards palliatives, Frend took a leading part in

[1] W.F. to A.B., 20.2.1836.

many charitable projects and discussed them in his letters to Lady Byron, herself a most active "do-gooder".

Housing and education were Frend's chief concerns, and we read of "a meeting of the Committee of the houseless of which I am a member" when "an animated discussion took place on the propriety of granting five hundred pounds for the relief of particular cases of distress . . . We who supported the grant were beat on a show of hands by about three to one." A little later we find Frend, undaunted by this defeat, discussing the problem of how to house and educate "15,000 young idle and dissolute vagrants" who were then "roaming the Metropolis":

"The idea of collecting these vagrants on board of ships & shipping them off to distant colonies is by no means a bad one for it is better that they should be there, whether instructed or not, than that they should run as they now do wild about the streets." But "supposing the lads well housed & well trained what is to be done with them afterwards? How are they to be restored to the world? These are considerations to be settled before the publick should be called on for its subscriptions." [1]

Workers' education was one of Frend's great passions and he describes with enthusiasm a visit to "a Mechanicks' meeting" at Hastings: "About twenty were present & the foreman, a shoemaker, gave us an excellent account of the origin of printing . . . I was highly gratified by what I saw & heard. The last Question was on Emigration. We are to discuss next Wednesday the effects of machinery on society. I think you will agree with me that this is a better employment of time than the wasting of it in an alehouse." [2]

His interest in adult education impelled Frend to help Birkbeck in organizing the Mechanics' Institute in Bloomsbury, and his name can be seen today among those carved on the stone at the entrance of Birkbeck College near Russell Square, where he lived from 1832 to '34.

[1] W.F. to A.B., 22.12.1830.
[2] *Ibid.*, December 1830.

As has been mentioned, Frend loved acquiring useful knowledge; he went to scientific lectures, and to exhibitions (which he recommended to Lady Byron as edifying for her daughter Ada, the brilliant mathematician and assistant of Babbage[1]); he collected learned societies as other old gentlemen collect antiques, and, being somewhat gregarious as well, he made a point of attending their conferences whenever possible.

His account of the 1836 meeting of the British Association at Bristol shows how much he got out of these jamborees, even at the age of seventy-nine. Bristol particularly appealed to him as a town, with its go-ahead attitudes and modern developments: "I am near a city rising out of its torpid state & holding out good prospects of increasing prosperity", he writes in August 1836. "Here is a princely merchant, his warehouses filled with tea of his own importation from China & I have had the gratification of being conducted over his numerous warehouses by himself." He tells Lady Byron he has visited an astronomer "who is building an observatory", and seen how "they are commencing the long talk'd of suspension bridge over the Avon . . . the person conducting the work is the son of a very intimate friend of mine." Then—symbol of technological progress—"there are two rail roads, one already commenced from this place to London, the other having the line prepared to go to the west of England and with my glass I see the flagstaff of one from my window."

Politically he approved of Bristol: "The riots in this place a few years back have been beneficial. They have roused a new spirit & there is in consequence an excellent police. The reform bill has done wonders. The place is said to be tory but it is now so mixed with the other party that good measures will be gradually adopted. The monopolising spirit of self election is done away with . . . "[2]

[1] Charles Babbage, F.R.S., inventor of computers.

[2] W.F. to A.B., August 1836.

Though in his eightieth year Frend was determined to enjoy every minute of his stay at Bristol, from his view of the railway and the steamers ("embracing a large vessel & kindly conveying it into port") to the scientific discussions of the congress and the social gatherings on the side.

We see him one evening "sitting quietly with our party between 9 and 10 when a gentleman call'd to take me in his carriage to a conversazione a mile off at the house of the late Mayor, who unfortunately held the office at the time of the riots." Here Frend found about a hundred people, and stayed well into the night enjoying the convivial talk and company.

At one of the British Association meetings he took the chair: "The principal feature was a dry mathematical subject very well explained to those who could follow him by Sir William Hamilton, into whose hands, by the way, I put a paper very prettily written out by Sophia & which has not return'd. Sir William had decided on the failure of an attempt of a very good mathematician, & it appear'd to me that the latter was in errour yet the errour lay deeper than Sir William imagined."

A member of seventy-nine years old might have been excused some of the evening gatherings, but Frend was undaunted, and deafness notwithstanding seemed to enjoy every moment. At "the grand meeting at the Theatre" one night, "I sat very much at my ease in the second row behind the president's chair, could see well, and the coup d'oeuil was very striking, but as to hearing, three fourths of what was said was lost upon me. This very hardy feat of mine led to its natural results." He caught a bad cold "and did not venture a second time into the theatre." Bravely, he went to his section the following day—"but colds are not to be trifled with" and he subsequently stayed in bed till noon, getting up only for the sections which especially interested him, "the geological and the mechanical". In the former, "a country gentleman gave an account of very interesting experiments he had made, which would never have been heard of if it had not been for the Association. All that is really valuable is done in the sections."[1]

"The business of the association concluded as it began, in the Chapterhouse", Frend tells Lady Byron on 1 September. "We met between 12 and 1 and did not separate till 5. The Marquis of Northampton was in the chair & performed his part to general satisfaction." After deciding on Liverpool as the place of the next meeting, members elected their new president: "Assuredly Lord Burlington had the strongest claims . . . There was an intention of bringing forward Sir Robert Peele", Frend says, but "this fell to the ground & the name of the Baronet was never mentioned."

At the final meeting in the evening, "the theatre was crouded. The philosophers were profuse in their compliments to each other & the Bristolians gratified by those bestowed upon them. Indeed they deserved these & I hope that each city in its turn will be equally attentive to their visitants."

Frend was, not unnaturally, somewhat tired by this time and did not feel up to attending the ceremony of "the laying of the first stone of the suspension bridge"; he tells Lady Byron regretfully that "it was a grand spectacle but too early in the morning for me", and he declined the invitation to the "subsequent dejeuner". However, later in the day he hurried up to the Avon Gorge on hearing that there had been an accident to the "bar", involving his friend Tate's son Charles. "The bar was brought up to its place and the basket was moved upon it", he wrote. "Mrs F. came home in great agitation in the evening for she was in a fright for Charles Tate who she was told was in the basket suspended over the Avon. I went up immediately and found that he was safe back again. A new bar will be put up this evening & we have had a letter from Mrs Tate his mother today expressive of her alarm. He is a fine spirited young man, the agent of Mr Brunell in this place. In spite of all my philosophy I cannot get rid of my feelings on his account but I trust he

[1] W.F. to A.B. 1.9.1836.

will not venture till the strength of the rod has been ascertain'd by the transit of the basket without a man within."[1]

* * *

In January 1837 Frend suffered a slight paralytic stroke. He had by 8 May recovered enough to write to Lady Byron that "after about 4 months confined to the house I last week enjoyed the fresh air & the sun in the garden of our square ... My complaint is far advanced on the decline." But it had been "very troublesome" and he had needed all his philosophy to endure the pain and the sleepless nights.

The illness aged Frend a good deal, and from then his letters grew longer and more diffuse; although they continued to mirror his interest in the outside world he discussed people and politics less, and books and ideas more. One subject which still roused him to debate was Malthus' theory of population. In 1829 recalling "a conversation I had with Malthus on the first publication of his work", he expressed his opinion that "were men guided by reason and instead of destroying each other, subduing the earth", population "would increase with decreasing increment, so that at the conclusion it would terminate with an equality of births and burials. Each generation possessing the maximum of happiness adapted to its state that the earth can provide."[2] Now, on 8 May 1837 he returned to the subject: "Malthouse's [*sic*] theorem occupied my attention very early, for he presented to me through his bookseller the first copy of his work & on visiting me about 3 weeks after confess'd to me that he was the author ... As to his propositions of food in an arithmetical, and population in a geometrical, there never has been nor ever will be such a case & what is more I defy any man to draw up a scale of births & deaths so that population should increase in geometrical progression."[3]

[1] W.F. to A.B., 1.9.1836.
[2] *Ibid.*, 27.2.1829.
[3] *Ibid.*, 8.5.1837.

Frend and his wife were now living in Tavistock Square, and, apart from Henry, studying law, surrounded by those of the children who were not out in the world. Richard, the delicate second boy had to their great grief died some years before. On 3 August 1837 Sophia was to leave home, to marry Augustus De Morgan the distinguished mathematician, who had often visited them and played his flute at musical evenings at Stoke Newington.

The wedding took place in the St Pancras Registry Office, and Frend wrote approvingly "I am very much pleased at this new mode of marrying." He would have liked to have a religious ceremony as well, as his nephew had had in Pennsylvania, and had hoped this could be arranged at Essex Street Chapel—but "from the bungling way in which the Act is drawn up this could not be accomplish'd."

It was considered very advanced and daring of Sophia: "The idea of the Registrar's office at first startled the females but by degrees they were reconciled to it . . . Our relatives, all Church people, some clerical, excepting the Americans, will be not a little shocked. Pray let me know your opinion." [1]

Frend's activity was still remarkable; in the autumn of 1837 he visited a workhouse about seven miles from Ramsgate; had long talks with labourers and artisans and reported them verbatim to Lady Byron (as in an amusing letter about a discussion on "teetotalling", "with a wheelwright and a hatter"); worked out a new Nautical Almanack. But age was beginning to tell on him. He was troubled by deafness and when Lady Byron offered suggestions for treatment, wrote "I am tempted to try the experiment. My deafness is not a very great inconvenience, though in mix'd parties I feel the disadvantage of it as if the voice is not directed to my ear & there is another voice at the same time their sounds are lost upon me", yet "given distinctness I hear very well." [2]

[1] W.F. to A.B., 4.8.1837.
[2] *Ibid.*, 9.11.1837.

His letters become more rambling and his hand is shaky: "My pen does not obey my hand as well as it used to", he admits; he also mentions "a complaint which has been very troublesome and given me many sleepless nights, made more bearable by contemplations on the past & future."[1]

Such contemplations also creep into his letters, with copious reminiscences of his past life, enriched by many philosophical reflections. Soon after his eightieth birthday he wrote to Lady Byron, almost for the last time:

"An octogenarian has the honour of addressing your ladyship—mind, this is a secret for I know not whether even my own family is aware of the fact . . . that a fortnight ago I entered the third decade of old age . . .

"What a difference between myself now & myself when I entered the third decade of my existence! Then, an object of ambition was before my eyes & I laboured hard to attain it, now the scene is closed & yet I have enough left to compensate me . . . I am near the end of my journey. I have seen enough to convince me that the whole system of human affairs is under the controul of a wise & good being & that this whole will manifest his wisdom."[2]

Frend had indeed lived through a period in which the highest hopes of such men, humanitarians and radicals, had seemed to be in process of fulfilment: human progress—social and technical—had been astounding, and there appeared to be no reason why it should not continue at the same rate indefinitely, provided free inquiry was not hampered by bigotry and obscurantism.

In 1823 he had written to Sophia, staying with her uncle in Somerset and reading Locke: "I am glad to see that Mr Locke points out to you the danger of entertaining prejudices on any subject whatever . . . For what is prejudice but a previous determination, without giving yourself the power of forming a judgment? We may talk against the truth, but all our talking does not alter the nature of truth—we are doing

[1] W.F. to A.B., 21.6.1837.
[2] *Ibid.*, 7.1.1838.

an injury to our own minds when we cannot bear contradiction on a favourite opinion . . .

"The reason that so much prejudice is in the world and so little of truth is that men love darkness better than light; they cannot bear to be told that they and their fathers have been in an error . . . Truth must be loved for its own sake, but error is adopted and maintained because it suits the purpose of certain sets of people to keep the rest as much as possible in ignorance."[1]

In the sixteen years since writing that, Frend had seen so much social and technical progress that, at eighty, he was much more optimistic, writing to Lady Byron: "Man shall run to & from & knowledge shall be increased. How far the moral state of the world will be improved we cannot say but we have every reason to believe that the one will accompany the other. Every prejudice removed makes way for the progress of truth."[2]

In late 1838 Frend suffered a second paralytic stroke; but even though he was hardly able to speak or to move, he managed to write a last letter to Lady Byron in which he discussed Mr Belsham's definition of Unitarianism with surprisingly vigorous disapproval in a wavering but perfectly legible hand.

The last years of his life were spent at 36 Tavistock Square, surrounded by his books and belongings (including the cabinet made for him at Little Paxton in 1795, and the marble bust which was later presented to Jesus College). His farewell to life cannot be better described than by Sophia, who was with him when he died, in 1841.

"He had been paralytic three or four years and for many months unable to utter two or three words consecutively. The day before his death he pointed to a Bible and made a sign for me to read to him. I read his favourite Psalm, 'The Heavens declare the glory of God' etc. When I was reading 'As for man, his days are as grass', he joined in and repeated

[1] S. De Morgan: *Three Score Years and Ten*, pp. xxvii–xxix.
[2] W.F. to A.B., 7.1.1838.

with me clearly and in a firm voice the verses following to the end of the Psalm." That was the last time he spoke, and the next day, 21 February, he was dead.

That morning a messenger came from George Dyer to inquire after him. "When the messenger returned, Dyer asked for the news, and was told Frend was rather better. 'I understand', he said. 'Mr Frend is dead. Lay me beside him.' He went into an adjoining room, washed his hands, returned and quietly sat down in his armchair, as it was thought, to listen to a kind friend who came to read to him. Before beginning she looked up to her hearer, but the loving hearted old man was dead."[1]

At that moment, Charles Lamb's poem, written years before, must have seemed unerringly appropriate:

> Friend of the friendless, friend of all mankind
> To thy wide friendships I have not been blind;
> But looking at them nearly, in the end
> I love thee most that thou art Dyer's Frend.

They were both buried in Kensal Green Cemetery. Several obituary notices testified to the love and respect in which Frend was held, but Augustus De Morgan's, in the *Christian Reformer*[2] was the one which the old Reformer would have liked best. De Morgan, who according to his daughter Mary "always spoke of Frend as 'the noblest man he had ever known'," wrote: "On February 21st 1841 he closed a life which is regarded, even by those who differed from him, as a splendid example of honesty in the pursuit of truth and of undaunted determination in the assertion of all that conscience required.

"Sincere regret . . . is lessened by the reflection that his extensive learning, practical wisdom in the affairs of life, chivalrous assertion of all that he thought true, and extraordinary benevolence of feeling, were permitted a long and

[1] S. De Morgan, *op. cit.*, pp. 83–84.
[2] *Christian Reformer*, Vol. ii, p. 642.

useful career, terminated only by natural decay, and followed by the love of many and the respect of all."

Frend's epitaph could hardly be better framed than in his own words written at the height of the Napoleonic holocaust in Europe. After crying out against the folly and wickedness of war, he declared "Yet cannot it always remain so: in spite of the infidelity of the present day, we look forward to the time when reason shall have its due influence with mankind ... In that case, differences of opinion will be softened by other modes than that of force; and the instruments of destruction will be converted to their proper purpose, the subduing of the earth to the benefit of mankind."

SELECT BIBLIOGRAPHY

The following have been the most fruitful sources. For background I have relied on eighteenth- and nineteenth-century histories by established authorities, on biographies too numerous for individual mention, and on many contemporary journals besides those specifically mentioned.

Unpublished Material:

Letters from and to William Frend, 1772–1840 (in the possession of Miss Philothea Thompson; now in Cambridge University Library)

Letters from and to William Frend, 1790–1838 (in the possession of Miss Joan Antrobus, now in Cambridge University Library)

Letters from William Frend to Lady Byron (Lovelace Papers) (W.F. to A.B.)

Letters in Dr Williams' Library, London (George Dyer, Mary Hays)

——University College Library, London (Frend to Registrar)

——Jesus College Library, Cambridge (A. De Morgan)

——Trinity College Library, Cambridge (Frend to David Ricardo)

——University Library, Cambridge—Ely Diocesan Records (Bishop of Ely to Master of Jesus) (E.D.R.)

——Bodleian Library, Oxford—Montagu Letters (George Dyer, Major Cartwright to Frend)

Ph.D. Dissertation (Columbia University) The Unitarianism of S. T. Coleridge, Dr R. Frothingham

Minutes of College Meetings, Jesus College, Cambridge

Periodicals:

Cambridge Chronicle, 1790–93

Cambridge Intelligencer, 1793–97
The Gentleman's Magazine, 1790–1841
The Anti-Jacobin, 1798–99
Christian Reformer, 1841
Monthly Repository, 1805–18
Universal Magazine, 1805

Writings by William Frend:

Thoughts on Subscription to Religious Tests, and a Letter to the Rev. H. W. Coulthurst. St Ives 1788
Address to the Inhabitants of Cambridge. St Ives 1788
Mr Coulthurst's Blunders exposed. London 1789
Peace and Union Recommended. St Ives 1793
An Account of the Proceedings in the University of Cambridge. Cambridge 1793
A Sequel to the Account. London 1795
On the Scarcity of Bread. London 1795
Principles of Algebra. London 1796
Principles of Taxation. London 1799
Animadversions on "The Elements of Christian Theology". London 1800
Effect of Paper Money. London 1801
Patriotism or the Love of our Country. London 1804
Evening Amusements. London 1804–1822
A Christian's Survey of the Modern World. (*Monthly Repository*) London 1808–18
The National Debt in its true Colours. London 1817
Memoirs of a Goldfinch. London 1817
Is it impossible to free the Atmosphere of London. London 1819
A Plan for Universal Education. London 1832

Books consulted:

Barlow, R. B. *Citizenship and Conscience*. Philadelphia 1963
Beverley, J. *The Trial of William Frend*. Cambridge 1793
Bellot, H. H. *University College, London*. London 1929

BROWN, F. K. *Fathers of the Victorians*. Cambridge 1961

CESTRE, C. *La Révolution française et les Poètes anglais (1789–1809)*. Paris 1906

CHAMBERS, E. K. *Coleridge. A Biographical Study*. Oxford 1931

COLE, G. D. H. *The Life of William Cobbett*. London 1924

COLERIDGE, S. T. *Letters* (ed. E. H. Coleridge). London 1895

DE MORGAN, SOPHIA. *Three Score Years and Ten*. London 1895

——*Memoir of Augustus De Morgan*. London 1882

DYER, GEORGE. *Complaints of the Poor People of England*. London 1793

——*Life of Dr Robert Robinson*. London 1796

——*Poems*. London 1801

ELWIN, MALCOLM. *Lord Byron's Wife*. London 1962

FARINGTON, JOSEPH. *The Farington Diary* (ed. J. Grey). London 1922

GILLAM, J. *The Crucible*. London 1954

GODWIN, WILLIAM. *Political Justice*. London 1793

GUNNING, H. *Reminiscences of Cambridge*. London 1854

HAYS, MARY. *On Public Worship ('Eusebia')*. London 1792

——*Memoir of Emma Courtney*. London 1796

HAZLITT, WILLIAM. "Life of Thomas Holcroft" (*Works*. vol. iii). London 1934

KNEPLER, G. *Musikgeschichte*. Berlin 1961

KNIGHT, FRIDA. *The Strange Case of Thomas Walker*. London 1957

LAMB, CHARLES. *Letters* (Everyman edition). London 1945

MCLACHLAN, H. *Letters of Theophilus Lindsey*. Manchester 1920

——*The Unitarian Movement in the Religious Life of England*. London 1934

MILNER, MARY. *Life of Isaac Milner*. London 1834

MINEKA, F. E. *The Dissidence of Dissent*. Chapel Hill, N.C. 1944

MOSELEY, MABOTH. *Irascible Genius* (Life of Charles Babbage). London 1962

NORTH, ROGER. *Lives of the Norths* (ed. A. Jessop). London 1894

OGBORN, M. E. *Equitable Assurances*. London 1962
PATTERSON, M. W. *Sir Francis Burdett and his Times*. London 1931
RODGERS, BETSY. *Georgian Chronicle*. London 1958
ROMILLY, SIR SAMUEL. *Memoirs*. London 1840
ROBINSON, H. CRABB. *Diary* (ed. T. Sadler). London 1869
——*On Books and their Writers* (ed. E. J. Morley). London 1935
ROCK CENTENARY YEAR BOOK. London 1906
RUTT, J. T. *Life and Correspondence of Dr Joseph Priestley*. London 1831
SCHNEIDER, BEN. *Wordsworth's Cambridge Education*. Cambridge 1957
SEYMOUR, A. C. H. *The Life and Times of Selina, Countess of Huntingdon*. London 1839
STEPHEN, SIR J. *Ecclesiastical Studies*. London 1849
THOMPSON, E. P. *The Making of the English Working Class* (Pelican Books). Harmondsworth 1968
WAKEFIELD, GILBERT. *Memoir* (ed. J. T. Rutt). London 1804
WALLAS, GRAHAM. *The Life of Francis Place*. London 1898
WORDSWORTH, CHRISTOPHER. *Social Life at the English Universities*. Cambridge 1874
YOUNG, ARTHUR. *Enquiry into the State of the Public Mind among the Lower Classes*. London 1798

INDEX